MICHIGAN PREHISTORY MYSTERIES

By Betty Sodders

Avery Color Studios
Au Train, Michigan
1990

Library of Congress Card No. 89-81356
ISBN - 0-932212-62-X
First Edition January 1990

Cover Artwork by Diane Tedora

Published
by
Avery Color Studios
Au Train, Michigan 49806

TABLE OF CONTENTS

Dedication

This book was written through a culmination of efforts on the behalf of many individuals, all dedicated to the study and introduction of primitive man's accomplishments in Michigan.

First and foremost this manuscript is dedicated to Carol and Sprague Taylor. Early research into the mystery of the McGruer's Gods and the Newberry Stone was undertaken by Sprague. (now deceased) His endeavor, in turn, resulted in the writing of this book as his total dedication refused to let the matter rest...keeping the 1896 legend alive.

The following people also donated much personal time, effort and expense towards this writing...it would not have been published without their able assistance: *Wm. W. Sodders*, my patient husband who sacrificed togetherness during my work on the book. *Mike McCollum*, my publisher, who believed in me. *Barry Fell*, President of the Epigraphic Society, author of America B.C. and Bronze Age America, whose help and research added professionalism to my efforts. *Robert E. Haltiner*, Chief of Resources, Jesse Besser Museum, Alpena. He generously shared his personal archaeological finds with me. *Charles Bailey*, my research contact from Duluth, Minnesota, who offered so much personal time helping to establish the authenticity of the McGruer's Gods. Through his efforts carbon-14 testing has been arranged. *Dennis Morrison*, an amateur archaeologist, dedicated to the preservation of prehistory. Dennis supplied local "input" through his newspaper articles for the Harrisville Review for which he served in the capacity of a reporter. He also is responsible for many of the photos that appear in the book. *Mary Thompson*, Glennie librarian for the Alcona Library system who kept me supplied with research material. *Francis Moses*, a young talented artist from St. Ignace who provided artwork needed for many chapters.

Introduction

Over a century past, three generations of Fretz's owned and operated a weekly newspaper out of the small Upper Peninsula village of Newberry. It was here, in *The Newberry News*, the first words of an extraordinary archaeological discovery were printed for a surprised and eager group of readers. The year was 1896. The startling find was the unearthing of three almost life-size statues of a man, woman and child plus a most remarkable clay tablet inscribed with hieroglyphics of sorts placed on 140 squares. Needless to say, speculation ran rampant!

But I am getting ahead of myself...In 1987 I took on the job of getting the John McGruer, turn-of-the-century farmhouse, north of Newberry, listed on the Michigan Historical record. During research the nearly one-hundred-year-old legend of "McGruer's Gods" and "The Newberry Stone" just kept popping up. Help arrived with the able assistance of Carol Taylor, whose husband had done extensive preliminary research on these prehistory artifacts. Sprague Taylor authored several articles on this perplexing discovery and then as the years passed, the matter was more or less simply laid to rest!

Research tracking turned up early photographs of the gods and tablet, showing them as they were discovered. To that point, all we had to work with were two hand-drawn sketches that appeared in an old 1896 newspaper clipping from an unidentified source. One was a detailed drawing of the man-idol, while the other gave an accurate replica of the engraved tablet.

At just about the same time I also found a letter dated May 12, 1958, written by the second Mr. Fretz, Editor of *The Newberry News*. Please allow me to quote his reply to a request for information on these mysterious archaeological relics:

Dear Mr. Boyer:

I will be very glad to cooperate in getting some authoritative information concerning the 3-figures and the tablet found north of Newberry in 1896. They have *itched me* for a good many years! My information comes from my father, the late Wm. G. Fretz, and follows:

The images were found by Robert McGruer, on his "40" four miles north of town, in a comparatively shallow depression under the roots of an uprooted hemlock. The lot was brought to town and a great hassle arose concerning them, which has not been settled yet. Some investigation was made by the parties you name, pictures sent to the Smithsonian Institute, but they could tie it up with nothing in history known at that time. Dr. Farrand, Crocker, McLeod, Trueman and Brebner were all intelligent men, but one or two of them were prone to rig up practical jokes, and town opinion was about equally divided as to whether they really had something, or were just giving the cracker-box boys something to chew on. Father was of the opinion they were sincere, that the find was no joke. One of his reasons was that McGruer was a rather simple-minded old coot with no capacity for such a stunt, and, when properly lubricated, told all he knew anyway. Father lubricated him, but got nothing more than the facts stated. Since McGruer made the find while clearing land, he must have been a charter member of the affair, whatever it was.

As a young boy on my way to the swimming hole on the Tahquamenon River, I remember these figures being stored in an open shed on the McGruer farm on the river. Somewhere in my musty old files I have pictures of them. My impression is that they were not made of sandstone, but of red clay, baked hard, with some kind of surfacing. The molded figures were very roughly made, but obviously human beings. There were 3 of them, about 4, 3, and 2 feet in height.

The tablet, at the time I saw it, about 1905-06 was starting to disintegrate from exposure and being kicked around, and was also formed of the same reddish material as the figures. The characters meant nothing to a 10 or 11 year old kid, but a number of years later I saw the tablet, and the characters impressed me and as being wedge-shaped, like a Persian cuneiform tablet, but these were separated by squares. In no other manner did they resemble Greek, Egyptian or any other ancient tablet writing, but of course my ignorance far exceeds my knowledge in that field.

This sketchy information is all I can offer, and now you have me *itching all over again!*

Yours truly,

W.B. Fretz

Yes, Fretz was *itching all over*, just as I did as the story slowly unfolded. My perseverance led to a possible solution of this ancient riddle of antiquity. It also led to the writing of this book. On getting together with my publisher, it was decided to include other little-known Michigan prehistory mysteries along with the gods and tablet. After months of research and personal contacts, we chose the material deemed most interesting for Michiganders, no matter which part of the state they herald.

It is this author's intent to make you, the reader, start *itching all over* as well. It is a book of many unanswered questions. One I hope will not only tickle your fancy but also spark your imagination. I am sure it will make you ask the five proverbial "W's": Why, what, who, when and where.

Enjoy!

Preface

You hold in your hand no ordinary volume! Welcome to the world of mysteries both rare and exotic. Indeed, you are about to sojourn down a path into Michigan's prehistory. An avenue that will leave you looking at our State's earlier times in a very different light.

Author, Betty Sodders, is no stranger to those of you who have been reading the popular magazine, *Michigan Out-of-Doors*. She has been writing about Michigan for years now to the delight of many. Her talents as a master story teller are showcased in this, her first book.

Betty examines the baffling culture that inhabited the Keweenaw area of the Upper Peninsula. A civilization that was one day there mining the precious copper, and the next, laid down their tools and just seemed to vanish from the face of the earth.

What is even more enigmatic are the stone slab ruins buried on Isle Royale, where not a trace of cultural material can be found by which these early dwellers can be identified.

In these pages, you will visit along with Betty, the unusual rock pits and walls at Black River, Michigan. Why they were built and by whom has never been discovered.

You will take a look at mysterious statues that seem to bespeak of ancient European cultures having visited our fresh-water shores. Betty also investigates mysterious rock petroglyphs, as well as cave paintings, that archaeologists attribute to the Indians, and yet have perhaps an even more ancient origin.

Among other oddities of long ago, Betty will tantalize you with the following mysteries:

*Remote Beaver Island is one of Michigan's newest archaeological puzzlers. There has been discovered on the island a ring of stones now thought to be an ancient calendar.

*How about a look at some pyramids here in Michigan?

Sounds far-fetched but it's true. One of these possible earthen pyramids near Ontonagon is 63 feet high, with a second at 57 feet. Who built them and why? Or, are they natural formations? Read on!

*The remote shores of Michigan have turned up some stone tablets inscribed with cryptic messages. Two of these have been translated by Dr. Barry Fell, author of "America B.C." and "Bronze Age America." In this chapter, Mrs. Sodders examines what may well be Michigan's oldest existing written records!

*At one time the ancient Great Lakes were guarded by great image stones, again attributed to the Indians. This seems rather odd since archaeologists say Michigan's Indians of the northeast did not sculpt stone! Betty looks at who may have actually created these megaliths.

*Near Alpena was a prehistoric factory where inscribed stone discs were turned out in abundance. Oddly enough, in the whole State of Michigan as well as the entire nation, it is the only such site to have ever been found!

Besides the tangible, you will read of antiquated, fleeting wisps that have touched peoples lives for but a brief moment on the pages of time. The mysterious stone with its remarkable appearing and vanishing symbols, a discovery of my own, has been thoroughly investigated and included here for your speculation. Was it some sort of communication from prehistoric times? Mrs. Sodders' insights will help you decide.

If you enjoy a good mystery, then light up the fireplace and close the curtains. Curl up in your favorite easy chair and partake of these truce anomalies of life in Michigan so very long ago!

Dennis M. Morrison

Amateur Archaeologist/Freelance Author

The Copper Culture Riddle
PART 1
Who Were The Copper Culture People?

Michigan's oldest prehistory mystery is certainly by far the evidence left behind by a virtually unknown race of people, thousands of years ago...the Copper Culture people! We must assume them to be North America's first copper miners. Over 5000 mined prehistoric copper pits were discovered on Isle Royale alone, not including thousands of others located on the mainland of the Keweenaw Peninsula in Michigan's Upper Peninsula. There are a good number of things scientists know (and admittedly, don't know), but they are in relative accord that carbon-14 dating methods put these ancient digs in a perspective of approximately 5000 years ago. To perhaps be a bit more specific, dates would more or less range from say 3000 B.C. to A.D. 900.

Since 1847 when Samuel Knapp discovered these prehistory copper pits, over 300 articles had been written on these ancient mining oddities by the early 1900s. In addition, each early author more or less offered his personal opinions as fact. Public sentiment was overwhelming and naturally rumors ran rampant. In the long run, this mysterious race of people were ascribed to be Egyptians, Phoenicians, Aztecs, Toltecs, Brazilians, Eskimos, Mongolians, and Russians, as well as Danes and Norsemen. Still others claimed the Copper Culture people were of European descent. By the mid-1900s writers were leaning towards this mysterious race belonging to the same group of perplexing pre-Columbian individuals responsible for building the strange and inexplicable mounds that not only dotted our Michigan landscape, but even more so, the surrounding States of Wisconsin and Ohio.

Recent assumptions by Salvatore Trento, author of "The Search For Lost America" and Barry Fell, who wrote "America B.C." and "Bronze Age America," indicate an abject possibility exists that fleets of ships of ancient Norse, Baltic and Celtic derivation made repeated trips across the Atlantic

Ocean in a trading capacity offering goods for raw materials to the Algonquians of North America.

Scientifically, Barry Fell has calculated that twice since the ending of the Stone Age, conditions were favorable for ocean crossings. The first occurred during the middle of the Bronze Age as the world's climates were warmer. Following that specific time period, the northern route to the Americas once more became icebound and remained so until perhaps A.D. 700. Warmer weather prevailed and travel was again possible. Based on current information it was during this former period that the Vikings landed on our east coast, worked their way up the St. Lawrence River and established a trading colony in Canada.. It is interesting to note, however, that the Vikings were not just Norsemen, but in turn included men from the Baltics, Lithuania, and Latvia as well as Celts from Ireland and perhaps even Wales.

This new wave of "open-mindedness" brought additional scientific theories regarding the Copper Culture people. It was further believed that a Norse King, named Woden-lithi left his mark near Toronto, Canada, in the year 1700 B.C. He left behind petroglyphs and writings to indicate his visit was a trading mission for a well-established copper trade that was known to have existed in the Lake Superior Region some 1000 years before his visit. Evidently the Keweenaw copper industry was well established when the Norse King paid North America a visit!

Fell also reports that near the Peterborough Petroglyphs (as the Toronto site is so called), over a thousand copper artifacts were excavated. Generally speaking, many of these objects received a cabon-14 testing producing a date, one thousand years before the sailing time of King Woden-lithi. Further evidence links the copper mines themselves with a prehistory date of possibly 3000 B.C. to 2000 B.C. Almost unbelievable!

It is indeed hard to fathom people, an entire culture, here in our State of Michigan, at this early date. Perhaps because over the learning years we have been pre-programmed to understand that up until the time Columbus discovered America, foreign trade and travel just did not exist here in the New World. Likewise, I am sure you will admit the study of archaeology and especially that of past civilizations, is also in retrospect, a study of mysteries. Who can anticipate what further changes the future may yet reveal regarding Michigan's prehistory mysteries!

Let's consider for just a moment why Old World travelers would have attempted excursions to this comparatively new continent. Just as it would be today, the object was perhaps money, personal status, trade, natural resources...yes, even copper. History relates that about the year 1000 B.C. during the height of the Phoenician Empire, copper was used perhaps more extensively than during any other time frame of history. Facts indicate the semiprecious red-gold metal was in great demand. The Phoenicians were well known merchants with excellent fleets of ships. Perhaps we have underestimated the achievements of the Bronze Age peoples. Ships that plied both the North Sea and the Baltic were aptly described or pictured in rock carvings called petroglyphs in both Europe and North America. As previously mentioned, it appears entire flotillas of Norse, Baltic and Celtic ships crossed the Atlantic to enter into trade wars with the Algonquians for rich mineral deposits. At a much later period many of these early visitors eventually settled permanently in the Americas. Some, it has been said, mingled with local native tribes migrating westward from say British Columbia, southward as far as the Pacific Coast, downward to California and Mexico. From a realistic point of view, the Bronze Age produced races of people that were definitely not only literate, but also well educated. Here in the New World they left behind a lasting legacy containing rock inscriptions and drawings in both Iberian and Celtic script. At the present time scores of North American inscriptions are being translated by the Epigraphic Society and perhaps the future will bring firm and complete answers to many of the age-old myths and mysteries that abound, including the riddle of the Copper Country Culture!

Let's take time now to examine the uniqueness of this region so graphically called the Michigan Copper Country. Truly it is a mythical land! Rocks here are reported to be among the oldest in the entire world. One might imagine it has existed since the beginning of time! An Indian legend relates that here on the Keweenaw, the sun sets on copper mountains and rises once again at break of day, to shine on huge copper boulders scattered about its ridges and valleys. Actually at first glance mapwise, the Keweenaw Peninsula appears like a large copper finger extending into Lake Superior, perhaps pointing towards far distant Isle Royale, the site of still additional Indian folklore. Let me add quickly that these fables more or less afford positive proof against the possibility that early Indian races were the original ancient copper mining people.

One legend in particular, you may find interesting, reads as follows: On the Isle of Michicopoten (Isle Royale) lived a "spirit manitou", known as "Missibissi"... A Chippewa god. Michicopoten was regarded not only to be made of solid copper, but in addition was also termed a moveable land mass. The early natives fully believed that Missibissi used this remarkable floating island as his personal copper canoe, paddling it up and down the Lake Superior Territory! It is reasonable to assume the Indians additionally felt this mythical god caused "thunder" to boom as a dire warning should the island or any of the ancient copper mining pits be needlessly approached.

A still later embellishment of the above legend states that a group of four Indians landed on the Island during a severe storm. Wishing to prepare a meal, they made some stones red-hot to put in their birch bark dish, in order to cook fish. Evidently some of the rocks were copper. After eating their food they re-embarked, taking some of the copper stones along. Shortly after reaching the mainland, three of the men died, poisoned most likely by the action of copper salts. The fourth native related to the others what had happened and in turn died shortly afterwards. In all truth this so terrified the rest of the tribe that they did not dare go to Michicopoten (Isle Royale) again. Not only did the Indians believe it haunted, the dwelling place of the "thunders", but many also regarded the Island to be free-floating due to the fog and vapors that always shrouded it, often affording an appearance of being nearer or further off. Albeit, additional deterrents, in the form of Indian mythical monsters lurked near Isle Royale's shoreline...being the feared "Memogoissiouis"...fishes in the form of men! With the passage of time it naturally became a custom for all passers-by to throw offerings of tobacco and other small gifts to the Island spirits as insurance for a safe passage.

Folklore mentions that the early Indians possessed magical copper rocks and pebbles, yet the old legends and myths held fast, making the prehistory copper pits of both Isle Royale and the Copper Country, strictly, absolutely, TABOO! Furthermore, they were so completely deemed off-limits, that all natives thoroughly believed if they but pointed out a copper site to an outsider, they personally would die within the coming year. Undoubtedly they were so convinced of this phenomena that it was all but impossible to convince an Indian to reveal the location of any of the mines. One documented example of this behavior occurred in the year 1820 when General Cass, Indian Agent Henry Schoolcraft and a party of men visited the south shore of Lake Superior in search of an oddity of solid copper termed...the Ontonagon Boulder. They could find no Indian willing to guide them in this endeavor. Finally beseeching and bribing an Indian named White Pigeon, they began their journey. As things turned out, their native guide unbelievably lost his way! Such unheard of behavior caused this particular tribe to ascertain the man was being punished by the gods for attempting to reveal a sacred trust. As a matter of course, time dealt White Pigeon a series of misfortunes! The Indian brave no longer was a great hunter...the animals of the forest avoided him...he was reduced to living on roots and berries. By and large the Chippewas expelled him from their village and a short time later, he died; a starving, emaciated Indian who obviously violated a tribal law.

The Ontonagon Boulder, mentioned above, that Cass and Schoolcraft were searching for, has been a matter of record since the Jesuits first entered the Canadian Territories. Actually as early as 1608, the explorer Champlain was presented with a large specimen of copper by an Algonquian chief, that was believed to have been chipped off the famous Ontonagon Boulder. The chief explained to Champlain that the copper came from the bank of a great river that flowed into a great lake. Historians maintain the Indian referred to the Ontonagon River and Lake Superior.

Some time later an early Indian called Yellow Beaver, when asked to describe just how large this copper boulder actually was, replied, "Rock is big...big, like moose!" Just perhaps, a more apt description would have been as old records state..."a large gray rock, half buried in the sloping edge of a bluff, traced with rich veins of copper." To all intents and purposes, early explorers found the metal actually protruded outward in jagged, irregular corners and knobs. Nevertheless, it was evident that human hands had worked away at the rock for ages. Additionally, the boulder was actually blackened in places by fire and was hewn, hacked and pounded on every side. In retrospect, it gave the appearance that perhaps all the tribes of the Northland had tried at one time or another to secure a bit of the precious metal.

In 1771 Alexander Henry, after the Indian massacre at Fort Michilimackinaw, organized a company which began mining operations in the vicinity of the Ontonagon Boulder. After one unrewarding season, this venture was abandoned. The rock was more or less left to rest until Douglass Houghton hacked more off this 2-ton chunk of freestanding copper boulder in the early 1800s.

By 1840 this freak mass of pure copper became a national curiosity. Competition for ownership occurred between 1842 and 1843, when Jim Paul and Julius Eldred vied for moving the big rock, in various moneymaking schemes. However, the United States War Department stepped in and finally, after years of arguments and discussions, the Ontonagon Boulder was moved to the Smithsonian Institute in Washington D.C. where it remains on display to this writing.

As previously mentioned, the Ontonagon Boulder showed obvious signs of being worked for years before the early explorers discovered it. From Ontonagon to the extreme tip of the Keweenaw Peninsula, copper pits were in strong evidence. We are not now talking of copper mines in the context of today's modern endeavors, but in turn, refer to round, hand-dug pits, varying in depth from 15 to 60 feet. Rudimentary mining activities existed with the use of crude 20-pound stone hammers. Oddly enough, the hammers found on the mainland were grooved, to be held in place by perhaps a thong of sorts, while those discovered in the Isle Royale pits, were nongrooved...perhaps handheld. Naturally this led to speculation that the Isle Royale mines predated those on the mainland. It is indeed evident that these mysterious people came to the Copper Country, worked thousands of these copper pits, over an undetermined number of years, took out vast hoards of copper, then as baffling as it may seem, mysteriously just disappeared, leaving their tools exactly where they lay. By and large, the old Copper Culture People left behind one of the major archaeological mysteries of North America today.

Let's just take a moment or two to take a look at the extent of their early mining operations. Drier and DuTemple relate in their excellent book entitled, "Prehistoric Copper Mining In The Lake Superior Region", that perhaps 500 million pounds to more than 1 billion pounds of copper were prehistorically mined at these Michigan sites. Once again questions surface: Where did the copper go? How many people were required to carry out such a large-scale mining enterprise? How long did it take to mine this staggering tonnage? Do you think they made use of slave labor?

For instance, history points out that the Egyptians worked copper as far back as 9000 years ago. The actual extent of their copper source remains unknown! As previously mentioned, the Phoenicians were known traders of the Bronze Age and they, as well as the Celts and Norsemen, were documented to have traveled to North America with this purpose in mind. Additionally, the Celts were known to be miners in their homeland. Although nineteenth century scholars were perplexed by the Copper Culture mines, it was not until the 1940s that Henriette Mertz raised an incredible question in a book entitled, "Atlantis - Dwelling Place of the Gods." She writes: "This incredible amount of copper has not been accounted for by American archaeologists...the sum total according to archaeological findings here in the states amounts to a mere handful of copper beads and trinkets...float copper. Five hundred thousand tons of pure copper does not disintegrate into thin air...it cannot be sneezed away...it must be somewhere and, to date, it has not been located in the United States."

It is interesting to note that recent carbon dating methods

taken from these early copper pits place many of them in the vicinity of 1000 B.C., which, incidentally, is about the same time as the major Phoenician trading flotillas achieved their pinnacle. Obviously Mrs. Mertz argues towards the copper being removed to foreign shores, especially to various Mediterranean civilizations. During a later time period, as a member of the Epigraphic Society, Henriette Mertz ties in other Michigan prehistory discoveries; namely, the McGruer's Gods and the Newberry Stone, to this same race of ancient culture. It will be further discussed in an upcoming chapter.

Relics of the Copper Age have repeatedly turned up in the spectacular edifices attributed to the class of people known as the Mound-Builders. Awls, knives and trinkets, all made of copper, were designated to have originated as Lake Superior copper. How can we be sure that copper artifacts found in so many areas, even as far distant as Mexico and Central America, all came from these far-reaching Michigan mines? Easy! Until recent years the Keweenaw Peninsula and Isle Royale, known together as the Copper Country, was the only place in the world where copper was found in a pure, unadulterated native state. All other sources of copper were, to say the least, impure; that is, containing sulphur, carbon and chlorine that involved worked copper to first be smelted or refined. Pure native copper proved malleable enough to be pounded or rolled into shape with very little effort. Needless to say, Lake Superior ore has assayed out as high as 100% pure copper.

Furthermore, another peculiarity of this unique Michigan copper was that it very often was additionally laced with silver, giving the finished product a natural hardness and durability. Implements of copper, showing the same characteristics, have been unearthed in the tumuli of the Mound-Builders. In fact, some time back near Crowley's Ridge in Arkansas a stone bust was excavated called "King Crowley", that had a solid copper heart and copper eyeballs with silver pupils. They are believed to have been made from specimens of this rare silver-copper mix so peculiar to our Michigan copper range. Believe it or not...King Crowley's estimated age is 25,000 years old! He now resides in a

Milwaukee, Wisconsin museum. This welding or marriage of silver and copper seems to definitely harden the finished product. For example, knives manufactured from this mix have an exacting cutting edge over those that are made solely from basically copper alone.

Still another classic example of an unusual Lake Superior copper discovery was reported by Robert Haltiner, Curator of the Jesse Besser Museum in Alpena. Robert, teamed with his father Gerald, over the years collected some 20,000 prehistory artifacts from the northeastern part of Michigan. Let me quickly add here that the Jesse Besser Museum contains one of the finest collections of Old Copper Culture artifacts in existence today. Their Primitive Man displays are superb, bar none! One of the more intriguing Haltiner finds occurred when this father-son team unearthed a cache of artifacts containing both worked and unworked copper, side by side. To date this remains unique! It is quite remarkable to note, this relatively good-sized cache of copper was found directly across the street from the museum on the campus of the Alpena Community College.

In the following section, Part II of The Copper Culture Riddle, we will take a look at the mining operations of this primitive mining industry. The huge scope of the task performed by the inscrutable Copper Culture clan becomes prominent and naturally once again, questions quickly surface. True, most are unanswerable! Besides discovering just how the miners extracted the copper, we will also look at existing copper storage pits and how they played a role in the obvious copper trade system that naturally evolved as a spin-off. Read on...

CREDITS:

Robert E. Haltiner, Chief of Resources, Jesse Besser Museum, Alpena, Michigan

Jesse Besser Museum, 491 Johnson St., Alpena, Michigan

ARTWORK:

Francis Moses, St. Ignace, Michigan

The Copper Culture Riddle
PART II
5000-year-old Mines Discovered!

The ancient prehistory copper pits found along the 120-mile Copper Range of the Keweenaw Peninsula represent one of the most unique aspects of prehistoric remains found in Michigan today.

When Samuel Knapp discovered the first copper working pit in 1847, it was strictly by accident. The prospector was in the process of making a small cave suitable for a night's lodging when he inadvertently noted unnatural rubble on the cave's floor. Certainly this evidence of prior occupation sparked his interest. On disposing of the rubbish, Knapp found several stone hammers simply lying about in a helter-skelter fashion. Surprisingly enough he came upon a mass of native copper some 10 feet long by 3 feet wide and 2 feet deep. He almost accurately estimated his find at an unbelievable 6 tons. At this particular point in time, Knapp readily realized other pits and trenches found in close proximity to this particular cavern were also not the norm!

Even more surprising, this magnificent discovery was recorded at the identical site of a modern-day copper mine, quite famous in its own right and known as "The Minnesota." Knapp's inexplicable discovery became known worldwide as simply...the "Mass Copper" find.

History records this glorified copper chunk weighed a staggering sum of 11,588 pounds and had shown evidence of being worked free of the Mother Lode or matrix. This mass was found resting upon billets of black oak supported by sleepers of a similar wood. To all intents and purposes, this cribbing was more or less manufactured in the style of say, a log cabin construction, giving the enormous copper mass great structural support due to the logistics of this unusual concept. Furthermore, it is interesting to note that the Mass Copper probably was originally elevated a few feet at a time from the slope of the main vein by the use of primitive wedges.

Additionally, it is recorded that one of the logs from the cribbing measured 6 inches in diameter, and still clearly bore signs of ax marks that in turn measured approximately 2 inches across. Perhaps a copper adz was used in this ancient endeavor. By means of this cobwork, the early miners raised the copper boulder nearly 5 feet with the use of three stacks of billets and two sections of sleepers. Unbelievable! Marks of fire used to detach this mass from the pit were indeed evident as well. It is further believed the rock was first superheated by flame, then doused with water, which caused the porous material to crack, chip and flake. Finally stone hammers were brought into action. Afterwards, the Mass Copper had been pounded and chipped until every single projection was broken away from the main body of rock. Then by far, adding to this prehistory puzzle, the magnificent copper mass was merely abandoned. To present time, the reason remains unknown!

It is reasonable to assume that at the time of Knapp's discovery, the timber billets or cobwork were actually preserved underwater over a period of say, several centuries. While it remains true that the wood beneath this enormous chunk of copper metal showed evident signs of rot, it was still preserved to some degree, due to the fact the timbers had been immersed in water. The most remarkable feature of this find was that although the wood was obviously dark in color, plus the fact shrinkage occurred during the drying process, the logs still marvelously retained perfect adz cuts.

What gang of primitive workers labored so diligently to raise this ponderous weight some 5 feet plus off the floor of that early mining pit? Better yet, one cannot help but marvel at the standards by which they accomplished this super-incredible feat. Questions just can't help but surface here!

Early field studies additionally coordinated similar pits at the same given location, gave up tons of stone implements...more exacting, 10 wagonloads. A late report indicated an early settler completely lined his deep-water well with hammer stones removed from this prehistory mine site alone. Additionally, other ancient digs showed intense intrusion of primitive man's handiwork, further indicating a major Michigan mystery. Stone hammers, mauls, wood

Rows of pits from which prehistoric workmen have mined copper. Triangle Island, Lake Superior.

A rare find! Examples of worked and unworked copper found in a single cache near Alpena, Michigan.

Known as "King Crowley," the bust has a solid copper heart and copper eyeballs with silver pupils. They are said to have been made from "half-breed," or specimens of native copper mixed with pure silver peculiar to Michigan. The King's age is a reputed 25,000 years, yet his heart is shaped in the relatively modern St. Valentine design.

The Copper Boulder of On-to-nog-on

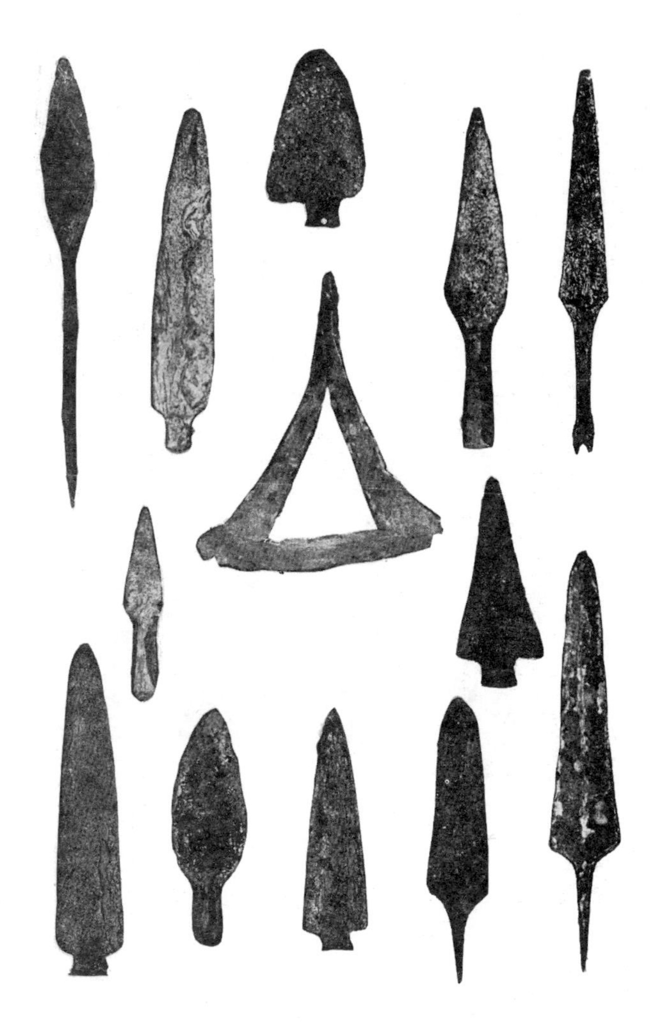

Worked copper from Michigan. Collection of Claude Hamilton, Grand Rapids.

Early Indian Mining.
5000 B.C. - Mining Pit Isle Royale

shovels, bowls or pans, buckets made from animal skins (believed to be walrus hide), and ancient wood ladders, as well as other crude working implements were discovered throughout the copper-bearing areas. Also found nearby was a copper gad as well as a chisel set with a socket.

It was most impressive that with minor exceptions, the wooden tools found were semi-preserved under water, as were the cribbing of the Mass Copper find. However, in the final analysis, many were indeed so ancient, that as soon as the air touched them, they simply disintegrated. In turn, many included attached withes or handles but once again upon going through the drying process, these leather or wood thongs crumbled into mere dust.

While discussing these stone hammers and mauls it should be noted the hammers averaged from 6 to 8 pounds and measured approximately 8 inches in length. On one occasion, a maul was recorded to have weighed a hefty 39½ pounds and subsequently was fitted with two grooves instead of the normal one. Furthermore, it was believed to have held two handles. Similarly, numerous hammers and mauls in the 20-pound range were uncovered. In fact, they seemed in good supply. It seems hard to fathom how one man could wield the larger implements alone. Furthermore, these bygone era working tools were all fashioned from a fine-grained basalt rock, waterworn to an exacting smoothness. As previously indicated, the grooved hammers appeared on the Keweenaw Peninsula while their non-grooved counterparts were prevalent mainly at the Isle Royale sites. On one occasion at the Island's Minong Mine location, over 1000 tons of stone hammers were found, representing a staggering tool count of some 200,000 to 300,000 items!

How many miners were required to carry out this extensive ancient copper mining industry? How many years were these old digs operable? Certainly one must tend to agree, this prehistory paradox is far more than merely mind boggling! The mystery of the relics left behind by a mysterious race of prehistory miners has survived over the centuries.

Sadly to say, early prospectors and subsequent mine workers literally destroyed most of these ancient pits and primitive tools. No one bothered to retain findings for latter-day teams of archaeologists and anthropologists, resulting in a real loss of valuable scientific evidence. Basically tons of excellent historical material from these mines were needlessly scrapped or destroyed. Additionally, most sites were in turn scavenged in the late 1800s by souvenir or artifact hunters, resulting in a loss of clues as to whom these prehistory digs should be attributed. Sad, but true...the ancient pit mines of the Ontonagon copper-bearing region now belongs to the distant past. The great "Minnesota" mine, located at the very site of the perplexing "Mass Copper" find, proved to be during its heyday, one of the richest lodes in the Copper Country complex. It too is now extinct! In retrospect, there are no more masses of virgin copper to be found. 5000-plus years have come and gone! Indeed it is wise for us to look back into the past, but now only the Copper Culture Riddle remains.

Surprisingly over the years, as each new copper mine was founded, ancient remains of prehistory copper workings were evident. Unimaginable as it may appear, these members of a long vanished race had mined every productive copper-bearing vein in the region, from Isle Royale some 50 miles distant in Lake Superior, to the copper ridges of the Keweenaw Peninsula, as well as the Ontonagon Range from the northwestern shores of Lake Gogebic to the village of Ontonagon. Ambiguous as it may seem, even hidden copper veins that did not directly surface as mineral outcroppings were previously tapped by these people from the past. When you stop and consider, every single modern-day copper mine located along the Lake Superior main trap region, had been previously pre-mined, one can but speculate as to this early race's inscrutable method of ore detection.

At this particular time it should further be noted that while our home State of Michigan was "THE" copper mining center of the New World, still other prehistory diggings for various minerals became clearly evident across our entire nation. Still more amazing is the fact that all other mining activities more or less mocked primitive Copper Country mining methods. For you see, mica was mined in North Carolina, serpentine in Pennsylvania, and lead mines were found in Kentucky, just to name a few. However, the most baffling endeavor was located along the Mississippi Valley where prehistoric oil wells were actually discovered. Additional oil operations can be noted in Ohio, Pennsylvania and Canada. These early oil pits averaged 10 to 15 feet across, were symmetrical in shape and roughly 3 feet deep. Many contained crude ladders that in retrospect were similar to those removed from copper pit workings. An apt description of ladders found at both the mine sites and the oil wells, pictures them as merely cut, single tree trunks, that contained stubs of hacked-off limbs, measuring 2 to 3 inches in length, which served as toe holds for the early workers involved in either operation. It is indeed interesting to note that scientists believe the oil was merely skimmed off these prehistory oil pits or shafts, leaving the water behind.

Are you, the reader, gaining an abject respect for these past prehistory miners? It is indeed an incredible saga, to say the least!

Nevertheless, it would prove remiss not to compare the Keweenaw copper mines to similar works found in Munster County, Ireland. Near the Killarney Lakes region, Old World copper mines were prevalent, believed by archeologists to have been worked by the Danes. The interesting comparison here is that similar grooved stone hammers and mauls used to extricate the copper, were also found. Fire was used to hasten the process, also water, in a manner not unlike the ancient miners. Since it is an established fact the Danes made numerous North American visits, both before and after the birth of Christ, is there perhaps a link to this race of people and both mining activities of the two worlds?

Many turn-of-the-century writers graphically described early Copper Country mining performed by the Copper Culture people. These ancient digs were the "talk of the times!" Henry Gillman wrote an excellent accounting in his book entitled, "The Mound-Builders In Michigan," published in 1879. His writings on this matter follow:

> "The pits which have been examined by being cleaned out, invariably had on top a large deposit, mostly of vegetable matter, the accumulations of many a fall of the leaf, beneath which lay a thick bed of charcoal and mud layered with fragments of copper-bearing rock. Besides this, they were partly filled with water. The removal of the contents was

consequently very dirty work. The method of mining pursued by those people was evidently, on turning back the overlying drift, to heat the rock through the aid of fire, then when by the application of water the rock was sufficiently disintegrated, to attack and separate it with their great stone mauls. What a slow, wearisome process! Even with a large force constantly engaged in this labor, it must have taken a long series of years to accomplish the work exhibited; and, if those people withdrew during the lengthy winter season, as had been supposed, it would more than double the period required...with their crude methods it does seem that hundreds of years would be needed for their accomplishment."

The extent of prehistory copper mined has been estimated by today's mining engineers at a staggering 1.5 billion pounds. Furthermore, it is believed that as many as 10,000 miners labored some 1000-plus years, in an estimated 10,000 Copper Range pits. Even at modern-day standards these figures prove astounding, to say the least! A puzzling riddle for subsequent generations to perhaps solve!

Questions pop up right and left again. Who were the common people who performed this almost impossible feat of labor? Once more, was slave labor employed? Certainly one of the most perplexing questions to date is how long the ancient mines were actually in operation.

While still on the subject of mining methods of excavation, another mass of copper was found at the Central Mine site near Eagle Harbor, Keweenaw County. In turn, it weighed a whopping 47 tons. Every single portion of the rock's surface was rendered smooth. It appeared as though it had been hammered by those who were responsible for detaching it from the original vein. Along these same lines, the Mesnard Mine in the Portage Lake region also produced a similar detached copper mass weighing in at close to 18 tons. These two unfinished copper works throw further light upon the manner in which the extraction occurred. Both masses were extensively hammered, chipping the main portion away from the Mother Lode, until just a thin neck or bottle-like piece attached the two sections. Some finds found this umbilical cord structure still firmly in place. Reports also indicate that the ancient miners first removed the rock from around existing copper veins. This matter was accomplished by the building of fires either upon it or around the mass. As previously described, water was introduced at this point, causing a crumbling of the main matter. By use of stone hammers and mauls, the copper was broken up into pieces and removed. When the vein was sufficiently exposed on all sides, a point was determined where the mass was the most vulnerable. Hence they commenced cutting the mass by patient and continued hammering until the vein severed into two separate sections.

Not only did these early prehistory miners seem to perform an unimaginable task but they met still other formidable problems head-on. Transportation at best would have presented insurmountable difficulties. Additionally, the obvious short seasonal working period, the need of an adequate food supply, the rugged topography of the mining range, plus availablity of proper housing, all added up to just some of the logistics that had to have been solved. When you stop and consider the vast enormity of the work force required to keep these mines in operation, many problems naturally surface in this regard.

Another intriguing aspect in the legend of the Copper Culture People was the abject discovery of prehistoric copper storage pits. They indeed are worthy of mention. For you see, many were discovered ranging from the Copper Country itself as far east as Sault Ste. Marie, clear across the upper peninsula. One generally accepted theory was that these storage pits lined the probable over-the-water routes taken by the early copper traders. One particular site was later utilized by the Calumet & Hecla stamping mills during more modern times. It seems as though copper was removed from these ancient storage areas, transported by boat across Torch Lake, and finally a 9-mile portage over hilly terrain to reach Lake Superior. An estimate of some 80 miles were saved by utilizing this age-old shortcut. The Torch Lake storage pit measured over 50 feet across and resembled a huge, scooped-out bowl. Additionally, a burrow some 20 feet deep extended around the pit's perimeter. The storage pit showed signs of repeatedly being both filled and emptied, so actually the pit must have been used quite extensively.

It is also an established fact that the Ontonagon copper miners employed a similar route regarding their respective copper cargoes. For sake of a name, we will call it the Portage Lake entry. At the extreme western end of what is now known as the ship-canal, a second storage pit is attributed to the ancients. Interestingly enough, many artifacts such as stone tools, spears and arrowheads were found in this vicinity. This route would have taken early traders through Portage Lake near present-day Hancock and Houghton. Early maps indicate a stream once existed connecting Portage Lake with Lake Superior, long before the ship-canal was dug. Obviously, if true, the Copper Culture people would have utilized this specific route.

Furthermore, a short distance below Sault Ste. Marie at the eastern end of the peninsula, additional storage pits similarly turned up. Credence afforded speculation that this past race of people transported copper past the "Soo", down the St. Marys River, finally branching out in either direction at the Straits of Mackinaw. Perhaps at this point the copper traders split up...one group may have progressed along the Lake Michigan corridor, while the other one pursued a Lake Huron route. Examination of the Sault pit sites offers further proof that they were basically used for copper storage, as it is a known fact that only sandstone is prevalent in this immediate area. A reasonable assumption would be that these Sault Ste. Marie storage pits were located at the headwaters of the Copper Culture trading network, which eventually wove its way along just about every main river and tributary in North America. When we consider the extent of this vast trading network, the sheer wonder of the copper mines themselves, plus the hoards of people needed to carry out this marvelous endeavor over an extended period of years...well the "Copper Country Riddle" remains one of the world's enigmas, even today!

Additionally, these ancient people left no dead, no household goods, no pottery, no written records or nearby petroglyphs...no apparent cultural evidence was discovered to provide clues to this timeworn puzzle. All that remains after thousands of years have come and gone, are simply stone implements and quiet copper pits.

Where, in all retrospect, did the bulk of prehistoric copper tonnage disappear? Why indeed were the ancient workings abandoned? Remember...workers just seemed to walk right off their jobs! Archaeologists are quick to agree on at least one point, that being that the Copper Culture people had in all truth intended to return to work the following day. Odd the crude tools lay in disarray as century after century quietly passed, until once again discovered by early explorers during the 1600s.

Three major unanswerable questions close this chapter on the secret of the ancient copper mines. Where did the workers live? Where did the copper as well as the miners themselves go? Why did they more or less simply just walk off the job? Perhaps this is the real crux of the mystery!

It should be brought to your attention that you can still view an example of this ancient pit mining at the Fort Wilkins State Park located at the tip of the Keweenaw Peninsula.

Part III of the Copper Culture Riddle will examine the only positive remains of prehistory habitation discovered on Isle Royale. Some experts regard this site as a prehistory cellar village, still others have yet more astouding theories. To say the least, the following data is especially intriguing...

CREDITS:

Prehistoric Copper Mining In The Lake Superior Region
Drier and DuTemple
Published privately, Calumet, Michigan 1961

Fluted celt, length 8 inches. Bay County. Fluting on one side only.

A mass of copper weighing 6,000 pounds, found on the Keweenaw Peninsula (at the site of the modern day "Minnesota Mine"), on which the work of the ancient is plainly to be seen.

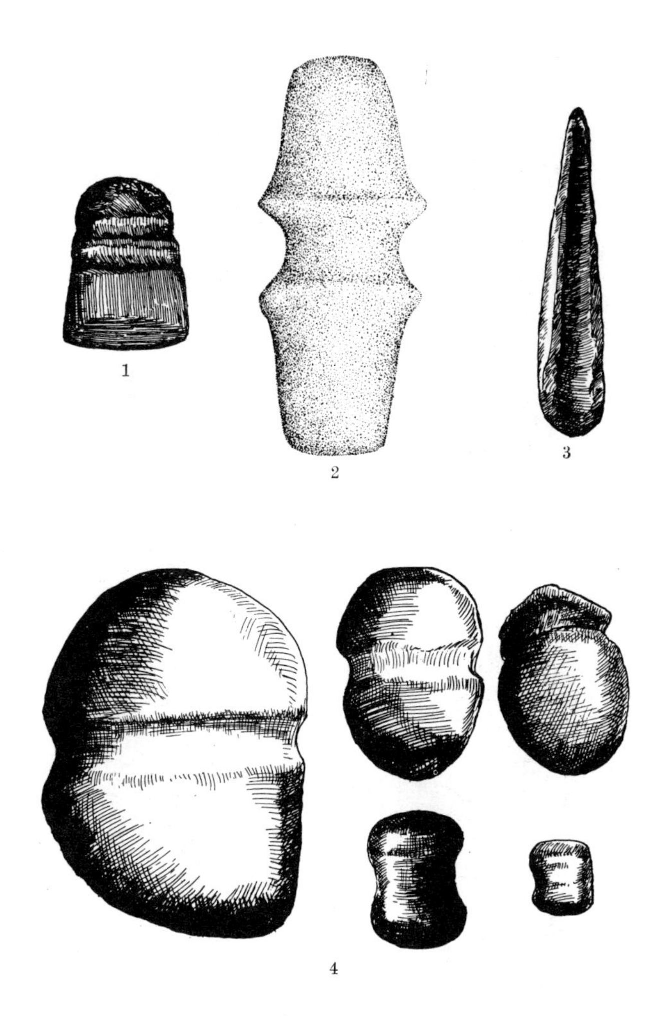

Fig. 1., Double grooved adze, length 2¼ inches. Washtenaw County. Fig.2., Double bitted axe about 8 inches long. Lenawee County. From Moorehead, Stone Age in North America. Fig.3., Gouge, hard stone, length 11 inches. Washtenaw County. Fig. 4., Mauls and hammers, weight varying from 12 pounds to 13 ounces. Largest from Lake Superior copper mines.

Fig. 1., Double grooved maul, length 6¼ inches. Branch County. Fig. 2., Double grooved axe, length 4½ inches. Calhoun County. Fig. 3., Axe with wide slanting groove, length 8 inches. Mackinaw County. Fig. 4., Fluted axe, length 10 inches. Charlevoix County.

The Copper Culture Riddle!
PART III
Prehistory Ruins - Isle Royale

From our 20th century perspective, theories presented by early writers of the late 1800s have drastically changed course. Conjecture may be giving ground to scientific proof. But before we examine modern thinking of the subject preconceived to be an early Isle Royale village site of the ancients, let's first examine this unusual discovery through past records. It is reasonable to assume approximately 95% of 19th century historians deemed the Copper Culture people summer residents only. Their perspective of the facts stemmed strongly from a lack of evidence of prior occupation, for certainly in retrospect no camp sites or skeletal remains ever surfaced. Strong research data from that former era adequately backed this line of conjecture.

Additional observations made this Copper Country riddle still more perplexing, as conclusions directly indicated the early prehistory copper miners were one in the same with the ancient race of Mound-Builders. Further turn-of-the-century accepted theories more or less speculated the prehistoric miners arrived at Isle Royale each spring by canoe from geographical regions to the south, commenced to labor at the mines throughout the summer months, and finally departing late fall before the harsh northern winter set in. Archaeologists point to possible stopovers for rest and supplies at both Beaver and Summer islands located in Lake Michigan. The recent discovery of a "ring of stones" located on Beaver Island adds fuel for thought in this regard.

Nevertheless, disregarding possible origins of these enigmatic people, they still had to live somewhere at least during the mine-producing months. Why then have temporary camp sites at least, never been located? Were these itinerant villages perhaps looted by a later race of people who in turn removed anything and everything they deemed of value, leaving behind just the cumbersome stone hammers, mauls and other mining equipment? Until the advent of more positive proof this fascinating historical puzzle simply leaves archaeologists, scientists and historians scratching their collective heads, each theorizing as to what might have been. Once again questions remain unanswered!

Despite the common agreement between writers of the time, one man dared to venture a conflicting theory: albeit, a permanent prehistory village had to exist on Isle Royale...perhaps out of the close proximity of the mines themselves. The man was Henry Gillman and believe it or not he hit pay dirt on an Island visit in the year 1879. Let's take a glimpse back in time and let Mr. Gillman describe his magnificent discovery in his own words taken from his book of that period, entitled, "The Mound-Builders Of Michigan!"

> "At an indentation of the coast on the southside of Isle Royale, where a stream about 40-feet in width had cut a channel through the rocks and formed quite a fall of water, was discovered what is taken to be the site of a town or the habitation of these ancient people. It occupies an elevated slope, giving an extensive view of Lake Superior and overlooking the intervening point of land which makes the little bay an excellent harbor. The remains consist of a series of shallow excavations, generally about 4-feet in depth, and occupying the successive terraces of the slope. Some of these pits are circular, others are quadrangular, and they vary from 10-feet to 30-feet in diameter. Indications suggest that timber or bark was used in their construction, the soil being thrown up around them to a sufficient height. But time did not permit a satisfactory examination of this interesting locality, which with other points on the island, it is hoped will afford, on a thorough examination, many valuable facts connected with the life of this remarkable people. They doubtless shipped the copper, the object of toil to the south shore of Lake Superior; the wonderful metal finding its way thence to other parts of the country, as is testified by the articles of copper found in the burial places of the mound-builders. This point, therefore,

was well selected as a town site. The good landing, the admirable harbor, the abundant stream and fall of water, the sheltered and yet commanding hillside, which enabled them to watch the return and departure of their copper-laden flotillas, were all strong recommendations even to those semi-savage inhabitants."

When Gillman wrote this early chronicle regarding the finding of a prehistoric village in close relationship to the copper pits of Isle Royale, it eventually caught the fancy of William F. Ferguson. The articles by Gillman so intrigued this man that even though some 50 years had passed since its writing, Ferguson felt compelled to rediscover this Copper Culture village for additional study and investigation. Actually he had few hard facts to go by. What he did know amounted to the combination of a waterfall, a good harbor and a bisecting stream. These three objects nevertheless proved to be a starting point acting as compass points to begin his quest for the lost village of Michigan's Isle Royale. One further clue was gleaned from the old articles, mainly the site was supposedly situated at the south side of the island. Armed with just this sketchy information, William Ferguson made two exploratory trips to the island in 1920 and 1921.

Actually the first journey started out pretty exciting for almost immediately Ferguson found a harbor, a stream and a waterfall. Ironically, however, the site proved unfruitful, causing the historian to return to the mainland with abject disappointment. All things considered, his next island visit proved far more successful. At this particular time Ferguson located still another waterfall on a small river recorded on old maps as the Sibley, on others as the Little Siskiwit. Here located on both banks of the stream, lying hidden from view under centuries of forest litter, was one of the rectangular pit cellars described by Gillman's accounting. You must agree here...one can't help but dramatically feel Ferguson's excitement at this point!

These ruins of an ancient civilization were aptly depicted as presumably hundreds of square or oblong pits, lined with stone, following along the natural ridge line of the embarkment. These holes or depressions oddly enough seemed to be aligned in a pattern to some degree. Additionally, the pits were not only faced with medium-sized boulders, but in turn were rimmed or banked with dirt possibly removed when the holes were originally excavated. It seemed conclusive the earthworked rims were designed to siphon off any accumulation of water, thus keeping the pits themselves in a dry condition. At this point Ferguson speculated on the possibility that this Isle Royale village site was perhaps quite comparable to ruins found in northern Europe.

William Ferguson's findings reported the pits ranged in size from 25-feet square to the largest rectangular one, measuring a more spacious 30 feet by 60 feet around its perimeter. It was quite obvious that many of the remaining excavations were nothing more than small holes or ground depressions. He also noted these pit structures were easily distinguished from the mining digs for they were excavated, not in rock as were the mines, but instead were dug from soft earth and manually lined with a single layer of rocks. Additionally, they were rectangular instead of round. In summation, the house pits were more or less tapered from top to bottom.

It is reasonable to assume the ancients chose this particular site because it not only offered a safe harbor, but in retrospect the rushing turbulence of the waterfalls provided an adequate water supply should some of the village inhabitants occupy the site during the winter.

An even more surprising observation turned up during Mr. Ferguson's last trip to the island. He was impressed to say the least, that at night his compass lined up with the true meridian of the North Star from the north and south sides of all the pits. Now understand this, observatory alignments are quite common in the handiwork of previous past races both in this country as well as the Old World. For nearly a century archaeologists puzzled over the origin of unexplained stone ruins found in the northeast section of the United States. Finally, in 1975, Celtic inscriptions were discovered on rock "cellars" presumed prehistory village sites in New England. Here once again it is believed that some 3000 years ago Celtic sailors crossed the Atlantic Ocean from Spain, establishing colonies or settlements in our eastern states. It is interesting to note that these inscriptions were often discovered in Phoenician, Basque and Celtic script. Some of these stone settlements similarly occurred in Pennsylvania and West Virginia as well as Massachusetts and Ohio. Many date back to the time of Julius Caesar for some excavations have turned up Latin numerals, calendar systems and astronomical steles dating from that time span. It is relative that many of these ancient stone pit buildings have been identified as temples or observatories.

The ancient prehistory ruins William Ferguson regarded as an early town site can be pinpointed on a present day plat of Isle Royale. Simply locate Sec 24 and Sec 23 of Township 64N, Range 37W. The village actually straddles the Little Siskiwit or Sibley River directly at a point dominated by a series of trap waterfalls. Actually in all essence, the site lies directly on the section line. At one point along the ridge, an earthworks of sorts was aptly described as perhaps a fortification. However, modern-day technology has redefined this outcropping as natural in context, resulting from an earlier prehistoric shoreline.

For the most part, Ferguson's second trip to Isle Royale in 1922 proved successful. Through his field studies he excavated several of the previously mentioned pit areas. Records indicate approximately 18 inches of thick vegetation and forest debris was removed from many of the pits. At one particular point, a dense mat of roots and decayed matter resembling a mattress in size was lifted from one of the pits. This slow process of rubble removal had to penetrate a depth of 5 feet. At this depth an unusual fire platform retaining traces of fire plus the remains of many small charred sticks was unearthed.

As a matter of course, Ferguson's crew excavated this particular pit down to a substantial 2 feet lower than the bottom of the exposed fire pit. He subsequently found the pit size at its lower extremity measured 15 feet east and west, 10 feet north and south. The walls were obviously more inclined or sloping at the pit's base, making it somewhat narrower than the top. Stones proved to be but one rock thick throughout the structure, with all the corners somewhat ill-defined.

Perhaps the most unique circumstance here was the discovery of the fire pits themselves. These edifices were raised some 2 feet from the pit floor and were manufactured from small boulders piled loosely together, forming a rectangle of about 3 feet by 4 feet. Classic examples were arranged diagonally upon a line from northeast to southeast corner of the units. Strangely enough there was little evidence of fire upon the cap stones, even though remains of charred limbs and charcoal were indeed evident among the rock piles. Some of the badly decayed sticks were analyzed and found to be spruce.

Certainly it appears once again the fire pits were but pieces of an unsolvable jigsaw puzzle. What actually was the real purpose of the fire pits? Were they simply used for creature comfort during the winter months, or do you think they were ceremonial in nature? Here once again questions need to be addressed!

Furthermore, William Ferguson made a thorough assessment of the fire pits in several different structures. His conclusion pointed out that all fires were built on the pit's floor, oddly enough up against the very sides of the rock platform, rather than utilizing the top of the platform. Strange to say, there was an indication of large fires set with less appearance of long usage burning. In other words, facts indicate huge bonfires occurred rather than small warming hearths and cooking fires. Surely you must find this information rather intriguing.

Still the strangest discovery of all, was that even the smallest of the pits also contained similar fire pits. Perhaps they were lit as signal fires or beacons facilitating night travel to and from Isle Royale. Prehistory data often indicates large unexplained fires burned atop secluded mountain tops as either ceremonials or guideposts, in both the New World and the Old World.

Now that we have examined Mr. Ferguson's observations on his marvelous discovery of the early 1920s, let's bring this remarkable find a bit more up to date. New interesting information has recently come to light supplied through investigations done by Greg Bambenek and Glenn Langhorst of Duluth, Minnesota. Together this pair have done considerable field work in Wisconsin, northern Michigan, and Canada on stone works of a similar nature. Glenn Langhorst likens the Isle Royale pit site discovery to a similar find in Canada, termed the "Puckasaw Pits." He believes pits of this sort were used by ancient races to observe the summer solstice and similar movements of heavenly bodies...sort of acting in the capacity of a rough calendar. It has further been ascertained similar pit arrangements have now been located at several other Lake Superior sites. Perhaps these findings also indicate a civilization with a sophisticated knowledge of astronomy who needed to keep track of time...to support their large-scale mining operations and religious beliefs.

Principally while on Isle Royale, Glenn and Greg experimented to some degree, checking the solar alignments of the pits by building fires in all of the dug-out holes. This practice enabled the two men to easily note the pits were definitely used as an observatory for solar studies. These modern-day explorer-anthropologists have visited several astronomical sites, including stone cairns and "rings of stone", from the north shore of Lake Superior near Thunder Bay, Canada as well as to points in Wisconsin and northern Michigan. Their cairn (stone pile) data will be further examined in a chapter addressing Michigan's Black River cairns and stone walls. They are one of our State's most recent prehistory discoveries.

As this publication progresses, perhaps you, the reader, will be startled and yet amazed at the extent and scope of the territory utilized by this ancient race, called the Copper Culture people. Signs of their visits crop up all over Michigan and the surrounding states.

While still briefly discussing rock circles, stone cairns, and cellar observatory pits, it should be mentioned here that a set of three separate stone cairns or organized rock piles have been reported along the Ontonagon River in close proximity to early copper mining sites. Newspaper accounts reveal a University of Wisconsin professor, James Scherz does not believe these stones were placed randomly by chance or natural means. Scherz further theorizes the rock cairns acted as calendars and were primarily constructed by the race of people involved in the copper industry...indicating possible routes between the Lake Superior mines and the Mississippi River via both the Ontonagon and Wisconsin River systems.

Professor Scherz teaches surveying at the University of Wisconsin. He fully believes his previous findings warrant further study. Additionally, Scherz speculates the possibility of large trade canoes being used from mine sites near the Ontonagon River, then traveling down the river as far as the first falls. From this point on, James Scherz speaks of the probability of smaller canoes being utilized via portages, eventually joining other water routes southward.

Over a period of years, early surveyors' notes and turn-of-the century writers both offered positive evidence that temple mounds were also in this same general Ontonagon copper-bearing region. These architectural wonders of prehistory origin also seem to fit in with the ancient aligned rock sites. These tumuli or mounds are located along the southwestern fringe of the copper range. Later in this book, a chapter titled "Who Were The Mound-Builders?", will once again take up the topic of these curious edifices, including two known as the "Ontonagon Pyramids." Perhaps future investigations will scientifically bring forth new and startling information offering a correlation between prehistory sites throughout the State of Michigan.

In more ways than one, the Old Copper Culture people riddle remains the most problematic of the Michigan prehistory mysteries. It is this author's supposition that all other ancient finds in our State tie in directly or indirectly with this unique copper industry phenomena. Try to picture past remnants of a vast and glorious civilization that depended solely on their astronomical prowess to allow sufficient travel time before a severe winter arrived that might possibly lock them into an inhospitable terrain. An entire race of people from an ancient culture that were not only accomplished miners, but in turn brilliant engineers, expert raw material transporters and traders. Remember also, all these mentioned activities, took place so far back in history that no tradition of its origin or its people remains. Surely you must agree, their influence bears out predominant in research carried out by their trading networks, forming an enigma that still flourishes today. But...it does seem we are getting closer to really substantial answers with each new exciting prehistory discovery.

After reviewing the facts presented here, what do you think? Was the Isle Royale ruin site an ancient Copper Culture village or was it perhaps a unique 5000-year-old solstice observatory? As existing evidence indicates...my advice to you would be...remain skeptical, but keep an open mind...trust the future will shed new light on this Old Copper Culture Riddle!

CREDITS:
Charles W. Bailey, Duluth, Minnesota
Greg Bambenek, Duluth, Minnesota
Glenn Langhorst, Duluth, Minnesota

SUGGESTED FURTHER READING
The Copper Culture Riddle

AMERICA B.C.
Fell, Barry
Quadrangle Books, New York, NY, 1976
ATLANTIS — DWELLING PLACE OF THE GODS
Mertz, Henriette
Published privately, Chicago
BOOM COPPER
Murdoch, Angus
Published privately, Calumet
BRONZE AGE AMERICA
Fell, Barry
Little, Brown & Co., Boston-Toronto, 1982
COPPER COUNTRY — GOD'S COUNTRY
Avery, Thomas
Avery Color Studios, AuTrain, MI 1973-77
MOUND BUILDERS OF MICHIGAN
Gillman, Henry
Michigan Pioneer Collection, Vol. 3, 1879-80
MYSTERIES OF MICHIGAN'S LONG-AGO PEOPLE
Haltiner, Gerald
Pamphlet, publ. privately

PREHISTORIC COPPER MINING IN THE LAKE SUPERIOR REGION
Drier and DuTemple
Published privately, Calumet, MI 1961-65
RIDDLE OF THE COPPER CULTURE PEOPLE
Haltiner, Robert
Published in the Weathervane, Spring, 1983
THE SEARCH FOR LOST AMERICA
Trento, Salvatore, Michael
Contemporary Books, Inc., Chicago, 1978

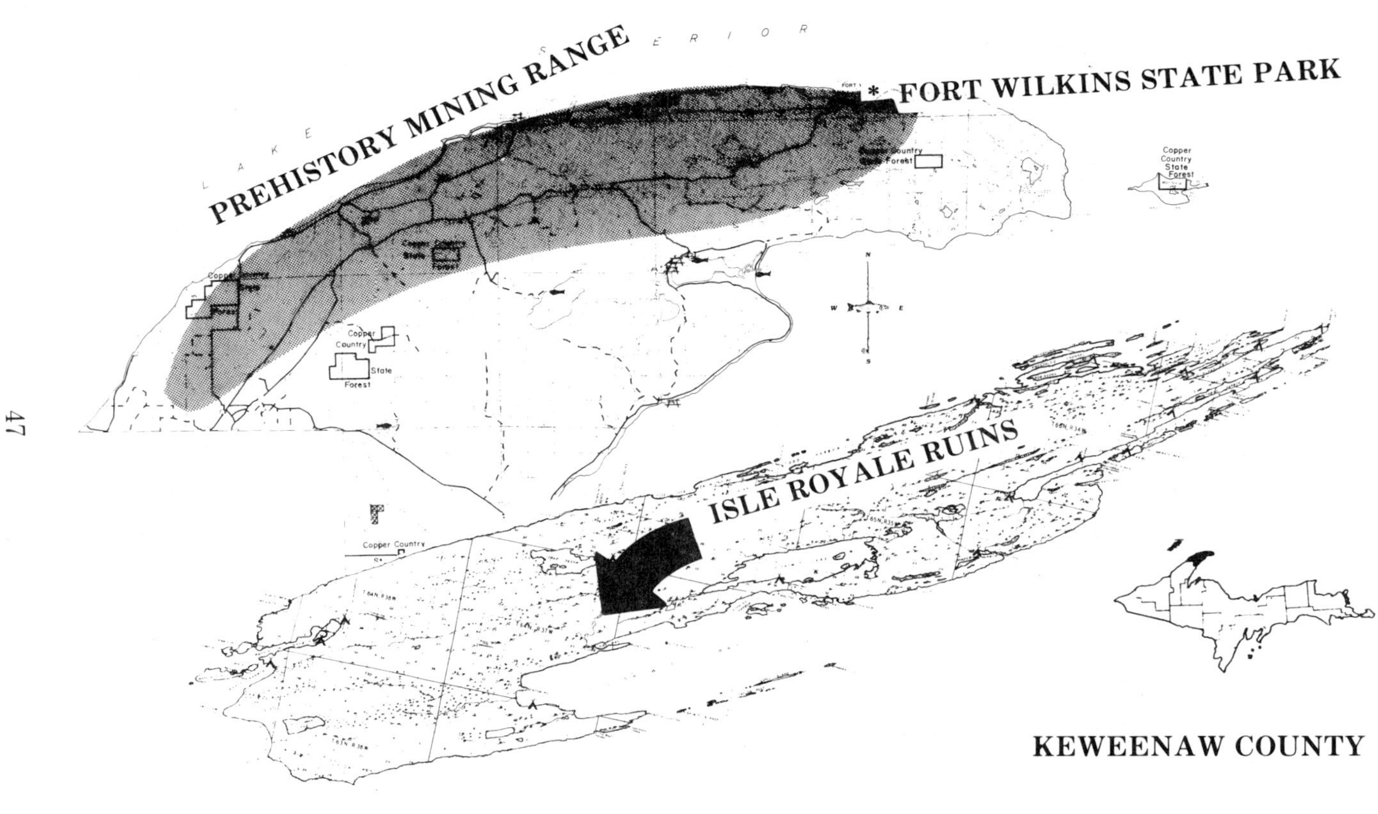
PREHISTORY MINING RANGE
* FORT WILKINS STATE PARK
ISLE ROYALE RUINS
KEWEENAW COUNTY
L A K E S U P E R I O R
Copper Country State Forest
Copper Country State Forest
Copper Country

A Puzzling Prehistory Disc Factory!

Imagine if you can.....Time: A.D. 1300.....Place: A disc manufacturing factory on the shores of Lake Huron near Alpena. Picture natives sitting cross-legged on the soft, sandy ground of this open-air, sun-warmed factory producing engraved discs in various stages of development: chipping, pounding, shaping, polishing pieces of rough shale supplied from a local source into round, smooth, expertly drilled, pictorial engraved amulets. An industrious scene? Yes, but back to reality......

Almost immediately questions surface. Why were over two hundred engraved shale discs found in just one particular northeastern section of lower Michigan? Were they actually manufactured at the site of the discovery? If historic dates have been scientifically assigned to these pictorial artifacts in a range from A.D. 1250 to A.D. 1400, what individual purpose did they fill? Additionally who were the prehistoric natives employed at this unique disc factory? Let's attempt to address some of these perplexing questions.

Allow me first to point out that material supplied for this rare and unusual discovery comes basically from Robert E. Haltiner, Chief of Resources, Jesse Besser Museum located in Alpena. Robert and his father Gerald, now deceased, were responsible for the disc discovery. Over a period of a lifetime this father-son team of amateur archaeological standing, have collected some 20,000 artifacts of prehistory origin from the Great Lakes area. Since Gerald's death, the entire Haltiner collection has been turned over to the museum where presently it is in the stage of being cataloged, although much is already on exhibit. Jesse Besser Museum offers one of the finest "primitive man" displays in the Nation.

Robert Haltiner was kind enough to grant an interview and you will find his quotes and comments throughout this chapter.

Based on current information the disc cache sites, and there were four of them, were located in the vicinity of the Thunder Bay River in Alpena County near the Lake Huron shoreline. A broader perspective mapwise would place the sites in an area between North Point at the far northerly edge of Thunder Bay to the Bay's southern extremity, namely South Point. Incidentally,.this latter section figures prominently in other important prehistory discoveries, such as the Black River stone cairns and walls, described in a future chapter.

Since the disc find took place within the limits of Thunder Bay, let's first take into account the particular attributes of this unique territory. To set the stage for this endeavor one must understand that Thunder Bay, as its name so indicates, was held in deep dread by early man. Folklore passed down from generation to generation more or less declared Thunder Bay a dangerous, fearful place...a harbor of violent unexpected storms, frighteningly overrun by evil spirits. In all retrospect, thunder and lightning were frequently accepted phenomena. Indian legends associate the Thunderbird symbol, found engraved on many of the Alpena discs, with thunder and lightning. According to popular belief the Thunderbird or "Ah-ne-mi-ke" of Algonquian mythology was an absolute, imposing, all-powerful figure. The impressive Thunderbird inhabited the space far above the western sky and here, high in the heavens, he is said to have not only produced the booming thunderclaps but manufactured lightning bolts as well. Albeit the "thunders" were indeed frightening, but legend has it that it was the "fire-balls" that this bird "Ah-ne-mi-ke" had the power to throw at will, that made up the sum and substance of this fable. Needless to say, conjecture was drawn making the Thunderbird a most powerful, awesome, image-figure in the life of primitive man.

What made the Thunderbird so all powerful, you ask? Well for starters, they were believed to be archenemies of the evil, ever-lurking water creatures that preyed on lake travelers. The main myth involved "Me-she-pe-shiw," the water tiger. Legend relates that the Thunderbird was capable of possessing physical powers to release huge balls of fire (actually lightning bolts) at "Me-she-pe-shiw" to disturb this malevolent beast beneath the waters of the Great Lakes. As early as 1636, Catholic priests reported in the *Jesuit Relations* that this uncanny feline was a sea tiger, while Algonquian mythology terms this crafty animal as a puma or mountain lion. In turn, both sources positively agree the animal lives under the seas and brings forth great tempests by merely switching its long, sinewy tail.

All things considered, it certainly is understandable that primitve inhabitants of this particular Michigan shoreline proceeded with great care and caution. Generally speaking, it was common practice for people traveling by canoe to first appease the "Manitou" with offered gifts. In an area just south of North Point, approximately 40 paces inland, a small worship place was located so voyagers could make offerings before setting out on Lake Huron. An ancient culture had provided a shrine of sorts in this obscure clearing, consisting merely of a cluster of stones plus several large boulders...identified by the Indians as the "Manitou." Custom dictated a gift, perhaps tobacco or other small personal offering. A word of warning...those not cautious enough...could pay with their lives! So be the custom!

Historical evidence indicates numerous sacred, worship spots were prevalent along the shores and river systems of the Great Lakes territory. Many of them will be discussed further in a chapter on "image stones."

Now back to the discovery of the perplexing discs. Robert Haltiner states his father began collecting archaeological artifacts from northeastern Michigan as early as 1915. In turn the elder Haltiner felt the Thunder Bay area offered much of interest regarding evidence of prior occupation of primitive man. Most of his collection resulted from simple surface gathering rather than excavation. The Alpena area provided prime pickings. By the 1940s Robert accompanied his father in these explorations. Together the Haltiner team identified scores of sites and our cultural heritage prospers because of their dedication.

What made these inscribed discs special and important? First, they were incised with symbols that appear in the rock art of the Canadian Shield, more specifically near Toronto...Peterborough, Ontario, Canada. On May 12, 1954 three geologists: Craig, Phipps and Davis, discovered a rare and immense petroglyph (rock carving) described as sacred artwork of the Algonquians. How fortunate indeed, the Canadian Government had the foresight to preserve this major find as an enclosed park for present and future generations. Many of the same symbols that appear on the Alpena discs are in turn repeated on their petroglyph counterparts. Furthermore, I might add at this time, that the earliest section of the petroglyphs dates back to seventeen centuries before the time of Christ. Scientific data released by Barry Fell, author of *Bronze Age America*, describes a visit to this Peterborough site by a Nordic King named Woden-lithi. It is believed his voyage took him across the Atlantic and up the St. Lawrence River, where he established a trading post as well as a religious center and an astronomical observatory. Some of his beliefs were inscribed in stone recording his visit, his purpose being to trade goods for copper ingots originating, as experts believe, from Michigan's Copper Country and Isle Royale. Fell clearly indicates this was not the first known visit of Europeans to the Americas.

Robert Haltiner indicated the discs have been assigned a name "Naub-cow-zo-win" which in the Ojibwa-Ottawa language means a charm of personal significance. He also stated their very restricted archaeological occurrence suggests that their manufacture and use was local, short-lived and associated with a specific sacred context. Actually Haltiner confirmed the possibility that they represent the first appearance of several Algonquian symbols in firm prehistoric context.

Experts entered the picture in 1969 and 1980. First, Professor Charles Cleland, an Anthropologist from Michigan State, studied the Haltiner engraved disc collection and expressed a close resemblance to the "Mide'wi-win-- birch bark scrolls of that ancient American Indian society. Cleland further stated the occurrence of these unusual discs and their respective symbols were unrecorded in other archaeological context.

Richard Clute, an anthropology professor at Alpena Community College, joined forces with Haltiner and Cleland. They co-authored an article in the *Midcontinental Journal of Archaeology*, Volume 9, Number 2, 1984 titled "NAUB-COW-

ZO-WIN Discs From Northern Michigan."

It is interesting to note that although hundreds of archaeological sites have been listed in the northern lower peninsula, only four specific areas have turned up engraved shale discs...all in the Thunder Bay section of northeastern Michigan. In the final analysis, the first Haltiner site proved the most productive. Here is where the discs obviously were manufactured. By and large the other three sites were relatively nearby, but strangely enough produced few discs.

Haltiner described the location of these sites. The first and foremost was called the Hampsher site, since it was the Hampsher family that first took note of articles of antiquity outcropping in their garden area. Located in 1950, worked quite extensively by the Haltiner team in 1971, then scientific excavations were performed in 1982 by Professor Cleland. These archaeological digs additionally produced pottery, chert points, a scraper, celts and numerous shale discs. Haltiner also drew my attention that at this time many odd jar-shaped pits were additionally discovered.

Robert Haltiner stated that the conclusion drawn regarding the Hampsher site was that during a period say between A.D. 1250 and A.D. 1400, shale discs were manufactured at this spot, believed to have once been a small village. Discs were found in all stages of development and were quite unusually surface collected. He also pointed out that this site was indeed the most productive of the four.

Subsequently, the respective names of the other disc sites were termed the Anderson site, the Van Lare Hall site and the Hooley Creek site. The Anderson site was discovered when a local resident excavated a basement while building a house. Haltiner reports this to be a small camping area since but 9 discs were recovered here.

Likewise, just 4 shale discs were located at the Van Lare Hall occupation site. Incidentally, this site is located directly across from the Jesse Besser Museum on the campus of Alpena Community College. Some relics of archaeological context may have been lost here due to the fact that construction proceses actually leveled off parts of this area.

Ironically, still a third disc site was more or less damaged, this time by sand mining. The Hooley Creek site itself, a mile north of the mouth of the Thunder Bay area, was drastically disturbed by both mining and limestone quarrying production. Nevertheless, Haltiner informs us that 16 engraved discs, chert debtage and pottery sherds were initially surface collected here before the site was literally destroyed.

Talking further with Robert Haltiner, he estimates the shale used for the manufacture of the discs most likely originated from DeVonian Age limestone probably taken from what is now called the Dock Street strata. This shale outcropping is located perhaps one mile south of the Anderson site along the Lake Huron shore. Note among other things that the excavated discs ranged in shale colors of black, grey and brown. Furthermore, 11 taken from the Hooley Creek area were all grey while those from the Anderson site were brown.

Haltiner strongly feels the manufacturing process occurred at the original Hampsher site, for he called my attention to the fact that here the artifacts were found in several stages of development. Additionally, the discs were believed to have first been roughed out, forming a more or less circular shape. Chipping methods most likely were employed here. As the rough object began to take shape then a form of sanding was employed to make the prospective amulet smooth. Indeed, it is unusual that just some of these discs were incised by the use of small chert drills to produce a smooth hole for possible suspension by a thong of sorts. Haltiner commented that the final stage of manufacture undoubtedly was the engraving of the design or symbol on one or both sides of the disc. Here he speculates a sharp instrument was employed. You must agree...due to the many stages involved in the production process, this venture was a factory of sorts...an engraved disc factory.

As a matter of course, the symbols on the "Naub-cow-zo-win" discs were signs of great importance to the culture of primitive man. All told, 7 different designs were evident as recognizable Algonquian mythology. We have already previously described the mythical moutain lion or sea tiger, "Me-she-pe-shiw" who so cunningly lurked beneath the turbulent seas of all the five Great Lakes. It is interesting to note that the discs depict the cat with a long tail, horns on its head and clawed feet. Once again, the chapter on "Image Stones" is given as reference, for it describes live sacrifices of dogs to appease the cat's appetite. Often times the beast is depicted with plates down the back affording it a dragonlike appearance. Here once again Haltiner states similar drawings appear in the "Mide'wi-win" birch bark scrolls. He also remarked that on several of the engraved discs the mountain lion is headless, this certainly being out of context to the rock art of the Canadian Shield. One can't help but wonder why!

In addition to the mystic cat we have also talked about the Thunderbird effigy. One must understand primitive man often prescribed "anthropomorphism", ascribing human characteristics to non-human things. It was quite common to apply human traits to the animal world. Other discs contained the following symbols: "Ne-gig" the otter, "Moz" the moose, "Amik" the beaver and a tree and star form.

For reasons unbeknown, holes were never drilled through the discs with pictures of the undersea mountain lion or the Thunderbird. Haltiner was very firm on this point! Perhaps these two signs were thought so powerful, that in turn they were primarily carried in a medicine bag along with the owner's most cherished personal possessions. His magic! His "good luck" charm!

Here again, Haltiner notes the discs once again usually depicted the Thunderbirds headless. Another classic example was the headless moose; however, there was no mistaking his obvious body minus the head. Bodies sans heads...an enigma!

Robert Haltiner further spoke of the animal signs, remarking the long-tailed water lion appeared 16 times, the otter on five, our headless moose but once, while the Thunderbird is represented 6 times, the beaver once. Furthermore, the drawing of the Medicine Tree occurs a whopping 19 times and the star is duplicated just 4 times.

Many of the above listed disc symbols were classed as water symbols, some feature in the story of creation. Legends offer much of interest regarding ancient cultures, in fact often times they appear to parallel other civilizations.

Let's take a moment to discuss the size of the engraved discs.

Surprisingly they are relatively small, say on an average just 25mm and perhaps a bit less than 3mm thick. As at any modern-day factory site, discs were found in varying stages of manufacture. Many were broken. Many simply unfinished. Many had drilled holes, others did not. As previously pointed out, the Thunderbird figure and the water cat symbol contained no drilled hole. Haltiner also believes the discs most likely were drilled after they were fully shaped. It seems strange but discs were found drilled both with and without designs. Why? Perhaps it was a late step in the manufacturing process. We were informed that 53 discs and disc fragments held some type of decorative inscription.

Though extremely small in size, the discs present one "big" mystery! In summation, we know first, the 4 sites mentioned are the only ones where this type of amulet has been found anywhere in Michigan or for that fact, North America. However, I should mention at this point two similar inscribed discs were reported to have been discovered on the Canadian Manitoulin Islands some years back, but research failed to turn up positive verification. Second, the "Naub-cow-zo-win" discs are unique symbols of Algonquian iconography dating back in history approximately 700 years past. Supernatural powers evidently were assigned the water cats and Thunderbirds, causing them to be carried in a medicine bag rather than worn amulet style. It is believed to be the reason for these two discs appearing minus drilled holes. Lastly, Haltiner was quick to point out that perhaps the discs are the first documentation of specific Algonquian symbols. They may provide a source of interpretation of other inexplicable symbols found elsewhere.

True, we may never learn the actual extent and purpose of the prehistory Alpena disc factory, but the discs are a relative part of our Michigan prehistory past. In the long run these Thunder Bay "Naub-cow-zo-win" discs will remain an unsolvable mystery of early man's cultural heritage...a mirror of a long, bygone, mythological era!

CREDITS:
Robert E. Haltiner, Chief of Resources, Jesses Besser Museum, 491 Johnson Street, Alpena, MI 49707

PHOTO CREDITS:
Robert E. Haltiner, Chief of Resources, jesse Besser Robert E. Haltiner, Chief of Resources, Jesse Besser Museum
Photo reproduction work, Dennis Morrison, Greenbush, Michigan

SUGGESTED FURTHER READING

"NAUB-COW-ZO-WIN DISCS FROM NORTHERN MICHIGAN", Midcontinental Journal of Archaeology, Volume 9, No. 2, 1984. Cleland, Clute and Haltiner.

Engraved discs.

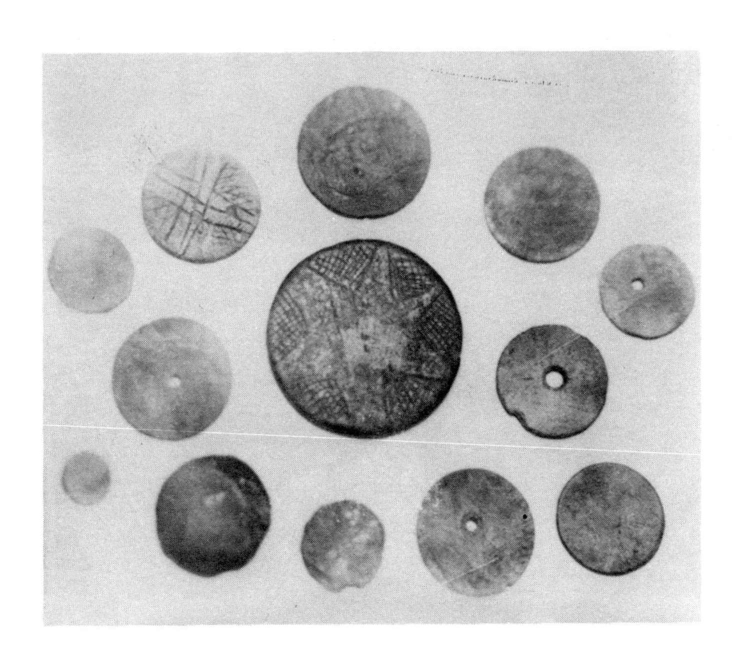

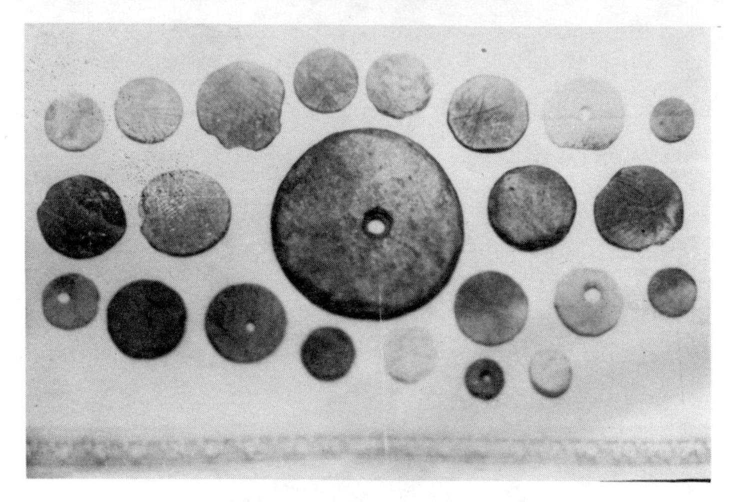

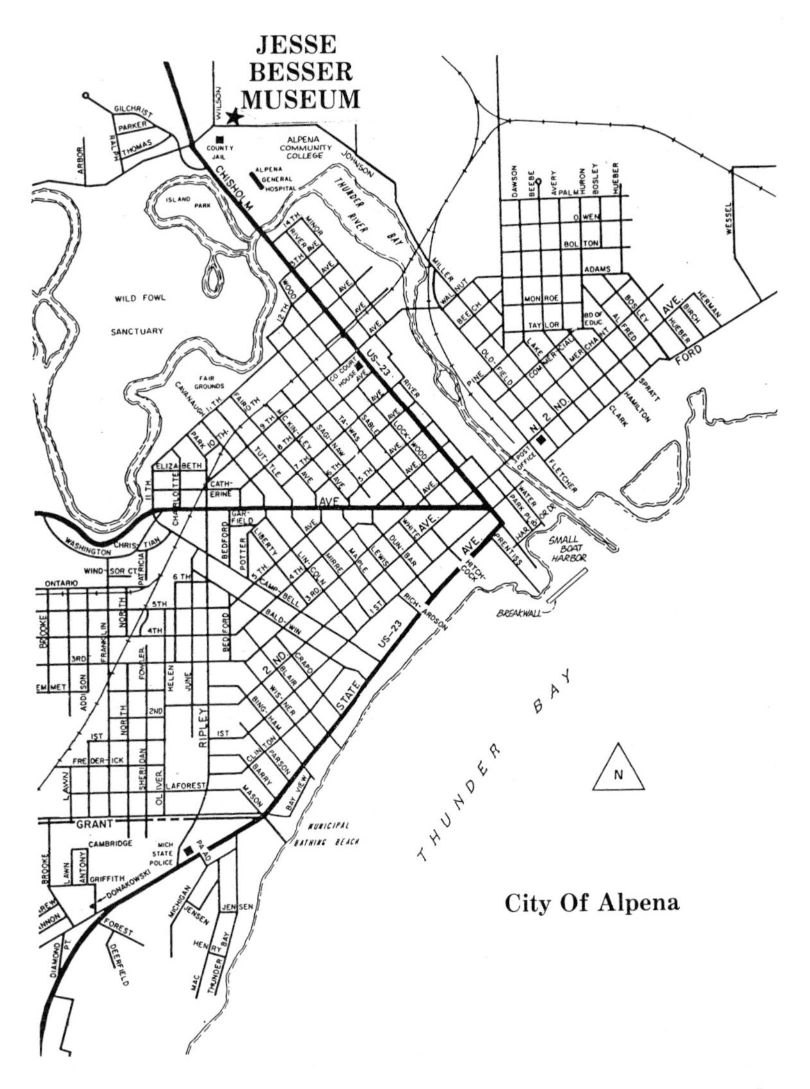

Jesse Besser Museum has an excellent "Early Primitive Man In Michigan" display.

Perplexing Pictographs & Petroglyphs

Petroglyphs and pictographs present perplexing possibilities! First, let's talk a bit about the difference between the two categories. Examples of both are considered in the range of Indian Rock Art. Actually the only two known types of this form of aboriginal rock art that exist in Michigan today are the Sanilac Petroglyphs and the Burnt Bluff Rock Paintings or pictographs. Research indicates most known rock drawings or stone carvings stem from the Rocky Mountain area with but a limited few found east of the Mississippi River. In retrospect, Michigan is deemed fortunate in having prime examples of both a petroglyph and a pictograph for it is a fact that most adjoining states are not as lucky.

Weather, rock material availability and terrain played an active role in the construction of these artworks by primitive man. Most North American examples to date have turned up along the Canadian Shield in northern Ontario. In fact an almost staggering sum of over one hundred petroglyphs and pictographs have been located in that specific region alone, the most famous perhaps, discovered near Toronto, at Peterborough. Experts attribute that a harsh climate literally destroys these types of artwork. Water seepage, freezing and expanding, in turn cracking and breaking art-worked rocks, caused irrepairable harm. By and large, it can further be assumed that many similar handiworks of primitive man may have been lost forever over the long span of years due to this natural phenomena.

How does a pictograph differ from a petroglyph? Well one might simply say one is painted, the other carved; but both artwork forms use rock as their medium. Pictographs were most likely worked as say finger painting with natural materials. Perhaps a crude brush was employed. Some of the interesting paint material utilized by primitive man in this endeavor included vegetable dyes, red ochre earth dyes, colors derived from iron and manganese oxides, as well as bird guano, and fish egg and animal by-product stains. To say the least, primitive man was quite prone to implore his ingenuity.

On the other hand, the petroglyphs were more or less carved or engraved on a soft rock surface with the use of a sharp instrument. Additionally, primitive rock craftsmen employed the skills of hammering, and chiseling, plus an ancient form of rock working termed pecking. The finished product was probably rubbed smooth with some type of abrasive.

Incidentally, pictographs and petroglyphs have been discovered in a variety of settings. Nature strongly influenced the artists. Caves, intriguing natural cliffs, and freestanding rocks all offered dramatic canvases for artwork displays. We must bear in mind, these drawings were in all essence not meant to be secretive. Perhaps they served as signs signifying good hunting omens, directions or other such messages.

Experts tend to agree that the enormous petroglyphs located at Peterborough, Ontario, Canada, were a product of many generations of artists covering a long period of time. One school of thought carries the belief that this artwork was first engraved as a record of visits by Norsemen around a time of 2000 B.C. For you see, some of these carvings have been analyzed, worked in Tifinag and Ogam consaine alphabets as well as other Norse-related drawings and carvings. It has also been determined that during this time period the Ojibwa Algonquians were already using an ancient form of Basque syllabary that is a form of Algonquian still in use today.

This particular petroglyph at Peterborough has been protected by the Canadian Government and today is one of their most popular parks, available not only to the archaeologist but the everyday tourist as well.

Some other petroglyphs discovered around the United States are fantastic beyond descriptive words. For instance, one located in the State of California depicts the entire "zodiac", but unbelievably, in a form that was individually special around 3000 B.C. Ironically, this petroglyph zodiac contained inscriptions done in an ancient form of Arabic. Furthermore, another rock-art carving found in a remote section of Nevada was again similar in design to the aforementioned Peterborough carvings. It too contained Tifinag inscriptions, indicating Norsemen possibly pressed westward.

Charles Bailey of Duluth, Minnesota recently found an unusual petroglyph near Kemmerer, Wyoming. It was an ancient "sun symbol" with a diameter of 11 feet. Due to a notch in the rock wall and a nearby trench, there is a possible solstice connection here. Also nearby is a natural platform rock which combined with the petroglyph and possible solstice activity, could in turn also indicate prehistoric solar worship.

The main point here is the difference in opinions existing between scientific circles as to the origin of this form of prehistory artwork. Were they solely the work of early Amerindian tribes, or did they date back to ancient foreign visitors of European ancestry? We leave this moot point for others more learned, to prove and ponder, for it is not the intent of this author to present a scientific report, but to merely present different viewpoints on this particular subject as well as other contradictory material present elsewhere in this book.

Most petroglyphs and pictographs were worked understandably near a water source, albeit a low cliffside overlooking one of the Great Lakes or on an unusual awe-inspiring shaped boulder along a swift-flowing stream bed. For you see, water routes were the favored highways of the early people. Inland paths and trails were a much later event. Additionally early man had a sense of magic about his surroundings. This aura will be dealt with more fully in a chapter discussing "image stones". The Native American held great store in certain objects, be they animal or mineral, as good or bad omens. Oftentimes the scope of their very lives revolved systematically around such specific "manitous."

One can almost feel the reverence and awe these pictographs and petroglyphs must have held for primitive man...a sacred place. While some forms of artwork featured mainly the animal kingdom, perhaps a good luck omen of sorts, others dealt with human forms, gods and goddesses perhaps. It is again interesting to note that some of the drawings contained life-size figures, while others were but a foot or less in height. Did this occur strictly by purpose or preference of the artist? We really don't have that answer. The reasons remain enigmatic. Perhaps it was a yearly ritual of, say, one specific group of people that annually made additions to the original rock art. But on the other hand, one gifted artist may have performed all the drawings with no specific "down the road" intention in mind. Then again yet another possibility arises. Some scientists believe it was a way of controlling the "kill." By drawing a picture of a specific animal, in a sense, you capture their soul. This belief can best be described by recalling at the turn of the century, many aboriginal tribes fully felt that if a cameraman took their pictures, their souls were forever trapped in that little black box!

Other learned scholars impart ceremonial symbolic shamanism and fertility symbolism to some of these petroglyphs and pictographs. Certainly religious purposes contributed deeply to these art forms.

The two specific Indian Rock Art sites located in Michigan are an excellent example of the two types of indigenous prehistoric art. The Sanilac Petroglyphs actually offer a hands-on type of experience. For many years both the Sanilac Petroglyphs and the Burnt Bluff Pictographs were open to the public. Unfortunately, only the petroglyphs remain in the public domain.

Let's examine the petroglyph first. The exact map location would read: Sanilac County, Greenleaf Township, S½ NE¼ and N½ SE¼ of Section 11, T14N, R12E. Early historical records place the site at the western edge of the ghost town of Holbrook. Actually the Village of Holbrook no longer remains. Foundations of a store and mill may still be traced. The more than one hundred rock carvings located here cover a smooth sandstone outcropping northeast of Saginaw, west of Forester near the Cass River. The petroglyph itself lies on the north side of the south fork of the north branch of the Cass. During the summer months this section of the river is a lazy, slow-moving stream but spring torrents show evidence of higher water marks. The land offers an abrupt slope from the river bed up to the level of the rock carvings perhaps 10 feet above the low-level period of the river.

An earlier history period indicated a former landowner unearthed considerable skeletal material while working a nearby gravel pit. To this author's knowledge, none were scientifically examined at that time.

Before discussing the rock carvings, mention should be made that in 1965 and 1967, 240 acres of land, including these unusual petroglyphs, were purchased by the Michigan Archaeological Society. In 1970, the land was donated to the State of Michigan for a cultural and geological attraction as well as for purposes of preservation. It is interesting to note the Michigan Legislature appropriated money for the use of providing a building to protect and better view these petroglyphs. Special lighting was to have been employed. Surely, as at the aforementioned Peterborough site, preservation would have benefited additionally.

Many scientists believed these petroglyphs were semi-preserved from weathering deterioration, as they were protected by humus and vegetation until the time the "Great Fire" swept through the Thumb Area in the year 1881. However, geologists feel that actually the ground cover of vegetation may have provided a detrimental effect. For you see, chemical weathering caused by humic and carbonic acids from roots, rhizoids and other microorganisms held in the soil, may have taken their toll. Frost action, as well as moisture, caused cracking due to temperature swings. It was indeed interesting to note that over the years, the bare spots on the rock surface, fared far better from the elements than the vegetational-covered sections. Time is continuing to extract its ultimate toll. Someday weathering alone will possibly destroy all past efforts of this ancient endeavor.

Scientists fix the date of the Sanilac Petroglyphs back to the Late Woodland Period of prehistory, specifically A.D. 800. Studies have also been done in the immediate area of the petroglyphs by both the University of Michigan and Michigan State University. Here, positive dates of 1000 B.C. are in order according to research carried out in 1970. But let me once again point out...nothing in the science of archaeology or anthropology is absolute. Time and methods, as well as interpretations, change. We may actually never determine the who, why, when of these petroglyphic records.

The Sanilac Petroglyphs consist of three groups of large flat sandstone slabs fairly close together. The first and largest is completely covered by aboriginal engravings. The carvings on the remaining two groups mainly contain geometric designs.

The petroglyphs present examples of scores of different figures...some are human, godlike forms...outlines of body parts, especially hands and feet...others represent animals and birds as well as animal tracks...many are strange nonexistent mythical beasts. As mentioned above, some oddly shaped geometrical forms are evident. Why? Many are abstract and unidentifiable. Some resemble gridwork found in Norse inscriptions, others resemble Ogam writing. Once again, the possibility of cultural intrusion reflects here. Were these petroglyphs first introduced by Norsemen and Celts? Did a later Native American tribe continue the inscriptions and pictures in their own specific time slot? Once again, more than one simply theory astounds scholars of today.

There are no clear-cut answers...just fascinating theories...perhaps the future will offer new clues in this regard!

Other interesting figures depicted here seem to be mythical in nature. Take for example, the bowman or archer, as he is also called. If you look closely, the carving resembles a stickman drawing of a hunter with a bow drawn back, presumably drawn taut in a hunting position. But why the odd-shaped, weird looking hat? It resembles an open-ended triangle sitting above the archer's head. This hunter measures approximately one foot tall. It is indeed a problematical carving because of the out-of-context headpiece. Absolutely nontypical.

It is interesting to note the Norse god Thor is often depicted with a hat of similar shape; that being, a triangle. Furthermore it is a known fact the Phoenicians also wore conical shaped headwear. The triangular inscription over the bowman's head might relate to foreign intrusion.

Other figures appear, including the elongated man who resembles one of the Norse mythology gods of the Peterborough Petroglyph. Many other carved figures impart a ghostly appearance. As a rule of thumb, depicted hands and fingers on the Peterborough site relate to time periods, namely months and days. In turn, one cannot help but wonder what both hands and feet represent here at Sanilac.

Archaeological evidence indicates many mythical animals are included at the Sanilac rock art site. For instance, five "underwater panthers" with long tails are depicted in the main group of petroglyphs. They seem to tie in with the underwater lion found on the engraved prehistory discs discovered near Alpena, described in a former chapter called "A Prehistory Disc Factory." The Chippewas called these unusual water cats a manitou with the name "Gitche-anah-mi-e-be-zhew," the great underwater wildcat. As previously mentioned, early Jesuit priests reported the Indians termed them underwater sea tigers, while at a later date other Native Americans called them undersea mountain lions. In retrospect, the similar terminology suggests the animals to be mystical in nature with extreme powers over life and death. Therefore, offerings were definitely the order of the day as far as water travel was concerned. In turn, primitive man left gifts of tobacco and small personal trinkets to appease these cats' insatiable appetites for it was deemed necessary to propagate a safe journey. For you see, the water felines had nasty tempers and with but a swish of their huge, sinewy tails lakes or rivers could be whipped into a frenzy of froth and waves...easily upsetting a traveler's canoe. What would you have done in this particular prehistory time and circumstance? Perhaps, paid the tythe!

While still discussing the mythological undersea cats, it is not surprising to learn other cultures transferred the cat image to that of a white bear. Furthermore, the Chippewas and Menominee Indians of Michigan and Wisconsin believed this "Michibissy" or underwater panther actually lived in the Great Lakes, and additionally protected the prehistory copper mining pits of the Keweenaw Peninsula, especially Isle Royale. So you see, the same mythical spirit occurs in many different cultures under many varied sets of curcumstances...but all simply relate to the same form and reason.

The main mystery of the undersea cats is quite obvious. Why were they depicted at the Sanilac Petroglyphs, some 25 miles inland from Lake Huron? Anthropology and archaeology once again prove to be studies of unsolved mysteries. Perhaps that is what makes them so fascinating; they leave room for mere dreaming and fanciful speculating. A nice feeling in a modern world of hi-technology where facts are simply facts, cut and dried, all sterile!

The nice part of the Sanilac Petroglyphs is you can pack a lunch, stay until dark, and use a lantern or flashlight to illuminate the carvings. The images then seem to appear as the sum and substance of what dreams are comprised of. You visit a seemingly mystical land where you can assume the position of the pictured archer, should you so desire. Pull the bow taut and follow the track of the bear, the deer, the otter. Take your soft-glowing lantern and hold it over the ever-milling water cats...feel the fear they impart to the total scene. In a sense you seem to acquire the very thoughts and soul of primitive man...a dull co-mingling of the ages!

Even the topography surrounding these petroglyphs provides an anomaly. Glacial action some 12,500 years ago scoured out unique potholes or depressions measuring some 2 feet across by 4 feet deep. These holes in the soft sandstone may have been used in more primitive times for grain storage or perhaps as mortars for grain grinding. Yes, it is a possibility suggested by anthropologists. Yet Native American legends offer still another solution, that being, giant footprints left behind by a huge spirit "manitou." By and large an Indian "Paul Bunyan" tall tale!

Researchers feel as though the Sanilac Petroglyphs provided a meeting place for various tribes. Certainly a viable theory. One can easily imagine a "rendezvous"-type setting with hunting tales swapped and adventurous journeys described. Perhaps the best of the lot were in turn added to the petroglyph. Due to the fact many animal forms plus animal tracks were depicted at Sanilac, scientists concur these particular petroglyphs relate to a hunting omen.

Many Native Americans feel as though these rock carvings are located near an ancient meeting encampment...a gathering place for all Indians living east of the Mississippi River or west of the Ohio River. Furthermore, they strongly believe the tribes met but once each decade. If the Sanilac property was such a meeting place, the pictures carved in relief on those soft, sandstone rocks were most likely done by many artists over a long period of time. There is sound reasoning behind this theory, for indeed many of the petroglyphs appear to be older than others. Surely some are not as well defined, yet speculation again rears its head...for this could additionally be attributed to the weathering process we formerly talked about. In essence, were some figures added at a more modern period than others, or did frost and atmospheric conditions play the major role here? Questions, always, unanswered questions!

What does the future hold for these unusual time-worn, chiseled drawings? In one respect, I can merely speak of the past, not the future. For you see, over the years unscrupulous people have actually stolen many of these prehistoric carvings. They chiseled them right out of the rock matrix, removed them from the site, no doubt to be sold or placed in private archaeological collections. What an atrocity! Thank goodness the "bowman," the "candelabra," the "canoe," the "horseheaded woman," the "graceful deer," the "bird of prey," and the mythical underwater lions are still evident.

Moreover, designs, dates and miscellaneous erotica of more modern times also grace these historical rocks of Michigan's ancient past. Graffiti does not belong here! Drastic efforts should be in order. Adequate protection is needed.

Archaeologists speculate future duplication of symbols found at the Sanilac Petroglyphs will perhaps offer new clues resulting in classification of similar designs and styles found elsewhere. In due course the riddle of the "bowman's" peculiar hat may be solved.

One should definitely take advantage of these extraordinary petroglyphs being open to the public. Visit the Sanilac Petroglyphs, but be sure to bring along a lantern so you can view them after dark. This is when you get the best showing...an old-time magic-lantern show. Past times surface to haunt the intruder...and here...you ARE the intruder!

Equally as exciting as the Sanilac Petroglyphs are the Burnt Bluff rock-art paintings. While the petroglyphs were carved or deeply etched in a soft sandstone medium, these ancient pictographs were painted with natural dyes and stains gleaned from Mother Nature's vast storehouse.

The history of the Burnt Bluff area has always been colorful. To set the stage for our prehistoric story, let's first talk about earlier modern times. Burnt Bluff is located about half way down the west side of the Garden Peninsula, situated on a 1,500-acre parcel of land jutting out into Big Bay de Noc. Its northern boundary overlooks Fayette State Park. Burnt Bluff's 200-foot towering cliffs impressively face islands to the west and Sac Bay to the south.

In the year 1867 the Jackson Iron Company purchased the Burnt Bluff Peninsula along with a large tract of forest land containing 26,000 acres. The company town complete with smelting facilities was located at nearby Fayette. By the time the furnaces were in full production, the peninsula now called Burnt Bluff was already completely cutover. No records exist, but legend indicates the land was burnt-over following the logging endeavor, affording this peninsula its unconventional name.

Fayette as a company-owned town allowed no taverns within its village limits. In 1870 one Alphus Bellinquette, a Frenchman, operated a saloon and bawdy house at Sac Bay just south of Burnt Bluff Peninsula. About 1874, the town fathers of Fayette deemed to rid the countryside of the temptations offered their workers at Mr. Bellinquette's notorious establishment. In turn, the Frenchman was run out of town, escaping by rowboat across the bay to Escanaba. Rumors over the years led to speculation that he had buried his gold in the area. The legend exists yet today, embellished further with each telling.

A few years later a small farming community named Burnt Bluff was established here on the peninsula. It was located in Fairbanks Township, 6 miles south of Fayette. By 1877 this village consisted of a store and a fishery operated by Mr. D.A. Wells. Today it is listed as a ghost town.

One can locate Burnt Bluff Peninsula easily on a map, just find Delta County, Fairbanks Township, Section 24 and you should be able to pick up the wording Burnt Bluff, just below the listing for the Fayette State Park. These described limestone cliffs are also known as the "red rocks." Here are found the Indian paintings or pictographs.

Over the years scientific endeavors to solve the riddle of Burnt Bluff included the following:

1. Dr. A. G. Ruthven of The University of Michigan directed anthropologists to the area in 1926.
2. W.B. Hinsdale, also affiliated with the University of Michigan, declared the rock-art paintings genuine in appearance.
3. Professor Cleland and Peske explored the Spider Cave area of the bluffs in 1963. They hailed from Michigan State University.
4. Dr. James E. Fitting, curator of Great Lakes Division of the Museum of Anthropology from The University of Michigan, explored additional cave sites in 1965.

It should also be stated here that for years the land above the rock paintings was privately owned by Henry and Ruth Lang. In 1960 the Langs erected a stairway from the top of the bluff to the water's edge. Steps were built from heavy timbers and concrete. At a point where the steep cliff drops sharply, the stairs more or less zigzagged back and forth from one landing to the next, affording an excellent view of the paintings. Furthermore, a lookout was built at the top of the bluff. Another stairway was constructed offering access to the main Spider Cave section.

Mr. and Mrs. Lang operated the Burnt Bluff pictographs as a tourist attraction for some 13 years. The property was recently sold to a man from Wisconsin. At this writing, the Indian rock-art paintings are off limits to the general public.

Ancient artists of long ago left some of their intimate selves here on these unique cliff and cave paintings. Several drawings are located along the bottom of the cliffs. During periods of high water they can be viewed from the water by boat. Some of the drawings resemble people with joined hands like so many cutout paper dolls. All told, 13 faded paintings appear at the base of this 140-foot cliff. The largest of these pictographs measure 2 feet in height, the smallest but 6 inches tall. Approximately 1300 feet to the north are located 6 more paintings, more or less scattered over the face of the cliff. At least 3 of them are unrecognizable due to aging and weathering. Besides these two widely scattered groups of paintings, four more are located near or in Spider Cave.

Incidentally, an estimated 200 caves are thought to exist in the vicinity of Burnt Bluff. But all evidence points primarily to the Spider Cave as the most productive and interesting of the lot.

Most impressive are the paintings termed "big man" and "spider man." It is quite obvious "big man" is the largest of the pictographs, standing approximately 2 feet tall; however, some of his limbs are fragmentary although body parts are still partially visible. The figure represents a shaded red-colored human with upraised arms, an extremely small-sized head in retrospect to his body, and contains a geometric covered torso. A fertility aspect is achieved by the depiction of a phallus projecting from the figure's lower torso. This painting includes shaped hands. Many of the other drawings found here do not...having either what is termed as "jug-arms" or merely handless stubs. It is important to note both the "big man" and "spider man" are the only figures showing fingers and thumbs. It should also be mentioned the zigzag, geometric designs on "big man's" chest may indicate clothing and/or amulet or gorget. Archaeological evidence indicates this particular figure represents a tribal chief or other leader, perhaps that of a medicine man.

The truly mystifying feature regarding the Burnt Bluff pictographs is shown in two other drawings. Both are figures caught in the act of urinating. To date this implication is not repeated at any known petroglyph or pictograph traditional artwork. One of the men is worked in a reddish-brown color and is depicted as "jug-armed." The other painting is done in a lighter shade of red and shows a male human with upraised arms, once again minus hands. Scientists account them extremely inexplicable, certainly most problematical.

As a rule of thumb, a large percentage of the Burnt Bluff paintings are problematic. One can easily gaze at them and depict fleeting, ghost-like shapes of one's own choosing. At a quick glance a ship becomes obvious or maybe it is a man riding a horse! Hmmmmm, now which is it? Yet another drawing looks like a figure out of the movie "Ghost Busters," while the one right next to it also resembles a spirit image, but that of a woman scepter. Presumably still another drawing must be a dancer or possibly an archer...look at it yet from a slightly different angle and the figure develops still another meaning. How do you decipher problematical paintings or carvings? Unofficially you could call it "Rorschaching." That being, like the proverbial inkblot test, you more or less read into the designs what you imagine, disregarding what actually may be indicated scientifically. Many of these specific paintings exist only in the mind of the individual viewer...like cloud pictures in the sky. Prehistory, as mentioned before, contains some fact...some fiction. Mysteries abound which make the subjects studied anomalous. Somehow the solutions seem just out of reach, one step away, always shrouded in mist.

While the rock-art work mentioned above seems to range in color from reds to orange to blues and browns, suggestions have been made that pulverized minerals of iron and copper were so employed here.

Now let's discuss the main figure depicted at Burnt Bluff...the one most famous in its own right. That would certainly be the "spider man." He is unique! Once again "Rorschaching" can be applied. This figure is painted in a blue-red range of colors that when damp or moist, take on a reddish-brown hue. It is thought to have been worked in red-ochre dye. As the name indicates, the picture seems to depict a giant spider at the lower extremity of the painting. In a most unusual circumstance, it seems as though the spider is attached to the man figure by a tether. The man himself, is quite a well-rounded figure, again appearing with a head way too small in proportion to his body. He too is depicted with hands containing fingers...one hand has four, while the other shows three. From his right knee and wrist a cord-like object trails around the man's head and ends close to his left hand. Another tether-like appendage seemingly starts at "spider man's" naval and winds around downwards until it attaches to the rear of the spider. Problematic, indeed?

For you see, there is yet another obviously accepted theory concerning this painting. Anthropologists feel it represents a "sweat lodge" concept. The spider figure then turns into a carefully arranged fire, with each specific log radiating outward from a central point. The object one sees as the spider's head takes on the appearance of a large stone being heated by the fire. When water is introduced to the rock, vapors arise that are indicated by the tethers. The rising steam acts as a purification ritual.

Once again it would be quite easy for us all to read a personal meaning into this specific painting. Mine would be as follows: in true ink-blot perspective...the spider -fire figure now would indicate a sun symbol. The tether attached to the man indicates he draws his strength from the sun. The sun is out of the sky region to indicate its relationship to the Mother Earth, from which all life springs. The second tether from the figure's wrist and knee returns the sun's strength directly back to the earth. The from "dust to dust" theory. It would be interesting to hear other viewpoints on "spider man."

Remember this point, "spider man" was not drawn on the red rocks or bluff, but in turn is found in what scientists call "Spider Cave." The cave itself is situated some 20 feet above the bay. Former prehistoric high lake levels formed this 90-foot-long cavern from limestone dolomite bedrock. A date of 2000 B.C. is roughly estimated. Henry Lang, the former owner of the bluff property, erected a stairway from the shoreline up to the cave's entrance. This gave tourists and other scientific individuals not only easy access, but prime viewing of the red-ochre painting as well.

Anthropologists have drawn a conclusion the cave was employed as a place where arrows were shot and spears thrown...perhaps for practice sake or maybe a ritual of sorts. A similar practice was recorded during the 18th century by voyageurs. Indians were known to have shot arrows into an overhanging rock crevice at a pictograph at Crooked Lake, Minnesota. Perhaps that is why so many chipped projectile points have been excavated from Spider Cave.

Some of the remaining caves have been examined by scientists turning up skeletal remains. At one in particular, human bones showing cut marks similar to those of a butchered animal were found. It is thought seven people may have been killed here. some of these other cave sites indicate a date of A.D. 375 having been carbon-14 dated, using charcoal taken from excavated hearths as a medium.

It is this author's fondest hope that someday in the future, the unique Burnt Bluff traditional rock-art pictograph paintings will again be "open to the public!" The State of Michigan should investigate and exhaust all possibilities of acquiring this property. It would make an excellent addition to the Fayette State Park, just to the north of the bluffs. For you must understand, it is the only prehistory example of an ancient pictograph located in Michigan. Until that time, we can but trust the Burnt Bluff-Spider Cave Indian paintings will stand the ultimate test of time.

You must agree...petroglyphs and pictographs both present perplexing possibilities!

CREDITS:

Artwork:

Francis Moses, St. Ignace, MI

Mysteries of Michigan's Long-Ago People, Gerald Haltiner, publ. privately, "Rock Carvings Tell Story of Early Indian Cultures."

Garden Peninsula Historical Society, Garden, MI

SUGGESTED FURTHER READING

Perplexing Pictographs & Petroglyphs

GREAT LAKES INFORMANT, "The Indian Rock Art Tradition In Michigan," by Donald Weston, Series 2, number 9.

THE BURNT BLUFF ROCK PAINTINGS, Douglas W. Lugthart, U.M. paper #34, ANTHROPOLOGY, 1968.

THE SANILAC COUNTY ROCK CARVINGS, by Mark Papworth, Michigan Archaeologist, Vol. 3, number 4, December 1957.

BURNT BLUFF AREA, by Grace Stern from OUR HERITAGE: Garden Peninsula, Delta County 1840-1980, publ. by the Garden Peninsula Historical Society, 1982.

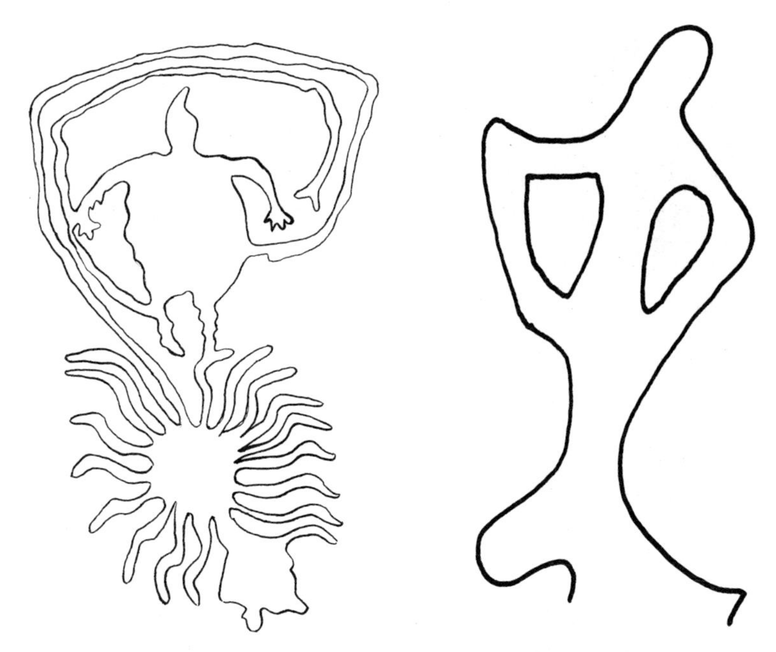

Burnt Bluffs drawing from Spider Cave, called Spider Man.
Problematical Burnt Bluff Pictograph

Burnt Bluffs pictograph...unique, one of a kind, showing two men in the act of urinating or perhaps fertilizing.

Sanilac Petroglyph depicting figure known as "The Bowman."

Sanilac Petroglyph depicting figure known as, "The Elongated Man."

Burnt Bluffs pictograph showing partial drawing of figure termed, "The Big Man."

Sanilac Petroglyph depicting a stylized grid.

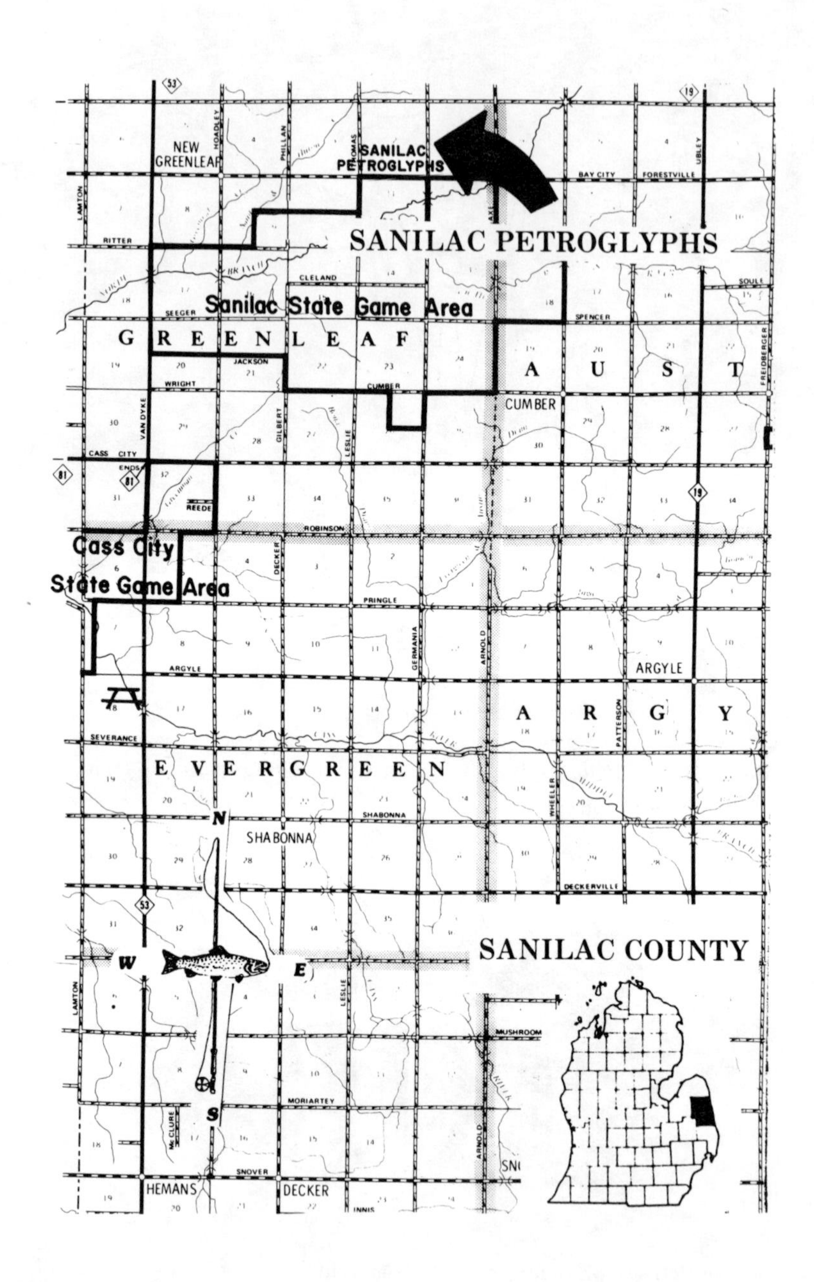
SANILAC PETROGLYPHS
Sanilac State Game Area
GREENLEAF
AUST
Cass City State Game Area
ARGY
EVERGREEN
SANILAC COUNTY
NEW GREENLEAF
CUMBER
ARGYLE
SHABONNA
HEMANS
DECKER
N
S
W
E

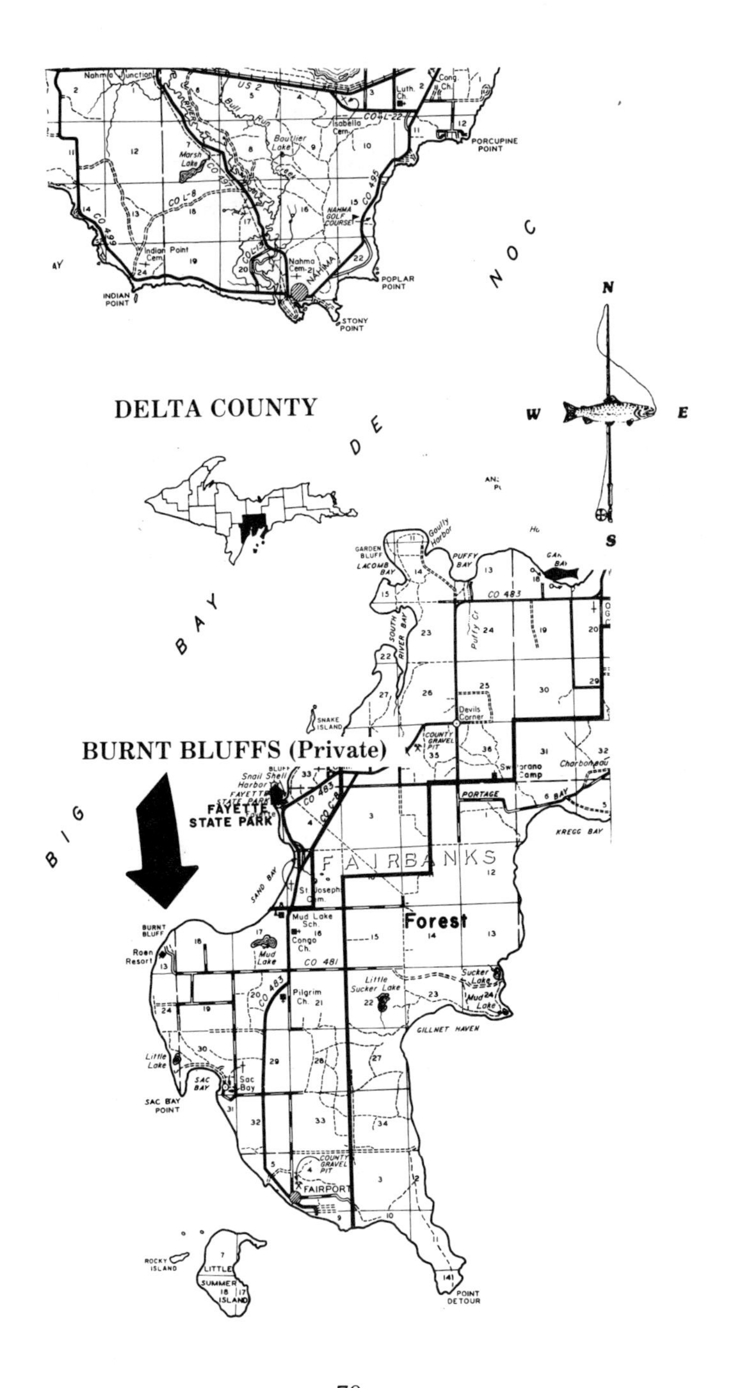
DELTA COUNTY
BURNT BLUFFS (Private)
BIG BAY DE NOC
N
W
E
S
Nahma Junction
US 2
Bull Run
Isabella Cem.
Boutlier Lake
Marsh Lake
Luth. Ch.
Cong. Ch.
PORCUPINE POINT
CO L-22
CO 495
CO L-8
CO 499
NAHMA GOLF COURSE
Indian Point Cem.
Nahma Cem.
NAHMA
INDIAN POINT
POPLAR POINT
STONY POINT
GARDEN BLUFF
LACOMB BAY
Goully Harbor
PUFFY BAY
CO 483
SOUTH RIVER BAY
Puffy Cr.
SNAKE ISLAND
Devils Corner
COUNTY GRAVEL PIT
Charbonneau
Snail Shell Harbor
FAYETTE STATE PARK
PORTAGE
KREGG BAY
FAIRBANKS
Forest
SAND BAY
St. Joseph Cem.
BURNT BLUFF
Roen Resort
Mud Lake Sch.
Congo Ch.
Mud Lake
CO 481
Pilgrim Ch.
Little Sucker Lake
Sucker Lake
GILLNET HAVEN
Little Lake
SAC BAY
Sac Bay
SAC BAY POINT
COUNTY GRAVEL PIT
FAIRPORT
ROCKY ISLAND
LITTLE SUMMER ISLAND
POINT DETOUR

Questionable Rocks With a Prehistory Past

PART I

Beaver Island - Ring of Stones

Some 30 miles out in big Lake Michigan, lies a tiny group of islands offering shelter to travellers, if needed. The largest of the complex, consisting of High, Garden, Pig and Beaver, is the 12-mile long by 5-mile wide glacier-carved outcropping of land we know as Big Beaver. Up until recent times the prime evidence of prehistory habitation on this island consisted of the discovery of three PreColumbian mounds explored in 1871 by Henry Gillman. The historian was sufficiently satisfied their origin was indeed ancient. They appeared to be of the same character as similar mounds found in the Detroit area, as well as along the St. Clair River and at the foot of Lake Huron proper. It was believed these archaic edifices were used for the purpose of sepulcher. Excavation turned up a generous variety of skilled stone products from awls, axes, unbelievable stone hoes and many other implements.

It should be mentioned here that the excellent museum on Beaver Island contains a grooved stone hammer very similar to the ones previously described from the copper culture mining era on the Keweenaw Peninsula. Professionally there has been speculation over the years, that Beaver Island was a way-station for those enigmatic ancient people that carried out the copper trade. The Beaver Island museum also has on display an enormous stone ax or celt similar to like objects found in Ireland. Once again the possibility of "Celtic" occupation dominates the Michigan scene. Makes one really wonder, doesn't it? Perhaps there is a tie-in here. Keep in mind the following objects: Beaver Island "ring of stones," the Escanaba Stone, the Huron Mountain dolmen...all "Celt"-related. Fred Rydholm, historian from Marquette, offers this theory. "The stone ring on Beaver fits so nicely into the Escanaba River stone and the Huron Mountain dolmen. It looks like these Celts stayed on the Island for the summers and traveled with the Ottowa (traders) up the Escanaba towards the Copper Country. Their calendar stone circle let them know when to return."

Before we discuss the inexplicable "ring of stones," Beaver Island's newest exciting discovery, mention should first be made of yet further evidence from an early culture known to have existed there. Centuries past, perhaps connected to the ancient mound discoveries, immense plotted gardens were evident. W.B. Hinsdale in *Primitive Man in Michigan* describes these early garden beds in the following manner: "Another conspicuous feature of Michigan's antiquities was the 'garden bed' construction. These symmetrical, low, earth ridges were laid out with precision and showed much artistic conception in their designs. Some were wheel-shaped with 'spokes' running out to a circular ridge from a circle within, but most of them were in well planned geometrical designs. They resembled beds in a formal garden, hence the name."

Hinsdale continues, "The garden beds of Michigan have been entirely destroyed, sad to relate. If one were to mention the outstanding peculiarities of prehistoric Michigan he would say the garden beds and the copper mines of the Keweenaw were the most conspicuous. The garden beds are gone, but the old mining pits may yet be studied especially upon Isle Royale and should be protected against unintelligent despoliation."

Over a hundred years ago, history relates the Beaver Island garden beds contained an overgrowth of trees found to be approximately 200 years old, proving without question these garden plots were not of modern pursuit.

Having discussed the presence of mounds, ancient gardens and discovered stone implements on the Island, it is not too surprising to learn of the "ring of stones" and accompanying "wagon wheel" rock designs that have proved so exciting in more recent times. As mentioned previously...they all seem to relate...they compliment each other!

Now perhaps your curiosity has peaked. What is the mysterious "ring of stones"? Well many have compared this perplexing Beaver Island find to a "miniature Stonehenge." We are all more or less familiar with the bizarre rock structures found at Stonehenge. The stone circles of the

Grampian region of Scotland were designed as a lunar calendar and were employed by the Druids for ritual and calendrical purposes. The axis of symmetry of Stonehenge is aligned on the point of midsummer sunrise. Less sophisticated circles have been determined to exist in Mexico and Central America as well.

The Stonehenge ruins were immense, the Beaver Island find..much smaller in scope but nevertheless important. If, as believed, the stones offered the ancients a form of calendar, it would be evident to their very existence. There has been speculation the ring of stones allowed not only tracking of the sun, but determining the seasons as well.

Still another question quickly comes to mind. What do Old World circles of stone have to do with ruins discovered in the Americas? We previously mentioned during the Copper Culture chapters the possibility of Old World settlers travelling through Michigan well before Columbus discovered America. So these are not new questions. The NIBC theory (no immigrants before Columbus) has not always been readily accepted in some scientific circles...but it is gaining ground.

It is accepted fact that stone rings and related rock monuments outcropped from the megalithic era. It is also known that there is a definite connection to edifices such as Stonehenge between these ringed structures and astronomical science. One of the best known sites here in North America is located at Mystery Hill, North Salem, New Hampshire. Here is found a stone chamber observatory together with a stone circle. (The chamber bears resemblance to the astroalignment pits of Isle Royale, while the stone circle relates to the Beaver Island "ring of stones".) At the Mystery Hill site, brush and debris was cleared, revealing that one stone marks the meridian and lies due north of the central observation point. Four other rocks indicate the sunrise and sunset points on the horizon for the midsummer and midwinter solstices.

All across the United States stone circles have been found, varying in size from small to large. Many contain massive boulders up to, say, 15 meters in circumference, involving great labor to merely position them properly.

Understanding just how stone circles and other forms of crude megalithic observatories work is important. During the course of a 12-month period, the sun moves across the horizon, a short measured distance each day. On the first day of spring (March 21), and autumn (September 21) the vernal equinox and the autumnal equinox, the sun rises due east and sets due west. With the approach of the summer equinox (June 21), the sun's northward journey comes to a slow stop and from that time on the process reverses. Half a year later the winter solstice (December 21), signals the reversal once again. The year is so completed. You can readily see the solstices are very important quarter-way marks along the equinox system. The results of the whole system might be that should a person place an object on the ground, lined up with a second, the shadows will indicate a functional guide if properly aligned. Once the two solstices are plotted out by a permanent marker, other points can then comprise the solar calendar.

Archaeologists maintain the axis of the Beaver Island "circle of stones" is aligned approximately on the point of the midsummer sunrise, and is believed to have been constructed by a cult of ancient sun worshippers or for use as a calendar.

This evidence of ancient man's endeavor was found on the west central side of this 53-square-mile island northwest of Charlevoix on the mainland. The circular structure is made up of 39 stones forming a 397-foot circle. Stones vary sizewise from 2 feet to 10 feet in diameter. Experts say the boulders are placed horizontally rather than upright. The center rock that occupies the middle position of the boulders contains a hole the size of a basketball, believed to have been chiseled by humans. Speculation indicates it may have once held a pole, probably serving in the capacity of a sundial. Furthermore, authorities attribute this rock circle to be man-made since there is little evidence of other boulders of that size-range in the immediate area.

This incomprehensible stone circle was first discovered in the summer of 1985 by Terri Bussey while searching for Indian artifacts. According to George Weeks, Staff Writer for the Detroit News, "Bussey came upon a large boulder on the west end of the island. The top of the rock had a large hole. Bussey remarked it resembled any other rock with a hole in it.

But on closer examination she became convinced the hole had been chiseled out and the rock had what appeared to be a man-made grid."

Weeks continues, "To check out a suspicion she had about its significance, she paced off from the rock to points of the compass, where she found more large stones, mostly buried. She charted the sunrise and sunset over certain rocks. For two nights she camped in the area noting alignment of the stars."

It should be stated here that Terri Bussey is part-Chippewa and presently is the director of the Grand Rapids Inter-Tribal Council's Michigan Indian Press. Excited over her discovery, she took her findings to members of the Grand Traverse Band of Ottawa and Chippewa Indians. She also tried to interest archaeologists in excavating near the site.

But based on what was previously known about prehistory culture in the Beaver Island area, archaeologists remarked that it would make little sense to suspect there would be anything resembling a "mini-Stonehenge" on the island.

Newspaper accounts, however, relate Dr. Donald P. Heldman, archaeologist in charge of excavations at Fort Michilimackinac at Mackinaw City, was intrigued. He made a trip out to the island, met with Ms. Bussey, and after preliminary examinations, determined Bussey had indeed discovered a circle of boulders placed by human hands. Since Heldman's initial findings, Bussey has had aerial photographs taken of the site with infrared film; however, results are not yet confirmed.

Once again, a similar question interjected in other chapters of this book, takes center stage. Who made this megalithic calendar from the far distant past? We have already discussed the inherent possibility the early primitive inhabitants may have stemmed from Celtic or Norse heritage. So in turn, let's explore two other avenues of thought.

Many archaeologists attribute both the mounds and stone rings to the people of the Mississippian culture...The Mound-Builders. It is reported their civilization stretched from Lake Superior to the Gulf of Mexico and from the Mississippi River to the Carolinas. In the chronology of the Upper Midwest, the Mississippians arrived in Michigan relatively late, about 1200 A.D., although they existed much earlier to the south of us.

Several distinct periods mark this era: Emergent Mississippian, 800-1000 A.D.; Early Woodland, 950-1050 A.D.; Middle Woodland, 1050-1300 A.D.; and finally the Late Woodland period, 1350-1541 A.D.

During the phase termed the Early Woodland Period, the Mississippians founded the town of Cahokia, near St. Louis, Missouri. It proved to be a major metropolis, a political and ceremonial center that grew in size to 6 square miles, with an estimated population near 40,000 inhabitants.

As time marched on, the middle phase of this culture group expanded into the Great Lakes region. Here their largest city was named Aztalan, located in present-day southeastern Wisconsin. Historians and scientists alike speculate this too was a way-station for transporting natural resources such as copper and animal skins to other Mississippian villages further south. It is indeed interesting to note that artifacts found at both the Wisconsin site and the location in St. Louis interrelate.

As we will point out in a chapter dealing specifically with the mounds, the Mississippians commanded resources from a vast and well-traveled, extended area. Excavations reveal conch shells from the Carolinas, lead ore from Wisconsin, cotton and precious gems from our southwestern states, chert from the Ozark region, copper from both Keweenaw and Isle Royale, and salt from the gulf coast. We have already established prehistory activity in the copper mining endeavor relating as far back as 3000 B.C....So we can pretty well establish whomever occupied the mounds may have also been responsible for other megalithic monuments, as well as the ring of stones. It is believed this culture ultimately succumbed to warfare and pestilence.

It is just possible once these stones are scientifically verified to astronomically align, the Beaver Island "ring of stones" may well represent one of the major discoveries of prehistoric earthworks in the Americas. This calendar, plus the possibility of a chamber observatory on Isle Royale, and the rock cairns at Black River in the northeastern lower peninsula, all point to a chain of early man's trade routes. It is exciting that important discoveries are still surfacing in our State during such modern times. Perhaps someday our

Michigan road maps will offer a new, unique symbol of identification...a stone ax...to mark and locate these primitive archaeological sites. Above all else, experts are in agreement these prehistory sites should be protected to prevent them from being lost from the ravages of time, greed and misuse.

At the time of the Beaver Island circle of stones discovery by Terri Bussey, it was also intrusively associated with early native Indian culture. The stone ring was further ascertained to be a "circle of life," an important part of Native American culture. The boulders were regarded to have held a spiritual significance. Several newspaper articles shortly after the discovery was made point out Indian artifacts had been excavated from the vicinity of the circle. Additionally, it is near an ancient Indian campsite that was located south of the ring of stones. Furthermore, according to archaeologist Heldman an Indian "sweat lodge" was found nearby. Actually, I might also add at this time, it isn't clear what positive purpose the stones held, but some experts estimate the age of this find at over 1,000 years ago.

George Weeks from the Detroit News also drew attention to yet another discovery made on Beaver Island, that was previously overlooked when the circle of stones was first discovered and being analyzed by archaeologists. Weeks maintains:

"Alvin Lafreniere, president of the Beaver Island Historical Society, also noted that about a half mile away from the stone circle he has located a smaller, moss-covered circle of stones with a diameter of about 200 feet and containing eight spokes extending from a center rock. He said he has seen others in the area, all with relatively small stones. Their configuration is similar to Indian 'medicine wheels' commonly found in the Northern Plains, but never before in Michigan. The wheels are believed to have been used as sundials and in spiritual ceremonies."

It is considered almost unbelievable according to archaeologist Donald Heldman that medicine wheels and rings of stone be located in such close proximity. They may well be one of a kind located in the Great Lakes region. Professor Heldman further indicated that if the confirmation of the stone circle is truly considered a "henge," this would indeed change current thinking about early civilizations in Michigan.

Research shows the wagon wheel circle is also considered to be a variant form of calendar stones in America. These smaller rock circles with radiating lines are quite prevalent in western Canada and adjacent U.S. states, principally Wyoming. Experts account the spokes are oriented towards points of the horizon, marking the rising and setting of obvious stars...north star for example. Once again these devices represent a rough calendar form for calculating the motions of the earth's axis.

It is obvious many sites containing rings of stone and/or wagon wheels probably have never been investigated. Overgrowth of forest floor rubble or debris can obscure them until a chance encounter makes discovery a reality. Then the "excitement" builds; the scientific communities become all stirred up, the archaeologists speculate, while the general public is awed by the shroud of mystery the whole scene presents.

Unbelievably at least six other satellite medicine wheels have been located on Beaver Island near the more dominant circle of stones. Lewis Johnson, a spiritual leader for the Grand Traverse Band of Ottawa and Chippewa Indians, attests this site as spiritually significant. Johnson is of Ottawa descent. It is told he found carvings in the center circle that led him to the other medicine wheel discoveries. Johnson states that near the north rock of the large circle are three stones (medicine wheels) of about 200 feet in diameter. About 300 yards from the west rock is a smaller wheel. Archaeologist Heldman is said to have only focused on the large circle of stones and in due process, missed the smaller wagon wheel patterns. Heldman believed, however, that the wagon wheel design is common in our northern plains area, but once again points out it is unique not only to find them here in Michigan, but also in context with the stone ring...it is almost unimaginable. As mentioned before, they possibly were used as sundials and in connection with spiritual ceremonies.

Historian Alvin Lafreniere offered the following information regarding the "ring of stones" discovery. We have already discussed the center stone that contained a large man-made chiseled hole that possibly at one time contained a post used as a sight alignment for the setting sun. However, the very same rock also holds a most mystifying petroglyph of sorts. Without question carved deeply on one face of the boulder is a map of lower Michigan in relief. To date its puzzling origin is unconfirmed. Indeed this is exciting!

Lafreniere also called my attention to the fact that another nearby circle contains yet a second center rock with unusual engravings that to date have not been scientifically deciphered. This circle is perhaps some 400-yards distant from the main circle. Dr. Luis Salazer, an expert in Native American engravings and artwork, from Beloit College in Wisconsin is scheduled to further examine these ancient markings. Hopefully they will be properly identified and deciphered.

Alvin Lafreniere told your author of still one more exciting find in the same immediate area of Beaver Island; that being, an oddly designed prehistoric painting or pictograph. Near the top of the stone appear to be paintings of "bird wings." Most unusual. He states they have been confirmed by Professor Jim Scherz of the University of Wisconsin as well as Dr. Donald Heldman, Director of Archaeology for the Mackinac Island Park Commission.

What a fascinating piece of prehistory Beaver Island offers us... both in the realm of the mysterious and the magnificent...A true anomaly that has survived over the centuries!

The evidence is clear...prehistory mysteries continue to surface in Michigan's modern high-tech world. Hopefully, as time goes on, all forces, ethnologists, archaeologists, geologists, epigraphists and historians alike will follow a common path...working together to better learn and understand Michigan's mysterious prehistory past!

Part II of *Questionable Rocks With a Prehistory Past* will deal with yet another form of rough observatory. We will examine the Black River cairns and rambling rock wall patterns...Michigan's latest addition to its prehistory mystery status.

CREDITS:

The Detroit News, Staff Reporter, George Weeks, Detroit, MI
The Beaver Island Historical Society, St. James, MI
Alvin Lafreniere, President, Beaver Island Historical Society
Phil Becker, photographer
C. Fred Rydholm, Marquette, MI

ARTWORK:

Francis Moses, St. Ignace, MI

SUGGESTED FURTHER READING

BRONZE AGE AMERICA, Barry Fell, publ. Little, Brown & Co., Boston-Toronto, 1982
PRIMITIVE MAN IN MICHIGAN, W.B. Hinsdale, publ. Avery Color Studios, Au Train, MI 1983,1986,1987

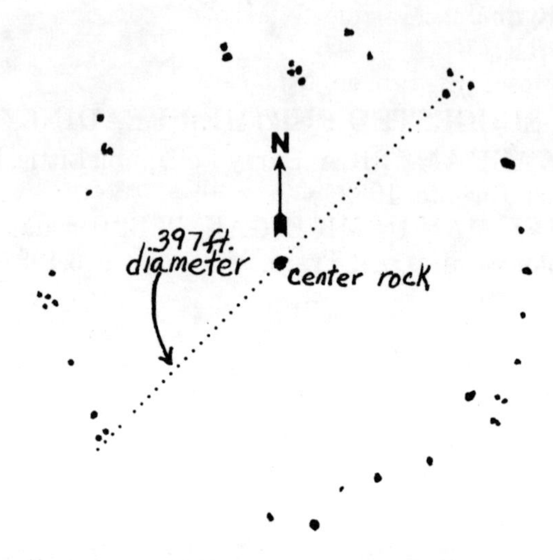

Diagram of ring of stones.

Archaeologists believe the circle of boulders that is located on Beaver Island might be a primitive calendar that allowed Indians to track the movement of the sun and determine the growing seasons. Many Indians believe the circle also has spiritual significance. The center boulder contains a hole that may have held a post, possibly serving as a sundial. The largest boulder in the circle is the eastern rock, which archaeologists say may line up with the rising sun at the seasonal equinoxes. The circle, similar in concept to Britain's Stonehenge, would be, if verified, the only one of its kind found in the Great Lakes Region.

Drawing of a "Ring of Stones."

Center stone of the Stonehenge, The hole at left was used to put in a post to use as sight alignment for the setting sun.

The right section of the same rock, with what appears to be a map of Michigan chiseled into it --so far unconfirmed by anyone.

A prehistoric painting we are referring to as the "Birdwings."

Center rock of another circle about 400 yards from Stonehenge. Near bottom of rock are man-made engravings as yet undeciphered.

The same rock from a short distance. Note the "wings" near the top.

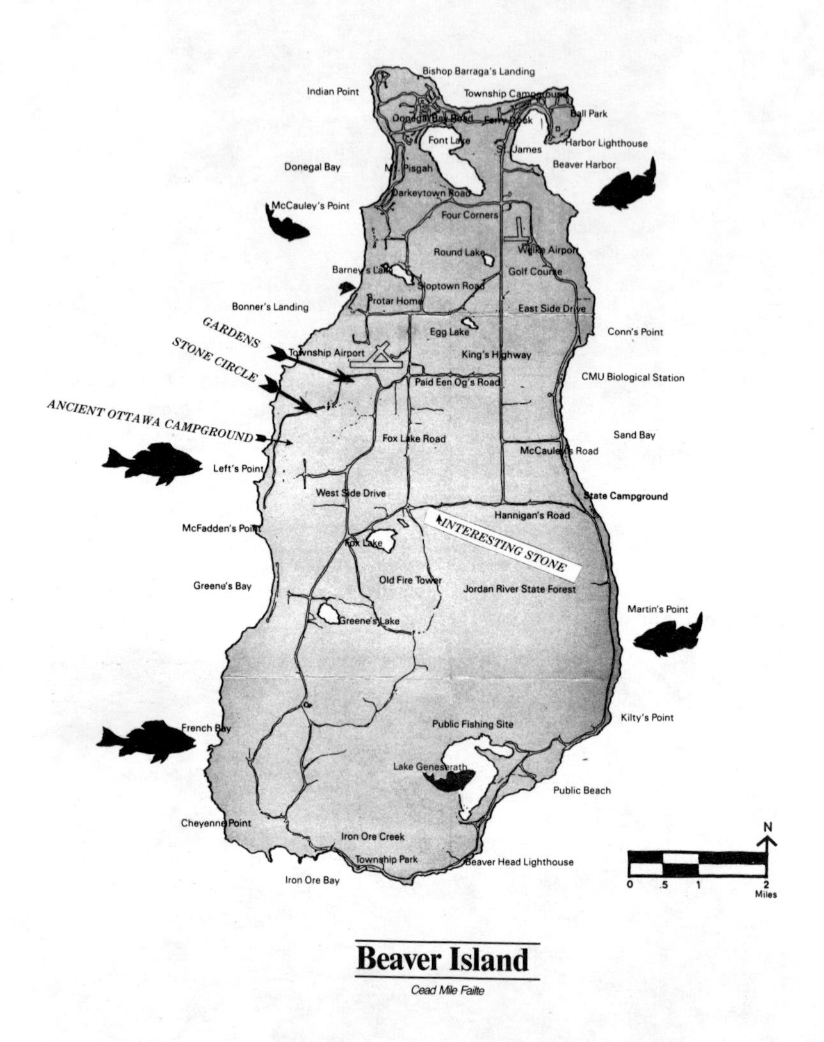

Note locations of 1) ring of stones, 2) ancient garden beds, 3) old Ottawa campgrounds, 4) unusual rock.

Questionable Rocks With a Prehistory Past
PART II
Black River Cairns & Walls

Of all the existing megalithic monuments, perhaps stone cairns and rambling rock walls have received the least publicity. In all truth, we know relatively little regarding them...they more or less simply present an enigma. Perhaps they present a fresh new frontier of ancient prehistory. Actually, a mystery yet to be solved scientifically at some future date. Indeed new breakthroughs seem to be surfacing yearly at a startling rate. Actually, the more cairns and rock walls that are discovered, the more clues introduced. In retrospect it is that "mystery" factor that makes the study of prehistory places and artifacts so anomalous.

First of all, just what is a cairn? A cairn or carn, as it is often termed, is defined as a mound of stones oftentimes used as a burial cover. Research also indicates some of these rock piles serve as markers or guides, while still others in more regimented forms, offer the probability of sighting points as for a prehistory rough calendar...compass...observatory, as the case may be.

Next question. Who built them and why? Many ancient races are well-known stone builders from balanced rock markers, slab-roofed stone chambers, standing "phallic" stones, dolmens, trilithons and cromlechs, as well as cairns and giant rock walls composed of dry construction...all puzzling man-made stoneworks. Early man believed rocks held the key to power, strength and fertility. A partial list of prehistory stone worshippers would surely include the Celts, Greeks, Romans, Egyptians, Persians, Hebrews, and last but not least, the South-Sea Islanders, namely the Polynesians and Fiji islanders.

Ancient history relates the Semites often built stone piles or monuments near a water source; albeit lake, river or merely stream. Absolution and consecration were two rituals that figured prominently in their lives. The Bible mentions stone cairns, pillars and idols on several occasions. An Old Testament story that quickly comes to mind relates to the Jewish people finding the Promised Land. At a place called Gilgal, a pile of stones taken from the bed of the River Jordan, marks the spot where the Jews crossed the river. This entrance to the Promised Land, Gilgal, actually means "a heap", taken literally, a pile of stones.

It is interesting to note that similar stone piles such as found at Gilgal had been discovered in the last century, along rivers in Ohio, in Perry and Ross Counties, causing speculation if perhaps the ancient people who erected them in a like fashion did not in turn come originally from Asia. Equally as intriguing was the fact that many prehistory stone piles found in New England also were located in close proximity to inscriptions of the Hebrew language. Rocks present multiple mysteries both here and abroad!

Furthermore, history records that in Europe during the Neolithic Period many early primitive people buried their dead under piles of rock and stone. Perhaps the practice began to keep wild animals away from skeletal remains; eventually, however, it became a tradition.

An interesting group of cairns or piles of stone were discovered in Massachusetts. They consisted of conical piles of stone, many of which contained inexplicable base openings. Similarly, several hundred were located in the State of New York, but at this particular find, only three of the cairns held these peculiar frontal holes. It should be stated here that all of these unusual cavities possessed crude hearths. Additionally, there were indications that burning was predominant over long periods of time. Since many rock cairns have been found situated high on a bluff or mountain top, once again speculation drew a relationship between this type of cairn and ancient altars of stone employed by early Israelites, for history records this race of people erecting mountain-top fire altars. Along the same line of thought, stone cairns erected in the Middle East, oftentimes included stone circles nearby. The cairns seem to trace their roots to Asia on many occasions.

Mention has been made both to discoveries in the Old World

as well as the New World, especially around the eastern states of our country. But now let's take a look at our home State of Michigan. How do the cairns fare here? In the 1800s Bela Hubbard wrote an interesting book titled, *Memorials of a Half-Century* in which he reported stone piles near Romeo in Macomb County. In several places in this area were found mounds made of stones, nicely piled up to a height of nearly 5 feet, similar to the fashion of a "haycock." They were entirely constructed of stone and more than a mile distant from any other group of earth-mounds. Interestingly enough, one of these mounds was opened. It proved to be 4 feet in height and placed in a circular excavation of 2 feet deep by 4 feet in diameter. The rocks were nicely placed and were preserved. Mr. Hubbard reported skeletons were exhumed. For all intents and purposes, the above is an excellent description of a cairn used as a burial marker.

Still another cairn possibility was pointed out by Hubbard. He recalled Henry Schoolcraft described stone piles or cairns on Mackinaw Island. While Indian Agent Schoolcraft was of the opinion these cairns were from earlier settlers clearing fields, Bela Hubbard strongly maintained they were heaped about bodies for protection from scavenging wild animals, until such time as a religious ceremony could be held. "The Feast of the Dead" was carried out in religious-festival tradition approximately once every ten or twelve years. At that time the skeletel remains were exhumed for a huge, common grave burial, while a ritualistic feast was held to honor the dead!

Now let's discuss Michigan's most recent prehistory revelation which just happens to be stone cairns and accompanying rambling rock walls. This important new discovery is located at a spot called regionally, South Pointe. It can be found near Black River, south of Alpena, north of Harrisville, on the northeastern side of Michigan, bordering Lake Huron's shoreline. Our Michigan Department of Natural Resources (D.N.R.) plans to incorporate this area into a 1700-acre park system which will be known as Negwegon. Newspaper articles will be quoted later in this chapter, regarding the development of this site, but first let's examine descriptive remarks on the Black River "Negwegon" find from an interview with local amateur archaeologist, Dennis Morrison of Harrisville.

Dennis expresses his eyewitness account as follows: "Well let's talk about Black River a bit. You walk up the lakeshore from Black River about a distance of 6 miles. Then you come upon a clearing in the pine woods. As you continue to hike inland, you come across an old stone well and next to that, a twisted ancient thorn-apple tree. Still further on there are the remains of what some historians consider to be a prehistory rock wall or stone fence. As you stand at this spot and listen, the waves striking against the rocky shore, seem to whisper of yet another time and the secrets that era has covered up at this very spot!"

"My wife Kathy and I first hiked up there during the summer of 1986. It was fascinating to say the least and we made many additional trips as time went on. We took numerous photos which identify both the stone piles or cairns as well as the unusual stone walls. We also photographed the unique old stone well that was constructed of small boulders without cement or any other bonding agent. Popular conjecture in this local area indicates this well was dug by the man who supposedly homesteaded this land; namely, Nigger Marshall. I have a problem however with seeing this rock-lined pit as having been used as a well. To start with, it is...or was, as someone filled it partially with boulders; only 4½ feet deep. I sincerely doubt that it was ever used in the capacity of a well. It has been pointed out to me that possibly the bottom had been filled in with dirt and that at one time it was perhaps deeper. This is of course a possibility, but I find that argument highly unlikely because it would have served no real purpose to fill the well in and then leave the top 4½ feet unfilled."

Mr. Morrison continues, "The stone fence and stone piles lie roughly 50 feet west of the above described well. The piles are of various sizes. I believe each of them is hollowed out forming a cone. At least most of them seem to be. In a number of the cairns, large birch trees have grown up through their centers. The argument some people are going to use against these stone works being Indian or Pre-Indian in origin, is that everyone knows Nigger Marshall lived back in there. However, having spent a great deal of time researching the "Negwegon" area, I can say with certainty, that there was a co-mingling of cultures at this site. True, we have found things made in the 1850s but also relics of antiquity have been recovered from the same immediate area. As an example, I picked up a small black stone celt that had been kicked up from the trail by perhaps a dirt bike. Also along the path, about 5 blocks from the stoneworks is a large boulder, the top of which had been without a doubt, used as a primitive mortar."

"Perhaps I should mention here that the stones or cairns are more or less arranged in rows and circles and cover acres of land. Another reason I have never accepted the "squatter" homestead theory offered is that these stoneworks are just far too elaborate. In turn they are well designed and cover far more ground than a mere "worked over" garden area would contain. Let me put it another way...if a farmer worked his entire lifetime building these formations, they would not have been completed. Perhaps it may have involved several generations."

"Another interesting feature is the stone walls. They ramble...run straight for hundreds of feet, then for no apparent rhyme or reason, unexpectantly veer off at acute right angles. They do not enclose, say a pasture or garden area in a rectangular form. Within their confines however, exist many, many stone piles or cairns. Some are 12 feet or more across and about 5 feet high. It is possible for a man to climb down into the center of these conical cairns and still remain upright. Most exceedingly strange! Believe me!"

Let's pause here just a moment and discuss the man who is said to have settled years back, at this cairn site. The now non-existing homestead at South Point was thought to have been occupied by a man known locally as Nigger Marshall. This man was colored, perhaps an escaped slave from the South. Since no actual records are in evidence to this fact, what is offered here is classed as "hearsay." Legend recalls the name "Nigger" meant no disrespect, for the man was well thought of. Calling him "Nigger" was no different than say calling him "Curley" or "Shorty" or any other nickname from that particular time. Stories relate that the negro man along with his wife were tired of running, and perhaps the land here at "Negwegon" held a special fascination for this runaway pair.

Maybe the old rambling stone walls or fence caught his fancy and he envisioned a small farm of his own on that exact spot. Nevertheless, they settled there, he in turn did a bit of blacksmith work and they lived on the land until he died. His homesite has long since crumbled and reverted back to nature. Only the cairns and enigmatic stone fence remain to supply missing pieces from this jigsaw puzzle of past lives and endeavors.

Dennis Morrison (previously mentioned) had been covering the "Negwegon" cairn site for the Alcona County Review of Harrisville, for which paper he serves as reporter. The following article appeared in his weekly column entitled *From The Top*, dated December 30, 1988.

> "This past week I attended the Negwegon Park Commission meeting. After listening for a little over 2-hours, I walked away with a few concerns of my own over the historic and prehistoric relics that lie buried beneath the soils of the land in question.
>
> The commission is bent on saving these historic areas no matter what, and for that I commend them heartily! However having dealt with amateur archaeology for some time now, I have noticed something. When the state comes in and conducts excavations, it seems residents of the area never get to see what was found. nor hear the outcome. I would hope that this would not be the case with Negwegon. It is a gross injustice that takes relics from the communities in which they were found, and also to just leave the people hanging. I have worked several sites in the Oscoda area. I have a deep-set interest in knowing about the other sites found there and how they relate to my own finds. Still if I were not a member of the Michigan Archaeological Society, I would never learn about these other finds, as there are no releases to the media. Again I caution the Negwegon Commission, you are spending tax money in creating this park. Make certain that the taxpayer is well paid with the information that you uncover from this site. There was a great deal of concern expressed at the

meeting about possible looters going in and digging the sites at Negwegon if much is published about them. This is a concern all over the country with prehistoric sites, and yet the people who are interested have a right to know. I suspect that this 'low-key' attitude on where these sites lie is perhaps why the press was not invited to attend a recent walk through tour of Negwegon, despite the fact that two members of that commission had promised this reporter that he would be taken back there. Unfortunate it is that we were excluded, as with as much local resistance that this project seems to be stimulating, the Commission could use all the good press it can get.

I have the satisfaction of knowing these sites inside out as I have camped along the stoneworks, and in the orchard that once belonged to Nigger Marshall. I have gone in and photographed extensively the area. If the Commission were not so dogmatic about being afraid people might destroy the site and consult people like myself, then they might gain some allies. For example, I have seen and studied relics from the Black River - Negwegon site that prove the existence of prehistoric Indian habitation along the shoreline and also homesteads from periods prior to the 1860s. If the Commission were to have asked the press to come along on their walk through, I could have taken them point blank to sites I am sure they don't know even exist."

Incidentally, after the Negwegon Commission meeting, the commission showed excellent judgement by appointing Dennis Morrison as a member of that commission.

Recent Department of Natural Resources proposals for the Negwegon State Park include the following: Use areas within the park's boundaries will be defined into four zone classifications. This D.N.R. park plan requires two distinct recreation areas which might comprise about 25% of the total park acreage. One of the areas is on high ground and might be the site of an historic interpretive center. The other is a stretch of beach south of the current parking lot.

The initial development calls for 80 campsites which hopefully will be expanded to 160 if the need arises. It is unknown at this writing if the campsites will be modern or rustic. Plans are yet sketchy. Other proposed zoning areas would include a natural area zone; the biggest area of the park would be left undeveloped and closed to all vehicular traffic. Also proposed is an historic zone where areas of possible archaeological importance are located. Finally, a general zone that would link other areas which may contain access roads, pedestrian trails as well as boardwalks.

Should the above Negwegon Park plans materialize, Michigan then will have two archaeological theme areas open to the general public. The stone cairns and rock walls of Negwegon and the Sanilac Petroglyph State Park in Sanilac County.

How does this discovery tie in with say, other cairn locations? Two men from Duluth, Minnesota, have recently been studying cairns and rock piles in Thunder Bay, Canada, as well as northern Michigan. Their discoveries have proved exciting beyond words. The finding near Thunder Bay was aptly called "The Osmic Cairns," mainly because this word means "a heap of stones used for a landmark." They were researched by Greg Bambenek and Glenn Langhorst. This brilliant pair of anthropologists took compass bearings from the cairns and put them into a computer program planned out by Langhorst. As reports indicated, the pits definitely were not arranged haphazardly. Langhorst stated, "We calculated that we did have a summer solstice alignment, both for the sunrise and sunset." The men made five additional trips to this site. On one specific occasion they lit torches in three of the pits, and sat back and waited for the summer solstice sun to rise. The men actually got goose bumps as the three torches, the three pits and the sun on the horizon all aligned. Glenn Langhorst remarked, "It seemed like we lifted the veil of mystery in a way. It was kind of like stepping back in time and experiencing what the medicine men would have experienced."

Eventually the two men drew conclusions that this ancient form of alignment was used by primitive man in relationship to the lake trout and whitefish spawning season. The shallows near the cairns would have shown up the spawning fish along a reef, where they annually spend from seven to ten days. The other 97% of the year the fish live in deeper waters. The present site of the Osmic Cairns would have been situated along the ancient shoreline of Lake Superior around 2000 B.C. Presently at the Osmic site, old beach levels appear as terraces in the cobblestones.

It should be mentioned here while discussing these stone cairns, that like the Black River find, they similarly consisted of a pit with a rim of rocks some four feet high. Once again, here a man could stand upright in the hole.

Langhorst and Bambenek have also done considerable scientific research (as previously mentioned in the Copper Culture chapters), on Isle Royale regarding the stone pits located there. If you remember correctly, this anthropologist team more or less determined them to be an ancient prehistory observatory.

Additional rock piles have turned up in Wisconsin and the Upper Peninsula of Michigan, and newspaper accounts indicate they are being thoroughly investigated by Professor James Scherz from the University of Wisconsin. These piles or cairns are slightly different from the ones already described. The stone cairns measured from 6 inches to 3 feet high and were arranged in giant circles divided into degrees. Perhaps the ancient people used them to determine the solstices as with other rough calendars previously described. Scherz mentions rock groupings have been found located in swamps, on islands, and along river banks. This man has found these unusual smaller cairns along both the Fox River in Wisconsin and the Ontonagon River in Michigan's Upper Peninsula. This researcher states that he does not believe the rocks were arranged naturally or by farmers of the past century or so. Scherz theorizes the calendars were constructed by early primitive man along the copper trade routes between Lake Superior mines and the Mississippi River.

It seems as though we have been discussing the perplexing stone cairns to the neglect of mentioning the curious rock walls. Such stone walls or fences, as they are often called, have been reported from time to time in the Old Country. Research indicates that oftentimes stone piles exist in mysterious conjuction with unexplained stone walls found nearby. In many specific instances these mystifying pair of stoneworks are located in wooded areas or mountainsides. The majority found occurred where no farm had ever existed. However, let me point out here that in most instances, a good astronomical viewing area was in evidence.

In many cases walls of stone were discovered from Illinois, Tennessee and West Virginia, often measuring 3 feet wide and 6 feet high. Many are believed to be ceremonial in nature. Like the cairns, the walls are of dry construction conceived without mortar. In some cases these abnormal stone walls have been discovered that run true north and south or towards specific points indicated by solstice sunrises or sunsets.

In closing I would like to mention a personal find husband Bill and I came across on private land in the eastern Upper Peninsula that we both strongly feel bears further investigation. It was an enormous slab rock wall, black in color, perhaps 8 feet high...that stretched through a well-wooded section of land for over a quarter of a mile. This was definitely a non-farming area. The location was inland perhaps a distance of say, two miles from a water source, that being the St. Marys River. This "great wall," as we called it, ended at a clearing in the forest. As we remember it, there was a huge pile of rocks here as well as large scattered black boulders...as though an ancient giant had just finished a game of marbles. Additionally, a lava field was also evident. At the time of this discovery, the wall, the unexplained large pile of stone as well as the scattered boulders, all seemed most unusual. But until researching the cairns described in this chapter, the spot held little significance in a prehistory regard. Believe me, we will see that it is thorougly investigated.

Ancient rocks do have problematical prehistoric pasts. Becoming aware of these unusual discoveries hopefully will provide future generations the opportunity to witness these stonework reminders that Michigan was once occupied by a mysterious, vanished race of people.

Part III of *QUESTIONABLE ROCKS WITH A*

PREHISTORY PAST will take up the subjects of dolmens and engraved "message" rocks. Examples of each have been located in the Upper Peninsula...two viable reminders of a time and place when perhaps the "Celts" and the "Norsemen" were once known as "Michiganders!"

CREDITS:

Morrison, Dennis, freelance writer-photographer, Greenbush, MI, Reporter for *Harrisville County Review*, Harrisville, MI

Bambenek, Greg and Langhorst, Glenn, Anthropologists, Duluth, MN

Scherz, James, University of Wisconsin, Madison, WI

PHOTO CREDITS:

Morrison, Dennis, freelance writer-photographer, Greenbush, MI

SUGGESTED FURTHER READING

AMERICA, B.C., Fell, Barry; Quadrangle Books, New York, N.Y., 1976

BRONZE AGE AMERICA, Fell, Barry; Little Brown & Co., Boston-Toronto, 1982

THE SEARCH FOR LOST AMERICA, Trento, Salvatore, Michael; Contemporary Books, Inc., Chicago, 1978

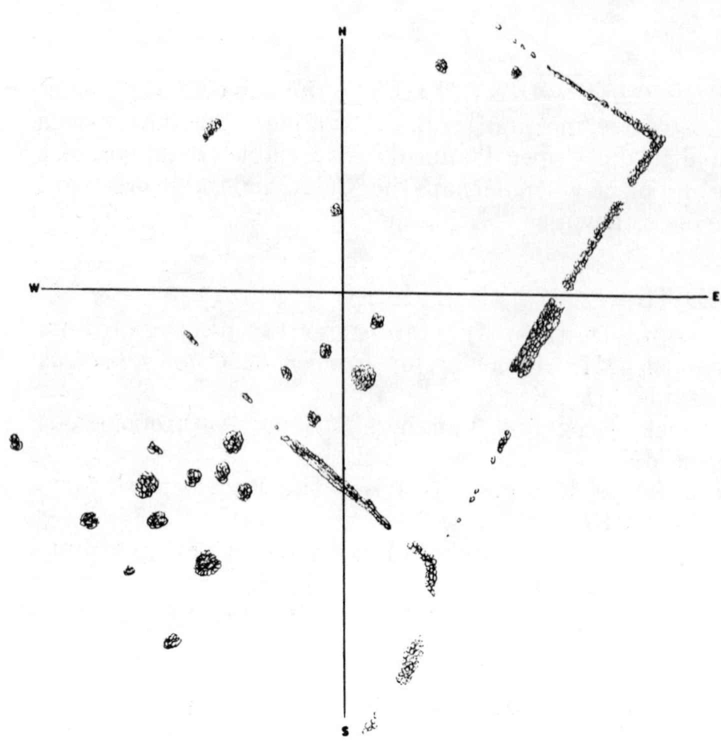

Diagram showing placement or alignment of stone cairns in relationship to the rambling rock walls. Note how walls seems to "take-off" at abrupt right angles.

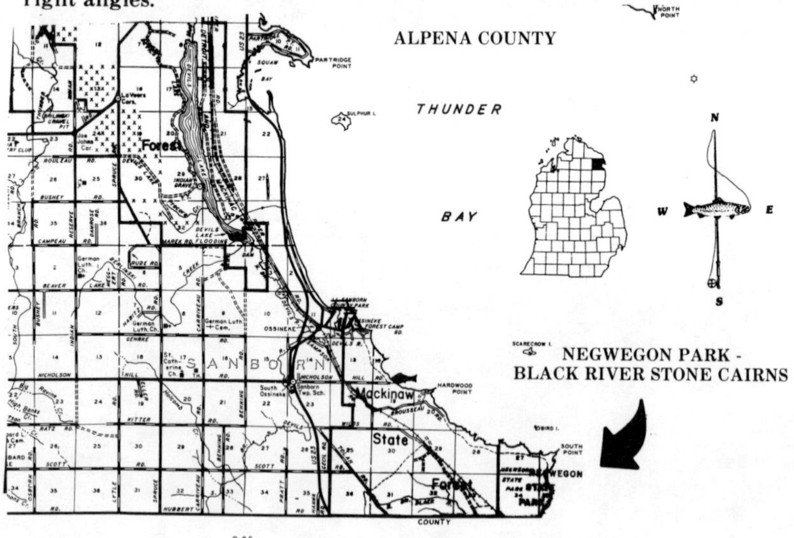

Black River Stone Cairns - Negewgon State Park.

Questionable Rocks With A Prehistory Past
PART III
The Huron Mountain Dolmen
The Escanaba Stone

It's too bad rocks can't talk, for certainly the Escanaba Stone and the Huron Mountain dolmen would have some "whoppers" to tell! For you see, these two Michigan megalithic monuments hold a definite relationship to Old World ties. In fact, these virtually unknown prehistory rock monuments or markers express the NIBC (No Immigrants Before Columbus) Theory more so than any other Michigan relic or ruin that has surfaced to date.

What positive proof of European influx is indicated here? Well first, for example, consider the case of the inscribed Escanaba Stone found in the Escanaba River in the year 1954. Sure, it more or less looks just like any normal-appearing, average-sized rock. But what definitely sets this particular stone apart from other rocks found in Michigan is a series of long, carved or etched, straight lines. Over the course of years, many experts in their field have simply dismissed similar rocks with inscriptions, as marks or scrapes caused by plowshares. Still others ironically attributed the writing to the action of salt crystals. Neither erroneous theory seems to hold water.

Extensive research indicates similar rocks to the Escanaba find have, over a period of years, been discovered in an impressive list of states, including: Arizona, New Mexico, Oklahoma, Arkansas, Missouri, Iowa, North Dakota, Minnesota, West Virginia, Kentucky, Tennessee, Georgia, North Carolina, Pennsylvania, New Jersey, Vermont, Massachusetts, Maine, Rhode Island and Connecticut. Needless to say, such a large number of these inscribed stones cannot all be dismissed merely as plowshare damage, or other such caprice of nature. This fact is especially viable, since over half of the script rocks were located a good distance from local agricultural pursuits. One field alone in Pennsylvania turned up literally hundreds of these specially-marked rocks. In due course of time, this discovery came to the attention of Barry Fell, President of the Epigraphic Society. Fell is also well known for his books, *America B.C.* and *Bronze Age America.* Both mentioned publications deal with Old World visitors to the shores of North America as far distant as 2000 B.C.

So now you are wondering, just what is the Epigraphic Society? It is in turn a non-profit group with a worldwide membership, dedicated to the study and preservation of ancient texts and inscriptions. Their findings and information is available through their "Occasional Publications" providing a bulletin on ancient inscriptions, writings, hieroglyphics and other related discoveries. It is the only publication of its kind, and the society often carries a large backlog for deciphering and interpreting inscriptions, not only in the United States, but around the world as well. The address for the society is as follows: The Epigraphic Society, 6625 Bamburgh Drive, San Diego, CA 92117-5105.

Back once again to the Escanaba Stone. It was found in the Upper Peninsula in the Escanaba River in 1954 by Joel Kela formerly from Negaunee, now deceased. Presently its whereabouts is unknown. For years it was on display at the museum in Marquette, but my investigation indicates it was removed a few years back. My extended efforts failed to track it down. However, photographs remain.

On November 16, 1957, Mr. Kela spoke to the Marquette County Historical Society, at which time his speech was described as follows: "Joel Kela, of Negaunee, showed a rock which had been carefully etched by some unknown hand, and had been found by him and a friend in the bottom of the Escanaba River. He told of the research he had done in attempting to find if it could have been Danish writing or done by the Vikings, either as a marker or religious symbol. He traced possible routes the Vikings might have taken in pushing westward."

It may just be possible that Joel Kela earned the distinction of being, "a man ahead of his time!"

As fate would have it, through some unknown means, a photograph of the Escanaba Stone came into the hands of Professor Barry Fell. In turn, Fell ascertained the etching or inscription was written in Ogam consaine script. Now what in the heck is Ogam writing? Well, before we reveal Fell's translation, let's talk first about ancient scripts.

According to Barry Fell, Ogam is a system of writing employing combinations of up to five parallel strokes set above or below a line or "stem." An ancient writing system that dates back to at least the Bronze Age in Europe. In turn Ogam Consaine script is very similar to Ogam but it does not employ the use of vowels. Naturally, as one would expect, Ogam Consaine, is harder to decipher. All ancient writings easily fall into perhaps but a half-dozen specific styles. It is also interesting to learn, that each known script was associated with perhaps several ancient peoples and cultures...not merely one. At the present time, new inscriptions are coming to light almost daily from all parts of the world...some localities as far distant as thousands of miles apart.

Additionally, it should be noted, most circumstances preclude fraud possibilities. Over the span of years, the Epigraphic Society has done an excellent job of also detecting fraud possibilities, and public denouncements appear in their *Occasional Publications.* They are a very well respected organization.

A good example of an engraved stone very similar to the Escanaba Stone was found off the coast of Maine and is called the "Manana Island Stone." Professor Fell translated this inscription to read, "Long-ships from Phoenicia - Cargo-lots and landing-quay." The script seemed to be relating a message to Phoenician merchant seamen that Manana Island (near larger Monhegan Island), was the designated landing to pick up raw materials from New World traders. It was written in a style of Ogam script only recently identified along the Iberian Peninsula, which suggests this message was left by Iberian Celts. Once again those "Will-O-The-Wisp" Celts feature in Michigan's prehistory.

Please keep in mind the Escanaba Stone was also incribed in Ogam script. At this particular point in time this author imagines you are excitedly awaiting Barry Fell's translation of Michigan's only incribed rock. So here goes...The Escanaba Stone written in vowelless Ogam or Ogam Consaine reads, "A prayer on my behalf, let me not drown on the waters." Fell considered the inscription to be a Gaelic prayer stone.

Here once again may you be reminded that a strong possibility exists that early people from the Celtic Race traveled from Beaver Island in northern Lake Michigan, up the Escanaba River towards Lake Superior. These routes tie in dramatically with the Copper Culture ore trade. Maybe they even relate to the Huron Mountain dolmen above the Marquette and the discovery north of Newberry known as the McGruer's Gods and the Newberry Stone. For you see, the so-called Newberry Stone in all essence is not a stone, but rather a tablet made of clay, on which appear 140 raised symbols, each contained in a square. Due to a translation by Barry Fell, it too is attributed to foreign intrusion via the Old World. It will thoroughly be discussed in yet another chapter.

It seems difficult to fathom, but all major rivers and tributaries as well as shorelines across the United States, have turned up evidence of a long-gone seagoing race of people. As previously illustrated, they have left behind evidence and reminders of long-past activity. A legacy comprised of a variety of stoneworks includes dolmens, stone cairns, cist chambers, inscribed rocks, giant rambling rock walls and prehistoric copper mining pits. One must tend to agree these facts are not fiction. They offer mute testimony to the fact that numerous small-scale groups of Old World traders possibly used widely diversified, well-established, trade routes scattered far and wide across the Americas from say Canada to South America. Almost unbelievable! The complex job of unraveling the complete scope of their travels offers progress with each additional discovery. The Escanaba Stone is but one small link in that immense chain of events.

Before going on to the next subject, that of the Huron Mountain dolmen, it should be understood the followers of Fell believe after the Celtic pioneers arrived in this country, they were followed by Phoenician traders from Spain. This ancient race of people spoke a language called Punic. In the written form, Punic entails a peculiar style known now as Iberian script. In time, some of these people stayed along America's eastern coast, but it is also thought many of these traders pushed into the interior, eventually mingling with the Amerindian tribes.

Meanwhile, research also indicates an influx of Egyptians similarly joined the Wabanaki Tribe of New England, which points the way to "why" the original American Indian birch bark scrolls so closely seem to resemble the Egyptian hieroglyphic style of pictograming. Additionally, Basque sailors left their mark in Pennsylvania, leaving behind monuments and grave markers to testify in their behalf. Still further southward, rocks and stones bearing names of Libyans and Egyptian sailors have turned up along the Mississippi River Valley extending directly to the Gulf of Mexico. Along the way, side trips were made into Iowa and the Dakotas for you once again find records of their progress left behind for posterity's sake. Believe me, generally speaking, people find it hard to fathom Old World travelers here in the United States before the time of Christ; but on the scope described above, the possibilities almost seem endless.

Since we have an idea of who may or may not have visited Michigan in prehistory times, let's take a look at Michigan's other artifact of ancient antiquity, possibly left behind by Celtic traders. It is called a dolmen and was discovered in the Huron Mountains above Marquette in the early 1800s. Perhaps you are curious. What is a dolmen? Well, a dolmen is a megalithic monument in which a capstone of up to 90 tons stands supported on three or more vertical stones or legs. Large examples appear to have been monuments perhaps in honor of a dead leader or chieftain. But in turn, many of these unusual, mysterious stone monuments featured mainly in religious ceremonies. Smaller versions of dolmens have been proven to serve as grave or burial markers. Perhaps you are more familiar with the strange rock structures at Stonehenge.

These huge megalithic monuments are not true dolmens, but are termed trilithons. Similar to a dolmen, except the capstone is found resting on merely two supports instead of three or more. This affords the structure a precarious look, as though at any moment it might collapse. Also the trilithon usually contains a smaller capstone, while the upright support stones are often higher...just the reverse of the dolmen.

Perhaps you would like to know prehistory dolmens range in the Americas from Labrador to South America. The most typical example can be found at North Salem, New York. this dolmen closely matches its counterparts in Europe. The relationship between the dolmens of the Old World with the New World indicates European contacts with the Americas, an almost unbelievable 2,000 years before Columbus.

Still holding descriptive thoughts regarding these Neolithic megaliths, it should be stated the name "dolmen" is a Breton word meaning a stone table. It so aptly describes many of the smaller structures, for in retrospect their capstones often resemble a flat, table-like slab, giving the dolmen an altar appearance.

An important correlation perhaps never introduced to the scientific community came about through research for this book. Early written records such as appear in the *Jesuit Relations,* 1636...mention slab-like rock altars placed in secluded spots throughout the Great Lakes territories. It is the opinion of this author that these so prescribed primitive Indian relics just might have been dolmens similar to the Huron Mountain find, left behind by yet a more ancient race of people. But now it seems all traces of these altars or dolmens, as the case may be, are gone. Lost forever...destroyed! History records false gods and altars of tribal worship were contrary to religious beliefs, and mass destruction of such articles was required to convert the red man to Christianity. Any form of such idolatry was considered sacrilegious. Destruction of idols and altars was the norm.

The following quote from *Michigan Pioneer Collections* written in the 1800s by Bela Hubbard illustrates this point. "Upon a swelling knoll overlooking the bay at the mouth of the Kawkawlin River, (Saginaw Bay 1837) in the midst of a tract of country from which all timber had been burned, was a spot which seemed to have been dedicated to the evil Manitou. Here an altar was erected, composed of two large stones, several feet in height with a flat top and broad base. About were several small stones which were covered with propitiary offerings...bits of tobacco, pieces of tin, flints, etc. all dedicated to the Indian's Manitou."

In all essence, the above description fits a trilithon or two-legged dolmen. Many other entries of altar stones can be found in the books of the Jesuits, as well as writings of other early Michigan authors. Perhaps someday this comparison will be worthy of scientific note...a new clue to one of Michigan's prehistory mysteries.

At this point two important facts should be brought to your attention. One that it has more or less become accepted theory that the American Indian did little or no stonework. He carved no stone statues, built no rock monuments. Secondly, on all documented occasions, Native Americans vehemently denied any knowledge of who actually built stone statues, dolmens, cairns, stone walls, mining pits, stone observatories, or in turn inscribed unreadable script on rocks.

Now let's talk about Michigan's lone dolmen. Information regarding this unusual rock structure comes from three sources: the Marquette Historical Society, Fred Rydholm a retired teacher and historian from Marquette, and a 1986 Marquette Mining Journal article.

In 1959, the Marquette Historical Society described this megalithic monument as follow: "Huron Mountain...On top of the mountain overlooking Mountain Lake is a large block of stone raised on three stone legs, each of them quite symmetrically shaped like truncated, three-sided pyramids, both stone and supports covered with fine lichen. The stone is roughly rectangular, about ten inches through. It shows no signs of having been shaped and is not set strictly according to compass points. It has been examined by John Longyear, an archaeologist, and he indicates it is not an Indian artifact but he could not say who made it."

At a 1957 meeting of the above-mentioned society, Fred Rydholm, was a guest speaker and meeting reports were as follows: "The mysterious altar stone, a huge boulder set on three legs in the Huron Mountains, was described by Fred Rydholm of Marquette. He also told of a huge Indian carving on the Huron Islands."

The Marquette Mining Journal in 1986 published an article written by W.H. Treloar entitled, "Did Norsemen Visit Upper Peninsula?" It appears here in its entirety with permission granted by Craig Swanson, Managing Editor of said newspaper.

Did Norsemen Visit Upper Peninsula? "Did people from the latter years of the Bronze Age dwell in Marquette County? Could it be that 3,500 to 5,000 years ago visitors from Norse countries came to our land seeking copper and other metals? Did Norsemen, who foraged afar, reach inland to the Huron Mountains in Marquette County?

A few years ago, questions like this would have been greeted with derision. In the past few years, however, there has been a rash of books on the travels of the ancients, which lends some validity to the questions raised above.

For years, it has been known that 1,600 feet atop the heights of Huron Mountain there rests a "mystery stone," a flat-bottomed stone resting on three smaller legs. The Huron Mountain Club at one time sold postcards depicting the stone. John M. Longyear, who founded the club in 1899, knew of its presence several years prior to that time.

Until recently, it has been considered a work of the Huron Indians who came here between 1615 and 1650, driven away from their eastern habitat by quarrelsome Iroquois. The Huron island, river and mountain were named for the Huron Indians. The reasoning was simple: Huron Indians came from the east, there are a lot of similar stone objects in the east. Some Huron Indians were driven inland and one tribe reached into Minnesota. There is a stone object atop Huron Mountain, thus it must be an Indian altar. For years this was accepted.

But now, with greater research, the stone is believed by many to be a true dolmen. The dictionary tells us a dolmen is a stone tablet, erected by the ancients at a burial site. The Huron Mountain dolmen is a ceremonial one, as it rests on solid rock.

C. Fred Rydholm, historian, has been interested in the stone for years. He was 15 when he was first told about it. Since then, he has guided scores of interested people to the site. "But whatever I did," he comments, "apparently was not enough to arouse a deep enough interest to excite research. I've talked about it, been taped, photographed, televised, and everybody just listened, murmured something about 'how interesting' and carried it no further."

"Rydholm made it clear he does not make any claims to solving the riddle of the "mystery stone." But in recent years, several historians have expressed views that could shed a different light on the Marquette stone. To start with, serious questions arise about the Indian theory. Several historians point out that the Indians did not build with stone, but with earth mounds. They built wooden shelters over their graves. They etched in stone, but did not construct with it.

Rydholm said, "Without question, the outstanding proponent of the Bronze Age theory is Barry Fell, now in California, a professor emeritus of Harvard University."

Fell, in his book, *Bronze Age America*, freely admits he has several detractors, but points out that the late Professor Robert Heizer of the University of California, the most vehement in rejecting all theories of Bronze Age visitation, later changed his views and collaborated with Fell on some further research. Fell has made a study of ancient alphabets and has been able to translate ancient inscriptions.

Most authorities agree that 3,700 years ago, King Woden-Lithi, a Norse, sailed the Atlantic and entered the St. Lawrence River, establishing a colony at what is now Peterborough, Canada. He left a small group behind when he sailed back to his homeland. While he faded into history, it is believed that some of his party foraged west in search of the source of copper.

Rydholm points out that, while many of these stone creations have been known for years, little importance was attached to them because of the flat denial, in the minds of many, that there was any important historical meaning to them.

While Fell has not visited Marquette, he sent a photographer here, one William Dexter of Vermont, who specialized in pictorial coverage of antiquities. After examining the Huron Mountain stone, he said, according to Rydholm, "That is a true dolmen."

Kevin Renfrew, an English historian, said these man-made structures which are found throughout the world, are the work of a megalithic people and they flourished in the latter days of the Bronze Age.

"So what I have done," Rydholm concluded, "is bring to the attention of all who will listen that there is just as much probability of this stone being a true dolmen, dating back 3,500 to 5,000 years, as there is that this is a more recent reminder of the Huron Indians."

"And while a controversy continues between historians, the "mystery stone" of the Huron Mountains rests where it was placed centuries ago, its mute message lost in the fog of time."

****

This author has corresponded with Mr. Rydholm and learned he is still actively searching Michigan's hinterlands for the truth. He has studied the recent Beaver Island "ring of stones" discovery, followed the progress of the investigation regarding McGruer's Gods and the Newberry Stone, as well as made several investigative trips to the State of Minnesota to check on other dolmens and engraved stones, along with other prehistory relics from that state. Fred Rydholm recently investigated a large dolmen in Minnesota at the request of Charles Bailey and Glenn Langhorst of Duluth. This dolmen was found on a small island in the boundary waters territory. This dolmen, perhaps related to the Michigan dolmen, was 6½ feet long, 4½ feet wide and 3½ feet high. It was a prolite basalt boulder of a granite outcrop. It is interesting to also learn here that immediately north of the dolmen was a perched rock situated on the shoreline which, incidentally, aligned with a natural ridge directly north and south.

Mr. Rydholm feels there is a common denominator between the Michigan dolmen, the engraved Escanaba River stone, the inscribed clay Newberry tablet, the newly discovered Beaver Island "ring of stones" and "wagon wheels" to perhaps other Lake Superior-Lake Michigan regional prehistory material and culture. In closing this chapter, it is this author's expectation that as future discoveries surface in yet unexplored areas throughout Michigan's northern lower peninsula and the entire upper peninsula...some of these seemingly perplexing mysteries from centuries past will in turn be solved. Perhaps this book will get things once again "stirred-up"...a new beginning in the right direction...a revival of interest...first step of a long journey towards the truth...I personally hope so!

CREDITS:
C. Fred Rydholm, Marquette, MI
The Marquette Historical Museum, Marquette, MI
Joel Kela, deceased, Negaunee, MI
The Marquette Mining Journal, Marquette, MI
Charles Bailey, Duluth, MN
Glenn Langhorst, Duluth, MN

PHOTO CREDITS:
Marquette Historical Museum, Marquette, MI
C. Fred Rydholm, Marquette, MI
Charles Bailey, Duluth, MN

SUGGESTED FURTHER READING

AMERICA, B.C., Fell, Barry; Quadrangle Books, New York, NY 1976.

BRONZE AGE AMERICA, Fell, Barry; Little, Brown & Co., Boston-Toronto, 1982.

THE SEARCH FOR LOST AMERICA, Trento, Salvatore Michael; Contemporary Books Inc., Chicago, 1978

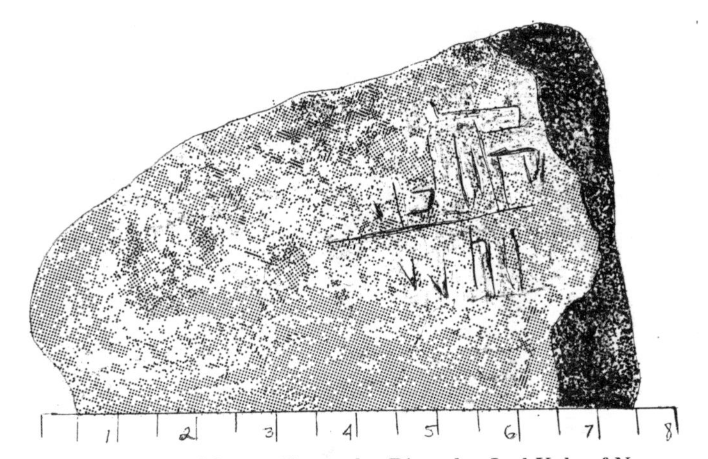

Etched stone found in the Escanaba River by Joel Kela of Negaunee. Translated by Barry Fell as a Gaelic Prayer Stone. Now known as The Escanaba Stone.

Huron Mountain Stone located on Huron Mountain Club property.

Minnesota dolmen located in northern Boundary Waters.

Data being collected by Glenn Langhorst, of Duluth, Minnesota.

MARQUETTE COUNTY

HURON MOUNTAIN DOLMEN

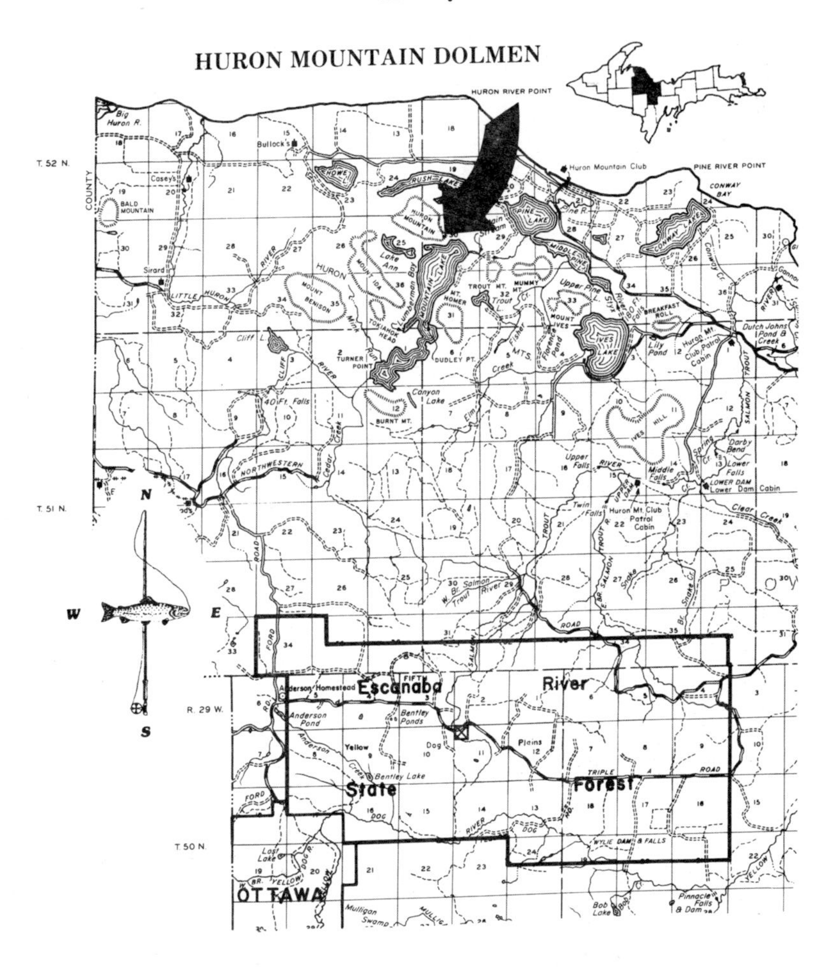

Image Stones - Spirit Stones An Enigma!

Rocks have always been considered sacred to Native Americans. Magical rocks, secret rocks, image rocks, spirit rocks...have all been wrapped in mystery for ancient races.

In many Amerindian nations the Indian word for rock means exactly the same as their word for "oldest god." Both the rock and the elder god were considered old beyond imagination, absolutely ageless and eternal.

Generally speaking, Michigan's forest people, our Native Americans, had no chapel in which they could summon their gods. In place of such, they revered rocks, trees, mountains, waterfalls, rapids, streams, lakes and certain secluded glens as venerable or sacrosanct. Strangely shaped rocks, especially those found along water routes, were worshipped as dwelling places of all-powerful spirits. Over the passage of centuries, customs developed of offering small token gifts including tobacco, at these quiet out-of-the-way, forest-water sanctuaries.

Whatever was mysterious and visionary was within the realm or scope of the Indian's religion. The activity of spirits more or less signified their deep beliefs in the supernatural. In turn, while practicing anthropomorphism, the Indians ascribed human or animal attributes to non-human objects, be they rocks, stones, statues, or idols and trees to name but a few. Furthermore, the Indians believed in an existence after death which prompted dreams and visions as part of their prescribed rituals. Spirits and ghosts often spoke to them through inanimate objects, as well as members of the animal kingdom. In turn, it was believed spirits often frequented their consecrated tabernacles of sacred rocks and altar stones.

Actually, their religion was quite simple...everything in nature possessed a "magical power." There is reason for supposing this strength was often introduced as a spirit which evoked awe and fear in the hearts of primitive man.

Ceremonies evolved over the years, making these sacred places even more worshipful to the Indian. As a matter of course, whatever appeared unusual in color, shape, movement or situation caused the Indian to stop, ponder, worship and perhaps offer a gift. An excellent example would surely be a "spirit tree." Should a specific tree at a given time, due to wind action, storm or natural happenstance, make a certain, unusual whispering or crying sound, it turn, it became known as a "spirit tree"...a place of worship. From that time on, all Indians knowing of its power, would not pass by without leaving an offering, perhaps a small amount of tobacco dropped into a trunk cavity.

It is readily agreed the early Michigan Indian wove medicine and magic very closely into his religion. He vastly differed, however, from the white man's beliefs for he offered gifts to the gods, not for favors desired, but out of gratitude for good fortune already granted. It is probable, however, that should his good luck fail him, then the Native American had recourse of a tribal medicine man to intercede in his behalf.

Actually, the word "manitou" among the Algonquians means a transfer of great power to an object. Oftentimes the "manitou" was considered a detachable property able to appear and leave at will. Many were felt to be permanent. Therefore, any specific property of nature that had an aura of unusuality, being different in any respect from its surroundings, could have been termed a "manitou."

Keeping this point in mind, the Indians actually did not have idols, per se. It is an accepted archaeological fact, early Michigan man did not work stone. How then did some of the early standing "manitous," composed of rock or copper described by explorers and priests of the 1600s, arrive in the Great Lakes region? Who then sculptured these idols? Actually in most instances the icons were adopted by the Indians as "manitous," yet records continuously indicate these specific regional natives had no prior knowledge of how the statues originated. True, no early written words existed among the natives at that time, but legends and tales were carefully passed down from generation to generation. The elders of the tribes were our equivalent of "talking books!" Thus these statues and idols present a unique and most compelling mystery.

Equally as perplexing, is it once again a possibility that early Indian alter stones were in essence really "dolmens" abandoned some 4000 years ago by wandering Celts or Norsemen? Once again, the same set of questions encompass the numerous ancient rock idols destroyed in anger by the Jesuits as sacrilegious icons. Additionally, this chapter will present a mysterious copper statue of a man portrayed with a beard, that entailed a unique Indian ritual. Was this effigy perhaps Mediterranean in nature? Questions arise regarding many of the Indians' spirit or image stones...do they actually go much further back into Michigan's prehistory than say, just the 17th century? Let's take a hard look at some of these worship areas and inexplicable rocks, stones and statues recorded around the State. They afford certain viable evidence that possibly open a new wave of speculation of foreign intrusion regarding subjects originally believed Indian. Once again, an open mind is in order!

Let's first examine the rite of sacrifice in respect to spirit stones. Many gods had to be appeased. Offerings of tobacco and small token gifts often times proved inadequate. Special evil"manitous" needed yet stronger medicine. It was common practice for offerings or sacrifices to be made to the spirits of various objects be they rocks, trees, rapids or other natural edifice. The Portal Rock and the Doric Rock, both located along Lake Superior's south shore, were two sacrificial areas. Here, along this beautiful, majestic and mysterious stretch of shoreline, early man threw dogs, with jaws and legs tied, into the water as gifts for the relentless undersea "watertigers" we have already discussed in previous chapters. These malevolent beasts lived at the bottom of the Great Lakes and were considered the "gods of the waters." The dogs were sacrificed for assurance of safe passage.

A similar example is written in the *Book of Jesuit Relations:* "I have seen an idol set up in the middle of a village; and to it, among other presents, ten dogs were offered in sacrifice in order to prevail on this false god to send elsewhere the disease that was despoiling this particular village."

Further documents revealed the Ontonagon Boulder, described in the Copper Culture chapters of this book, was also regarded by the Chippewas as an earthly "manitou" connection. This huge copper rock had always been consecrated as a native shrine. Legends state angry "manitous" often spoke during religious ceremonies through the voice of "thunder."

One historical accounting states that Father Charlevoix wrote in a letter to the King of France, that war captives were often sacrificed upon this big boulder. On one specific occasion he described a 15-year old girl was offered up to appease the "manitou." The Indians tied the maiden to the stone, built and lit a huge fire all around the rock. Then as the flames climbed higher, the leader or chief fired an arrow into the girl's heart. Almost at once the warriors rushed forward and dipped their arrowheads in her blood to make themselves invincible!

Generally speaking, spirit-image stones mainly evoked reverence and small offerings.

Let's examine the relationship between early man here in Michigan and his relationship to copper veneration. Writings of the 1600s indicated the Indians strongly worshipped copper. Once again, a passage from the *Jesuit Relations*, 1666-67 by Father Claude Allouez reads as follows: "One often finds at the bottom of the water pieces of pure copper. I have several times seen such pieces in the savages' hands; and since they are superstitious, they keep them as so many divinities, or as presents which the gods dwelling beneath the water have given them, and on which their welfare is to depend. For this reason they preserve these pieces of copper, wrapped up, among their most precious possessions. Some have kept them for more than 50 years; others have had them in their families from time immemorial, and cherish them as household gods."

Still additional references to copper comes from W.B. Hinsdale's book titled, *Primitive Man In Michigan*. "A farmer, living in Houghton County, unearthed a piece of float copper which presents a striking resemblance to a human profile. It was an accidental find. There is no positive evidence for thinking so, but it had probably been an object of veneration. The greatest diameter of the specimen is 40 inches, the weight was 484 pounds. It being a spirit object is conjectural."

Mention is made of this copper image to the extent that few

Indian effigies have been discovered over the years. However, Dennis Morrison of Greenbush has turned up two: one of clay, the other of brown shale. In turn, your author, has also excavated an effigy head worked in green scriptite.

To date, definitely the most bizarre of copper objects idolized, was an absolutely mystifying pure copper statue of most unusual propriety. This intriguing pagan deity is perhaps the strongest argument in the relationship of image-spirit stones and idols of the Lake Superior territory, relating back to European influence of a much earlier time. Once again, we quote Father Claude Allouez and the *Jesuit Relations* 1666-67, from a voyage made to the Outaouac country. This Outaouac country took in territory from the eastern end of the upper peninsula to parts of adjoining Canada, including the twin cities of Sault Ste. Marie and the early mission of St. Ignace. "There is observed in those regions of the Ottawas, a kind of idolatry which is most unusual. They have a grotesque image of "black bronze" (copper), one foot in height, which was found in the country, and to which they give a beard like a European's, although the savages themselves are beardless. There are certain fixed days for honoring this statue with feasts, games, dances and even with prayers, which are addressed to it with diverse ceremonies. Among them is one which, although ridiculous in itself, is yet remarkable in that it embraces the statue and, in order to pay homage with tobacco smoke, which they have in their mouths...which may be regarded as a mode of offering incense and performing sacrifice." (LeMercier's Relation 1664-65,p. 164, Vol. 2)

Many perplexing questions immediately come to mind at this point. The statue was said to be found in the country...who left it there? Was it perhaps buried by the Celts or Norsemen? For the most part, Indians were not known to have manufactured statues either of rock or metal...let alone one that contained a Mediterranean-style beard. Certainly it appears to have a tie-in with European prehistory visitors. Just one more addition to the already bizarre prehistory riddle!

Based on past information, many natural wonders or works of nature conceived in the shape of animals or human forms, were also revered by primitive man. One in particular was located four miles north of St. Ignace and was called "Rabbit's Rock." From a distance it had the complete outline of a sitting rabbit. Actually, it is an immense rock of high outcropping. Due to its shape it was believed to be inhabited by a manitou. When the natives paddled by, they stopped and made offerings of tobacco. Legends indicated this "manitou" once presided over all their ancestors. Today a newly established Indian Reservation has been located in close proximity to the Rabbit's Back" rock.

Unusual rock formations or fortifications termed "red rocks" located one on each side of Keweenaw Bay, were again held in reverence by the Indians. Doric Rock near Marquette and Portal Rock along the Pictured Rocks shoreline were two others.

Similarly, the Huron Islands, jagged, rocky and barren knolls of land protruding from Lake Superior at the mouth of the Big Huron River, also in retrospect conjured Indian inspirations. This time, however, in the form of a mammoth Indian statue that erroneously appeared to be carved in the side of a cliff. This unique structure was described by Henry Schoolcraft in his historic writings.

At a much later date it was thoroughly investigated by Marquette Historian, C. Fred Rydholm. His interesting story follows: "The Huron Island carving eventually turned out to be but a natural rock formation. I was asked to check on reported pictographs located on these islands by Mrs. Carroll Paul, vice-president of the Marquette Historical Society. I had been to the very spot several times but had seen nothing of interest. That year (1956 or 1957), her son and I made a special trip to the location and climbed all over the cliffs that were mentioned...nothing! Before leaving, we took a trip around the main island about 1½ miles out in the Bay. In the waning sunset there stood this huge Indian, exactly where we had just been searching earlier. Were we excited!"

"Some years later we went back once more and wondered what we had been looking at that day for we examined the place closely, with no positive results. The trouble was, that to experience seeing the figure, you had to be some distance from it and of course lighting conditions also had to be adequate.

Later, we again went the same 1½mile distance offshore and sure enough, we saw him once again, as plain as day. But...the closer we approached, he merely turned into a rock configuration. It was a natural formation, not manmade."

Can you imagine the awe primitive man must have felt on viewing this spectacular event? Close your eyes for but a moment, and imagine the wonders the entire Lake Superior coastline must have held for early man, from the spectacular Pictured Rocks to the huge, "on-again, off-again" natural Indian relief figure.

History records the Pictured Rocks area was never passed by without sacrificing a dog or two plus an offering made of tobacco or small tokens. In one particular hallowed place, a stone altar was described by Father Wm. F. Gagnieur of St. Ignace. He claims the altar was placed in a cove and used for religious ceremonies. Here once again, mention must be made that these stone altars possibly could have been dolmens left behind by the Celts, instead of being mainly Indian in origin.

As previously mentioned in the chapter on the Huron Mountain dolmen, a relationship seems almost imperative between the dolmens and altar stones found around the Great Lakes region. The altar stone on the Kawkawlin River in Saginaw Bay, mentioned in that specific chapter, plus the one just pointed out existing at Pictured Rocks, are perhaps two of many. Possibly they bore connections to the Old World travelers...now they are gone...lost to posterity!

Still another prime example of European intrusion possibly would have been a large stone statue that once stood along the Detroit River between Lakes St. Clair and Erie. Here again, mention comes forth that the Native Americans definitely did not work stone statues. So in essence, who again carved this one?

A description of the events comes once again from the *Jesuit Relations:* "In 1669 two Supician priests, Galinee and Dollier, set out for the upper lakes. They reached Detroit in the spring of 1670. Here after various misadventures, resulting in the loss of a great part of their baggage, including the altar service, they relate their adventure: "At the end of six leagues we found a very remarkable place, in great veneration amoung all the savages of these regions, because of an idol of stone which nature had formed there, to which they say they owe their good fortune of their navigation on Lake Erie, and which they propititate with presents of skins, provisions, etc." The stone was hideously painted, and bore a rude resemblance to humanity. The face was dabbed with red paint." They were convinced that this was the devil, to whom they owed their former shipwreck. The relation proceeds: "I leave you to think whether we avenged on this idol the loss of our chapel. We also attributed to it the scarcity of provisions we had been in up to this time." The priest tells us that he consecrated one of his axes to break this stone god; then having lashed two canoes together, they carried the fragments to the middle of the river, so that no one should hear of it ever again.

This idol was thought to have been located within the city limits of Detroit. It is most regretful the 17th century priests smashed what they believed a "false god" for perhaps if it existed today, facts may have pointed to who actually sculptured it. One thing that should be brought to mind at this point is that large rocks or natural boulders were not the norm in this part of southern Michigan. Doubt then remains that the idol was a work of nature.

Yet another report of a stone statue is noted in Volume 55, pp 193-4 of the *Jesuit Relations*. It tells of a statue near the Bay of Pauns. Research indicates the "Bay of Pauns" turns out to be Green Bay. The rapids one days journey up the river which in turn empties into the bay are possibly the ones on either the Oconto River which has some Ancient Copper Culture mounds at its mouth or the Whitefish, which was a known shortcut through the Keweenaw to Lake Superior. My research source, Charles Bailey of Duluth, Minnesota opts for the latter. The article found in the *Relations* follows:

> "One days journey up river from the Bay of Pauns there are three or four leagues of rapids. At the falls is an idol the Indians sacrifice to, a rock shaped by nature in the form of a human but in which one seems to distinguish, from a distance, the head, shoulders, breast, and, more especially, the face which passersby are wont to paint with their finest colors...To remove this curse of idolatry, we had it carried away by main force and thrown to the

bottom of the river, never to appear again."

I might mention here that is the first recorded stone idol or statue that has surfaced during my research, that was located along the Lake Michigan side of the state. Others have turned up along Lake Huron's shoreline as well as inland and in Lake Superior country, as well as the idol previously mentioned believed to have stood near Detroit along the Detroit River. This Lake Michigan discovery is most intriguing and exciting.

How many other statues were destroyed in a similar fashion? A replica of idols quite similar to the Newberry McGruer's Gods find turned up in a private indian museum near Oscoda. The McGruer's Gods were large and made of clay, but the facial structure of the man-idol to statues found in the Relations bear a definite similarity. So take the statues listed so far in this chapter, plus the perplexing copper bearded effigy and what do you have? Unfathomable mysteries of the first degree. My big question, however...were there a lot more of them? Did a series of mammoth statues exist, scattered about the shores of the Great Lakes as markers or gods for European travelers? Do they also tie in with the dolmen-altar stone connection previously cited? Evidence indicates many of the Indian worship stones were certainly not in my estimation "natural". Doubts are in order here.

We still have another stone image or god to add to this growing list of indisputable facts. This particular idol was an absolutely inexplicable relic that stood for years at the south shore of Hubbard Lake in northeastern Michigan. Many of the early Indian people had been quizzed by early white settlers and later by historians, as to the statue's origin, but to no avail. Let me tell you about it!

Hubbard Lake is the largest lake in Alcona County. Commanding a bird's-eye view of the lake, a weird monument of stone called the "Indian Worship" stood. It was deemed to be a relic of early aboriginal days. It is said this stone was erected to mark the burial place of a Chippewa Chief, Sedonikato. Offerings of beads and tobacco were left here at the monument as an act of worship. The statue was most unusual for it contained a removable hollow head piece. You took off its hat (which resembled that of a fisherman's sou'wester), and placed the offerings in the head. It was reported that oftentimes after the Indians left this spot, trappers would remove the statue's hat and take out the offerings the worshippers had left behind.

Jerry Wagner, who operates and owns a private Indian museum near Oscoda, gave the following accounting on this Hubbard Lake idol: "My information on the South Hubbard Lake image stone is scanty. It was a cavity-anthro sculpture. I will give you what I have, hoping you realize it to be primarily passed down through the years from human to human with, for the most part, no real regard for precise documentation or real scientific analysis. To begin, it was grey-green or grey-white in appearance except for the broad "hat" which was of a brownish darker color. The "hat" or "lid" was removed to place offerings down into the statue. The whole sculpture stood no more than 5-feet tall. At its base, slab type rock (probably layered limestone) was piled in such a fashion as to support and stabilize the idol in an upright position. While, as you know, it is not uncommon to Michigan Indians to have cavity dolls where ceremonial items are placed,it is somewhat uncommon for them to erect such a large anthropomorphic figure of stone for these offerings. Being next to water does, however, give this sculpture a legitimacy, but I feel Hubbard Lake was no real threat to the people concerning water travel. Therefore I at least partially subscribe to the theory advanced by Henry Mauw, that the sculpture was out of respect for the "short coat" medicine men (anglo) that came into the area or, even the Jesuit missionary who had such an awesome influence in Indian culture. Early on, the offerings either in reverence or in defiance, were put into the figure's cavity and were withdrawn and taken away. Evidently the placement, the touching of the offering to the stone, was sufficient to accomplish whatever was intended."

Some time during the late 1800s the idol was removed by white settlers and it is believed the remains were shipped to various museums. Some reports indicated they left the state for the east coast. Further research failed to track the statue parts down, sad to say. One cannot help but wonder why the Indians would have placed a stone idol here. Again, remember this fact...Indians did not carve rock! Another point, why did this peculiar statue have such an unusual headpiece or hat? Conjecture comes quickly to mind...was this false god possibly of European origin too...left behind centuries past? Could the sou-wester brimmed hat have in turn been a Celtic warrior's helmet? No pictures or drawings seem to exist for comparison's sake. One more fact would be that this unconventional idol actually was not far from the Black River cairns and walls also mentioned elsewhere in this book. Perhaps there is a relationship between the statue and this possible primitive observatory. Is this ignomatic icon just one more link of that chain of questionable events? Again and again, questions without answers!

In retrospect, mystery stones were common along the shores of Lake Huron. The Devil River flows through southern Alpena County near Ossineke. In 1839 a surveyor by the name of David Oliver discovered two large stones standing together near the mouth of the river. One was a gneiss rock with quartz banding and most crudely resembled a human figure. It weighed approximately 300 pounds. The other image stone was yet more unusual, as it was in the form of a human body, sans head, arms and legs. This statue was hard and crusty on the outside, crumbly on the inside. It seemed as though it was molded from lake sand with a hardened outer surface similar to cement. Once again, wonderment sets in...two more carved or formed rock image stones or idols. Similarly Ossineke is close to Black River, with its perplexing stone piles and rock walls. Connection?

Furthermore, history relates a large earthen mound once stood nearby at the river's mouth. Over the years it was looted by scavengers and scientists alike until it was literally destroyed.

But now back to the history or legend of the unusual Ossineke image stones, and believe me it is a fascinating one. The Native Americans called this sacred place "shinggawbawawsinekegobawat, Wawsineke," which in turn signifies "image stones." Wow, what a mouthful! Over the years the name became anglicized until present day Ossineke evolved.

The legend relates the two stones were once captured by a war party of the Iroquois. These hostile Indians took several captives plus the two sacred rocks into their canoe and started across Thunder Bay. When they reached the middle of the bay, suddenly a fierce storm occurred and the wind-tossed waves upset the canoe, throwing men and image stones into the boiling water. The Iroquois drowned, but the Chippewa braves escaped safely. When they reached the shore at sacred Ossineke, the two mystic stones were mysteriously found in place.

Sad to say, but in the 1940s a fisherman needing anchors for his nets reportedly took the two sacred image stones, and it is thought today they rest on the bottom of Lake Huron.

Once more Jerry Wagner supplies further insight into these spirit stones found at Ossineke. He states, "The Ossineke image stones are mysterious in as much as references to them are often confusing and vague. Early on by area Indians I was told the anthro-stone was of abraded (scraped) limestone, headless and used by the shaman or "chess-a-kee men" to nullify powers of opposing medicine men. One stone (anthropomorphic) was smaller but both were fashioned for the Mide'we-win or Grand Medicine Society rituals. (The Mide'we-win Society ceremony consisted of four stages or degrees by which one was advanced from mystery to mystery and received progressively spiritual insight and power.)

An early resident believed they were taken to be displayed in the "Big City," perhaps Detroit. I was also told these stones were common in the area wherever "sacred earth" spots existed. I took this to mean wherever visions were seen or religious happenings took place. Also of deep significance, the impression has been that the people connected by belief or whatever, were not of this specific Great Lakes area. But instead they are thought to have come from the north. Also the stones themselves could not be touched and were not handled by tribal members, but only by special people having the POWER!"

Once more questions pop up! Who designed these two crude statues? Surely not the early Indians who did not work stone. One can't help but wish they had not been lost to posterity, whether as reports indicate, either at the bottom of Lake Huron or moved elsewhere downstate, possibly to someone's private collection. Is there once again a relationship to the large McGruer's Gods found above Newberry? Always, unanswered questions.

Mr. Wagner's private museum contains many replicas of early Indian origin, including a statue bearing a vague similarity to the man idol of McGruer's Gods, which Mr. Wagner states he duplicated from a sketch found in the Jesuits Relations.

Other less important mystery stones have been reported around Michigan. They, in turn, may prove less significant than those already mentioned, but nevertheless they are a part of the heritage of our earlier Native Americans and merit mention.

One was called Black Rock. It too was located in the same general Lake Huron area as those previously mentioned. When the first fishermen began to frequent the shoreline along what is now called Alcona County, they were met by Chippewa and Saulk Indians. The axes, skinning knives and arrowheads found by local farmers confirm Indian presence in the past, as do the remains of an Indian fortress near Mikado and burial mounds around Hubbard Lake. Occasionally, one hears stories of the "black rock" along Alcona's shoreline. Indians traveling down the big lake would stop at this rock to leave gifts for the "manitou." This rock may still be examined near Springport.

Another sacred rock could be found 6 miles north of Rogers City near the Ocqueoc or Swan River located in Presque Isle County. Legend tells of two warring Indian tribes sharing a common boundary. The rock, during a skirmish, tumbled down the embankment and crushed the chiefs of both tribes. The centuries-old tale states the earthen banks at this particular spot have trembled ever since. The rock was immense, being a conglomerate 20 feet by 6 feet by 8 feet. During periods of high water the rock would perhaps be 100 yards offshore. This spot also is said to have been used to sacrifice dogs and offer gifts to the "black rock manitou."

Still traveling along the Lake Huron shoreline, other interesting image-stones turned up on Thunder Bay Island. These two stones were unique. One had a flat circular base and a long slender arm. It was set up under a tree. The other worship stone was thicker and seemed to resemble a head complete with neckline, sitting on a pedestal. Most unusual! One can't help but wonder what these weird-shaped stones indicated.

The Manitou Islands, located offshore of Leelanau County in Lake Michigan, also have legends attributed to early man. It was believed these islands were the dwelling places of spirits who worked evil deeds. They were avoided by canoes or simply circumvented, and propitiatory offerings were offered.

All over the State of Michigan ancient image stones have been reported. Moving along further south between Grand Blanc and Flint, where an Indian trail went through a hilly section, the natives had cleared and planted fruit trees. The spot was large, attractive and deemed sacred. Beside the trail stood a very peculiar stone, standing about 4 feet tall. It was called a god or idol and was named "Bab-o-quah." This "manitou" was removed in 1823 by a white man, but Indians forced him to return it.

Also mentioned in early records was a most sacred rock that was situated on the banks of the Pine River near St. Louis in Gratiot County. It was a large, very smooth boulder on which Indians left tobacco and other gifts. The unusual practice here was that pieces of copper were situated on the boulder. They were believed to have come from the famous Ontonagon Boulder mentioned in the Copper Culture chapters of this book. Still another baffling mystery!

Just a few years ago, a smiling sandstone sculpture that oddly resembled a carved face of an idol, turned up near the Saginaw-Tuscola County line. It was picked up from a nearby excavation area. Its origin remains a mystery today. A Michigan State anthropologist estimated it possibly could be 500 years old, and not carved by man's modern tools or methods. Was it too, yet another part of an idol...a head broken from an image stone? Interesting!

In closing this chapter on image stone-spirit stones, let me quote from the Michigan Pioneer Collections, written by Bela Hubbard: "Sacred stones were not uncommon in these parts. (Michigan) I have seen several such altars, sometimes in the most wild and lonely situations, invariably covered with bits of tobacco and other petty gifts."

For sake of review, once again there may be a shred of truth that many of these forsaken altars of veneration may still exist today in far removed, remote areas. There could be a possible chance that further archaeological wonders will be brought to light. Who knows, perhaps new rings of stones, rock walls, stone piles, image stones, old idols and altar stone dolmens may surface. By being more aware of what has already been discovered in Michigan, perhaps you, the common citizen, being either outdoorsman or amateur archaeologist, may just happen across the next important prehistory discovery. Keep you eyes open and the next time you stumble over a half-hidden rock, take a good long look at it...possibly it might just be a long lost image-spirit stone!

CREDITS:

Research: Jerry Wagner, owner, private Indian Museum, Oscoda, MI.

BIBLIOGRAPHY:

THE JESUIT RELATIONS AND ALLIED DOCUMENTS, selected and edited by Edna Kenton, Albert & Charles Bone, publ. NY 1925.

THE FIRST PEOPLE OF MICHIGAN, W.B. Hinsdale, publ. Geo. Wahr, 1930 Chapter VII, "Spirit Stones", pages 102-115.

IMAGE STONES OF OSSINEKE, Harrisville Review, Feb. 28, 1980, Robert E. Haltiner.

SUGGESTED FURTHER READING

MICHIGAN IN FOUR CENTURIES: F. Clever Bald, Harper & Bros., NY 1954

MEMORIALS OF A HALF-CENTURY, Bela Hubbard, G.P. Putnam's & Sons 1888.

THE INDIANS OF THE WESTERN GREAT LAKES, 1615-1760 by W. Vernon Kinietz, Ann Arbor, University of Michigan Press, 1940.

Piece of float copper weighing 484 pounds. This presents a striking resemblance to a human profile. The edges about the mouth and nose appear to have been folded back to bring out the features more strikingly. Greatest diameter 40 inches. Keweenaw Peninsula.

2

A full view of Jerry Wagner's replica. Upper torso and head are similar to a degree to McGruer's man-idol; however, the lower torso is completely different. Furthermore, the McGruer's largest figure is approximately 4 feet tall while Wagner's replica measure perhaps 24 inches. McGruer's man-idol is full-figured in a seated posture. The replica is not.

This hand-carved replica of an early Great Lakes idol bears facial resemblance to the male McGruer's Gods statue discovered near Newberry in 1896.

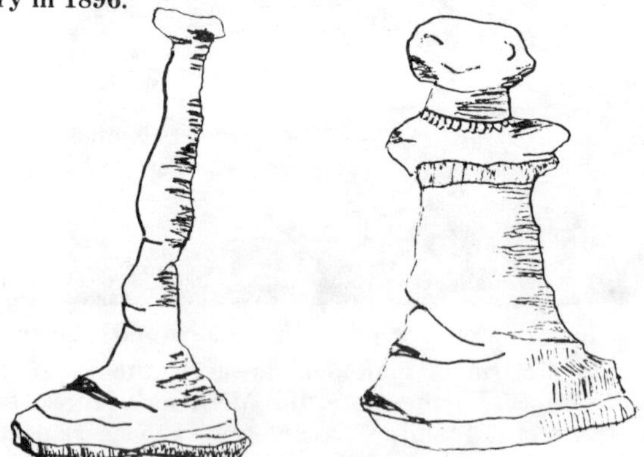

Spirit stones from Thunder Bay Island.

Smiling sandstone sculpture found near Saginaw-Tuscola County line. Stone idol (head only) estimated to possibly be 500 years old.

Prehistory Mounds - Pyramids - Earthworks - Gardens

PART I

Who Were The Mound-Builders?

Actually more is known today of the ancient past of Europe, Asia and the Near East than of our Nation's own prehistory developments. Here in Michigan, the same holds true. Many unsolved prehistory mysteries still exist today. Nevertheless, thousands of years ago this State was just a modest part of a mega-network of a succession of societies that not only engaged in extensive trade but also rose to magnificent heights, then mysteriously faded away, leaving a trail of monumental mounds in their wake.

The Mound Culture, as it could be ascribed, flourished some 2000 years ago, extending from the Great Lakes region to the Gulf of Mexico. Their vast trade routes encompassed copper from Michigan's Keweenaw Peninsula and Isle Royale, obsidian from Yellowstone, galena from Wisconsin, mica from North Carolina, chert from the Ozarks, salt from the Gulf of Mexico, flint from Midwest sources, furs from the Nation's northern limits and finally sea shells from the coastline of both oceans.

Just who were these Mound-Builders?

Actually many of today's archaeologists and anthropologists fully believe the culture that constructed the earthen mounds were the ancestors of our present day Indian tribes. They strongly accuse other historical and scientific writers of perpetuating age-old Mound-Builder myths. Claims have been made indicating these less sophisticated authors simply lacked the knowledge to fully explain the mound phenomena in the proper context.

Contrary to the above hypothesis, historical writers as well as those involved in more specific scientific endeavors, find the Indian theory just a bit hard to swallow. For it has been documented that as early settlers moved into these mysterious mound areas, local "savages" were deemed incapable of such an organized effort to have manufactured mounds and effigies of such complex geometric abilities. Furthermore, the natives had absolutely no concept of who built these structures or when they were manufactured. In other words, no prior knowledge traversed the generation to generation chain. A link in that chain of events seems to be missing! This fact alone spawned the initial hue and cries of a "vanished race" or a "lost civilization" from the writers of the 1800s. From that time on, journalists of the day capitalized on the subject and these inexplicable mounds were attributed to just about every class of immigrant from the Mexicans, Incas, Toltecs, Aztecs, Vikings, Egyptians, Phoenicians, Persians, and Greeks, right on down to the survivors from the lost continent of Atlantis as well as refugees from the ten lost tribes of Israel. One could truthfully agree just about every known nationality got into the act.

However, it is interesting to note that as far back in history as the year 1785, a map-maker, one John Fitch, wrote about existing mounds in Wisconsin in his reports: "This country has once been settled by a people more expert in the art of war than the present inhabitants. Regular fortifications, and some of these are incredibly large, are frequently to be found. Also many graves and towers like pyramids of earth."

Similarly early Jesuit priests of the 17th century mention mound discoveries. Here again they did not believe the native inhabitants capable of building such monumental structures and furthermore stated the regional Indians lacked any specific knowledge of prior occupants.

The mysteries of the Mound-Builders have fascinated Americans from the first discovery. Will a positive solution ever be forthcoming? Hopefully, yes. But with the everyday destruction brought on by modern development, chances remain quite slim.

Let's divide the mound culture into three distinct time periods. These far-ranging dates span some 4,500 years (3000 B.C. to A.D. 1500). The three main chronological groups include the Late Archaic, the Woodland and the Mississippian periods. The Late Archaic which occurred from 3000 B.C. to A.D. 600 was the onset of the development of cultural patterns. While the Woodland period consumed dates ranging from

1000 B.C. to A.D. 900, it was far more sophisticated and stylized and took in both the Hopewell and Adena cultures. The final phase or Mississippian Age was spread from A.D. 700 to A.D. 1700 and in turn was known to be a highly organized society, ruled by Chiefs holding divine powers. Mention should be made here that no Mississippian mounds were located in Michigan proper, but many artifacts from that period were located on Beaver Island. The discovery of these artifacts is considered rare and unusual. In 1978 the Sand Point Mounds of Baraga County also revealed Mississippian artifacts. Excavation reports follow in an upcoming chapter.

To appreciate a broader scope of the Mound-Builder's activities it has been recorded that over 100,000 mounds were built before and after the decline of the Hopewell culture. Hard to imagine, isn't it? These were pretty well spread out across the United States east of the Rockies. The State of Ohio alone contained 10,000 tumuli, some of which were termed as "colossal." Michigan had less, but nevertheless over 1,000 of these earthen mounds have been recorded. However, no mound building took place here or in the entire Midwest after say A.D. 1000.

Around A.D. 1200 an amazing city developed near present day St. Louis, Missouri that was known as "Cahokia." It contained a sacred temple mound called Monk's Mound that measured 1037 by 790 by 100 feet...it is known as the largest earthen mound ever built in North America. Incidentally, over one hundred additional mounds were located in close proximity to the temple. All in all, Monk's Mound together with its satellite mounds covered over 13 acres. Eventually "Cahokia" grew in size to a proposed 6 square miles and sprouted a population of some 40,000 people. It was regarded as a major political and ceremonial center. This sacrosanct tumuli was recognized as an archaeological wonder...a work of art!

Let's take a few moments to discuss mound structure. Some were found to be little more than simple humps of dirt piled up some feet above ground level, while others at the far end of the spectrum reached enormous measurements as described at "Cahokia." They are more or less divided into related categories of temple mounds, burial mounds, ceremonial enclosures, earthworks and finally effigy mounds.

Generally speaking, mounds were not constructed of brick, stone or mortar but rather of simple earth. The bulk of the labor was carried out by the common man with primitive tools. It is thought the workers dug up the ground, filled baskets, then carried them to the mound area to be dumped. Like the Egyptian pyramids of old, these earthen monuments were also built with immense work forces. With all our modern-day technology and equipment, often this is a hard fact to grasp, let alone imagine.

Structures varied from one location to another. Pointed pyramids, flat-topped pyramids, stone or conical mounds, cone-like earthen mounds plus truncated earthen mounds have all been discovered. Many were observed that employed designs including circles, squares, triangles and other geometric shapes that simply boggle the mind.

Actually these earth and stone mounds fell into several classes, albeit mounds bounded by enclosures, walls or embankments. Still other enclosures were supposedly designed for the sake of defense or religion, plus sacrificial mounds and mounds used for the purpose of sepulture and cremation were additionally evident.

The first and foremost wonderment of the Mound-Builder Culture was their affluent affiliation with the arts and sciences, for certainly they left behind examples of perfect circles, squares, octagons and parallel lines, as well as unexplainable geometrically-designed, formal garden plots. Mysteries abound and only naturally so! Unexplained facts and perplexing scientific data that just cannot be fully explained leave stubborn doubts clinging to the probable race and origin of these enigmatic mounds. The absolute Amerindian theory remains clouded.

As mentioned earlier, the Jesuits fully described mounds in the 1600s. The following description might give you, the reader, an insight into just what a truly complex, magnificent structure some of these edifices were. The account comes from the Jesuit Relations of 1610-1791 and appeared in a letter from Mathurin le Petit to D'avaugour, dated June 12, 1730, from New Orleans: "They have a temple filled with idols, which are different figures of men and of animals, and for which they have a most profound veneration. Their Temple in shape resembles an earthen oven, a hundred feet in circumference. They enter it by a little door about four feet high, and not more then three in breadth. No window is to be seen there. The arched roof of the edifice is covered with three rows of mats, placed one upon the other, to prevent the rain from injuring the masonary. Above on the outside, are three figures of eagles made of wood, and painted red, yellow and white. Before the door is a kind of shed with folding doors, where the Guardian of the Temple is lodged; all around it runs a circle of palisades, on which are seen exposed skulls of heads which their Warriors had brought back from battles.

In the interior of the Temple are some shelves arranged at a certain distance from each other, on which are placed cane baskets of an oval shape, and in these are enclosed the bones of their ancient Chiefs, while by their side are those of their victims who had caused themselves to be strangled, to follow their masters into the other world.

Another separate shelf supports many flat baskets gorgeously painted, in which they preserve their idols. These are figures of men and women, owls, pieces of crystal and jaw-bones of large fish. A perpetual fire is maintained in this room."

The above description offers a clear, concise picture of a mound's interior. The Jesuit accounting went still further, indicating the Chief lived in a small hut-like structure built on the top layer of the mound. When he died, he and his servants were entombed and once again the mound structure was enlarged, with a new hut at the top for the next leader.

Records indicate mounds first occurred in the midwest about 1000 B.C. These earthen structures were a logical outgrowth of traditional burial practices and special religious ceremonies. It became custom to place artifacts alongside the interred individuals. Oftentimes these Late Archaic burials were termed as "red-ochre" or "glacial kame" culture burials. These mounds were often built predominantly on natural earth rises or small hills. As a matter of course, skeletal remains unearthed were usually either in a flexed position or were found in what is termed, "bone bundles." Many contained common burials.

Artifacts recovered from Archaic mound sites would have included pottery sherds, projectile points, chert, flint, knives, gorgets, birdstones (throwing stick weights) and possibly some axes and tools. Additionally, some ornaments manufactured from sea shells may have also been found. Normally, large amounts of red-ochre were also included in these burial mounds. Red-ochre was a recognized feature of religious ceremonies of that era.

The Woodland period produced low dome-like mounds usually seving in the capacity of burial structures. Some cremation mounds were evident throughtout the Adena culture. Woodland burial mounds ranged from Illinois to Ohio. Excavated tumuli across the country provided a wide range of artifacts, many of which were not only termed unusual, but in all events, weird. One that quickly comes to mind was a skull that the Mound-Builders had constructed a replica of a nose, created of copper. It was thought to have been a skull of a chief. Other finds included spectacular copper and antler headdresses that were probably used in religious ceremonies. Bird effigies, cutouts, earspools, all created from copper, were common artifact finds. Pipes with interestingly carved animals, birds and humans were also considered unique. Pottery vessels along with serving bowls and cups made from conch shells were also the norm. Still other articles excavated during this Woodland period were designed bones, combs, masks, adornments, mica cutouts, stone carvings and some painted textiles.

Without a doubt, the most perplexing of the mounds during this time period, were the effigy mounds. Many were designed in unusual shapes of animals, birds and numerical figures. The "Great Serpent Mound" of Adams County, Ohio was by far the most famous. Many of these effigy mounds contained skeletons but seldom offered viable artifacts other than occasional pottery, shells and a few working tools. Reasons for these inexplicably shaped figure mounds remains a mystery today. Absolutely no purpose was ever determined; however, clan totems were deemed a possibility. Most of these effigies were located in Wisconsin, Minnesota, Iowa, Illinois and yes, northern Michigan. It has been written two effigy mounds were found in Michigan's Ontonagon County in the 1800s.

Both were in the shape of numerical figures. Strange but true, the figure "7" has occurred over the centuries in many, many varied cultures at various established prehistory time periods and has always stood, as it does today, to mean "sevan."

As previously stated the Mississippian period was definitely the "Cadillac" era of the Mound-Builders. However, it should be so noted, by that particular time the culture had moved much further from Michigan, with examples of their handiwork discovered along the Mississippi River Valley to the southeastern areas of the United States. Midwest artifacts and edifices were located in Illinois, lower Wisconsin and parts of Indiana. Once again it should be brought to your attention, Michigan was not included...these Mound-Builders had moved elsewhere. However, it has been reported that rare Mississippian artifacts have mysteriously turned up in excavations on Beaver Island in Lake Michigan and Sand Point in Baraga County near L'Anse. Furthermore, this was the age of spectacular cities such as "Cahokia" near St. Louis, "Aztalan" in southeast Wisconsin and the spectacular "Angel" site in Indiana. These cities more than indicate a highly sophisticated, well-governed society.

While it is true, our State of Michigan lacks in the elaborate edifices of this Mississippian Era, we were still considered to be a direct offshoot of their activities. We must keep in mind the vast scope of their trade network that existed across the length and breadth of our entire nation. The Great Lakes territories had much to offer in this regard. We all know by now, Lake Superior copper found its way along this trade chain. Additionally, pottery styles excavated here in Michigan showed positive influence of other specialized and stylized Mississippian cultures. This pottery could have been bartered for Michigan furs or copper.

In the year 1540 explorer Hernando DeSoto discovered mounds in Georgia and South Carolina that contained copper axes, maces and battle axes. Furthermore, mounds excavated near Cincinnati opened in 1815, revealed sheets of copper plus two copper plates and several very elaborate copper breast plates worked in complex designs. Still traveling further southward to Mexico and the land of the Toltecs, Aztecs and the Incas, copper tools, axes, chisels and wedges were found at abandoned stone quarries. Yes, indeed, copper was in demand!

Perhaps it should be mentioned here that artifacts of foreign intrusion also turned up from mound excavations. Michigan's Henry Schoolcraft investigated a curious stone tablet discovered in 1838 at a mound termed "Grave Creek" located near Moundsville, West Virginia. Schoolcraft made a mold or cast of the tablet that was described as an oval white sandstone disc which contained three lines of an unknown alphabet. At that time the writing was believed to be of Asiatic or European origin. The "Grave Creek Tablet" was later deciphered as Iberian script, more or less indicating foreign penetration into North America. Old World inscriptions have turned up in mounds across North America.

In the fourth volume of Schoolcraft's *Indian Tribes*, he termed this sandstone tablet as perhaps "intrusive antiquity." Schoolcraft felt it was added at a later date than the original Grave Creek mound period. While this early historian did not deny possible Phoenician visitors to the Ohio Valley, he did positively state that this tablet had no cultural connection whatsoever with the Indians believed to have built this particular mound.

Once again we are reminded of Michigan's own Newberry Tablet, similarly inscribed in a foreign script. If relics bearing Iberic script were located in mounds in other states, then how did a similar inscribed clay tablet come to be found in Michigan's Upper Peninsula in the year 1886?

In conclusion, the popular Amerindian theory of Mound-Builders is a strong one, but the unknown element is also a fact to be reckoned with. Possibly we will never know just who the Mound-Builders really were. Were they Native Americans? Were they unknowns...a mysterious race of people? Were they perhaps foreigners? Certainly additional scientific study is in order here, for no absolute or positive conclusions can yet be drawn.

Part II & III of Prehistory Mounds - Pyramids - Earthworks - Gardens will deal more specifically with some of these mystifying earthen structures discovered right here in Michigan. Read on, for who knows, maybe there used to be a strange, puzzling, curious mound right in your vicinity.

Makes one just "itch" all over in wonderment! Doesn't it?

BIBLIOGRAPHY: MOUNDS, PART I

THE FIRST PEOPLE OF MICHIGAN, by W.B. Hinsdale, Geo. Wahr, publ. Ann Arbor, 1930
PRIMITIVE MAN IN MICHIGAN, by W.B. Hinsdale, Avery Color Studios, Au Train, MI 1983-87
MEMORIALS OF A HALF—CENTURY, by Bela Hubbard, G.P. Putnam's Sons, 1888
PREHISTORIC COPPER MINING IN THE LAKE SUPERIOR REGION, by Drier & DuTemple, publ. prvt. Calumet. Refer to: "Ancient Copper Mines of Isle Royale," Winchell "The Engineering & Mining Journal Vol. XXXII - 1881
THE JESUIT RELATIONS & ALLIED DOCUMENTS, 1610-1791 compiled by Edna Kenton, Albert & Charles Boni, NY 1925. Data used: from a letter of Mathurin lePetit to D'Avaugour, dated July 12, 1730, New Orleans
BRONZE AGE AMERICA by Barry Fell, Little, Brown & Co., Boston, 1982

SUGGESTED FURTHER READING:

INDIAN MOUNDS OF MICHIGAN & THE MIDWEST, by J.R. Halsey, publ. in "Great Lakes Informant".

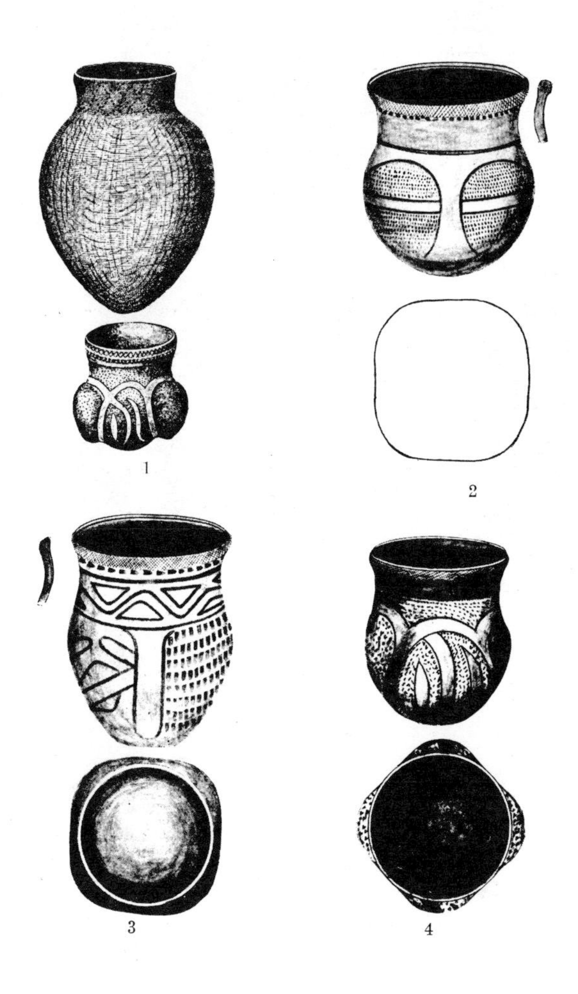

Fig. 1., Pots from mounds near Grand Rapids. From Hubbard, Memorials of a Half-Century. Fig. 2., Clay bowl. Kent County Mounds. Fig. 3., Clay bowl, Norton Mounds. Kent County. Fig. 4., Clay bowl. Kent County Mounds.

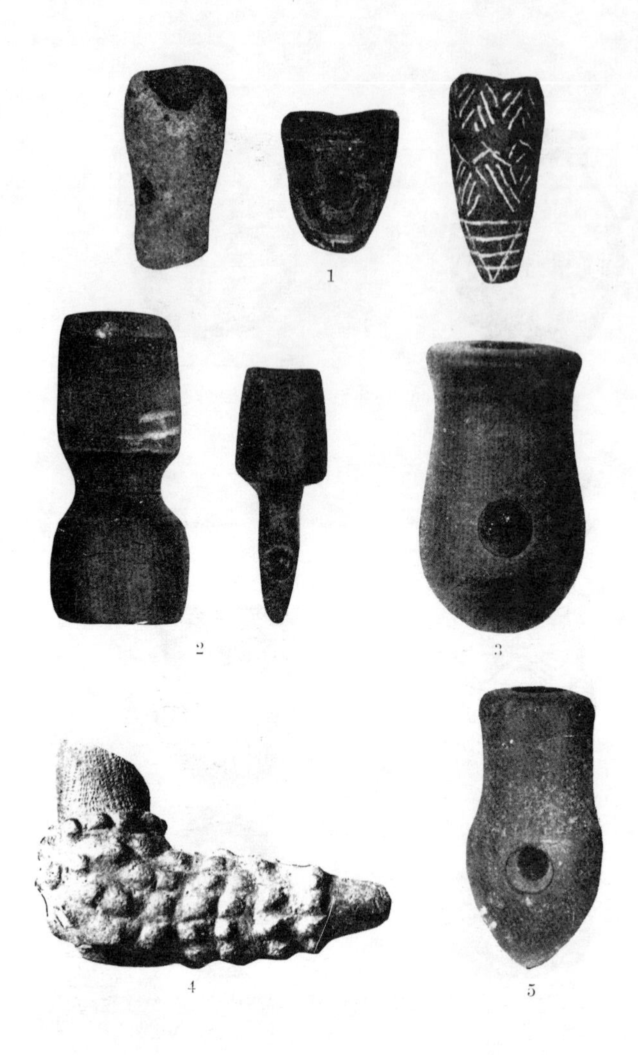

Fig. 1., Crude stone pipes from grave. Saline, Washtenaw County. Fig. 2., 'Micmac' pipes. Washtenaw County. Fig. 3., Fine grained granite pipe. Washtenaw County. Fig.4., Heavy clay pipe, length 5½ inches, found 2 feet below the surface. Missaukee County. Fig. 5., Fine grained granite pipe, length 2½ inches. Washtenaw County.

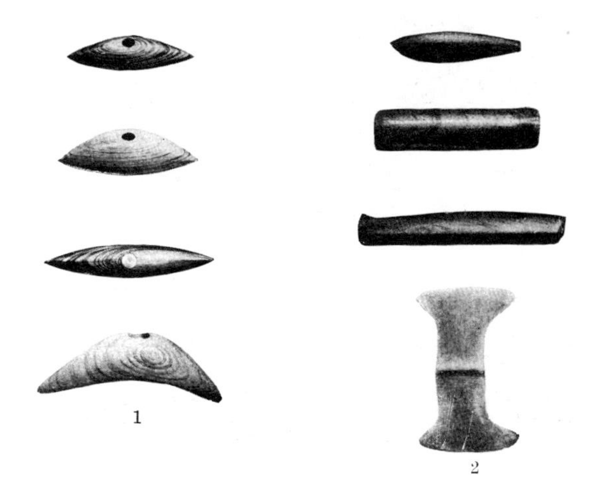

Fig. 1., Objects loaned by various collectors. Michigan. Fig. 2., Plummet, tube, bar amulet and hatchet; loaned by various collectors. Michigan. Fig.3., Miscellaneous collection of stone and slate objects, mostly ceremonials. Michigan.

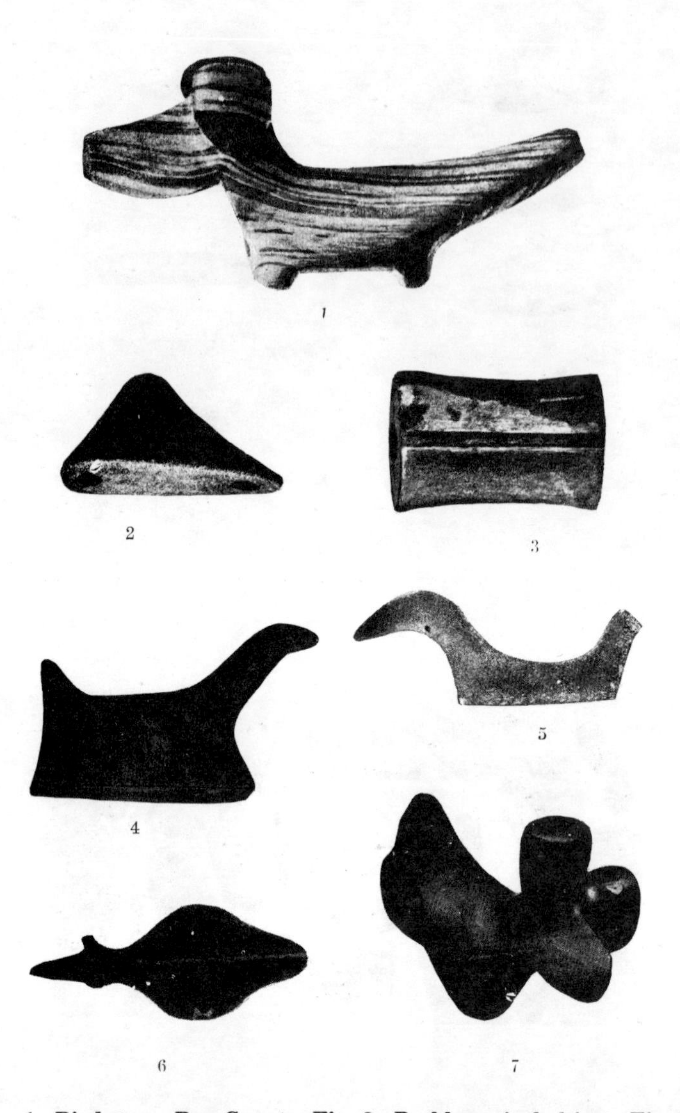

Fig. 1., Bird-stone. Bay County. Fig. 2., Problematical object. Fig. 3., Problematical object, slate tube. Fig. 4., Banded slate bird-stone, length 4 inches. Kent County. Kent Scientific Museum. Fig. 5., Bird-stone. Washtenaw County. Fig. 6., Bird-stone. Washtenaw County. Fig. 7., Bird-stone. Genesee County.

Prehistory Mounds - Pyramids - Earthworks - Gardens
PART II
Were There Really Pyramids in Michigan?

First let's summarize actual Mound-Builder Culture facts. It has been affirmed this group of people occupied the main part of the entire United States from Lake Superior to the Gulf of Mexico, as well as from the Alleghenies to the Sierra Mountains. This statement is shored up by the presence of Michigan-made copper artifacts having been found in countless numbers of mounds across the country. Another proven report is that the mound culture people were an agricultural race with similar habits and customs both of religion and government. Each specific tribe carried on a trade or barter system with surrounding groups as well as some more distant. They worked copper in merely a "cold" state, basically by pounding. They were known to be responsible for building extensive earthworks and mounds. It is further believed the Mound-Builders manufactured pottery of hardened, fired clay. They also worked stone hammers, axes, arrow and spearheads, as well as produced knives, wedges, pestles and mortars, pipes and copper personal adornments. Crude sculptures of stone and a form of burned clay often resembling human and animal figures were also attributed to this mysterious race of people.

Over the years, documentation shows some 1100 mounds were discovered here in Michigan. Some may have been pinpointed right in your own backyard! As civilization encroached the wilderness areas, urban sprawl and development caused numerous mounds to be literally destroyed. Furthermore, many a tumulus fell beneath the farmer's plow or the highway's heavy road-building machines. It was thought that as many as 500 such mounds were demolished with little or no regard for excavation of relics or scientific facts. These in turn were totally absent from later documentation.

However, in the early 1930s W.B. Hinsdale tabulated over 500 mounds in Michigan, listing them numerically by county. Since that census took place, many mounds not mentioned in the Upper Peninsula have surfaced. Example: two mounds were found on an island in the Montreal River that borders Wisconsin and Michigan in Gogebic County. Additionally, six have been described as having existed in Ontonagon County and five in Baraga County. Please note, all of the above examples were more or less located relatively close to 5000-year-old copper mining areas. Perhaps there is a direct relationship here.

Please find listed below a county by county numerical listing according to Hinsdale's report. This listing will give you, the reader, a better idea of not only where these mounds were principally located, but also a chance to learn if any once existed near where you live.

Alcona County	*27*	*Lake County*	*7*
Alger County	*n/l*	*Lenawee County*	*51*
Allegan County	*8*	*Leelanau County*	*1*
Alpena County	*6*	*Lapeer County*	*12*
Antrim County	*8*	*Livingston County*	*6*
Arenac County	*n/l*	*Luce County*	*n/l*
Baraga County	*n/l*	*Mackinaw County*	*1*
Barry County	*n/l*	*Macomb County*	*25*
Bay County	*2*	*Manistee County*	*10*
Benzie County	*2*	*Marquette County*	*n/l*
Berrien County	*17*	*Mason County*	*2*
Branch County	*7*	*Mecosta County*	*8*
Calhoun County	*6*	*Menominee County*	*n/l*
Cass County	*20*	*Midland County*	*5*
Charlevoix County	*n/l*	*Missaukee County*	*3*
Cheboygan County	*3*	*Monroe County*	*6*
Chippewa County	*n/l*	*Montcalm County*	*n/l*
Clair County	*n/l*	*Muskegon County*	*6*
Clinton County	*57*	*Montmorency County*	*n/l*
Crawford County	*n/1*	*Newaygo County*	*18*
Dickinson County	*n/l*	*Oakland County*	*2*
Delta County	*n/l*	*Oceana County*	*16*

n/l NOT LISTED

Eaton County	*8*
Emmet County	*10*
Genesee County	*13*
Gladwin County	*n/l*
Gogebic County	*n/l*
Grand Traverse County	*18*
Gratiot County	*n/l*
Hillsdale County	*8*
Houghton County	*n/l*
Huron County	*12*
Ingham County	*n/l*
Ionia County	*2*
Iosco County	*3*
Iron County	*n/l*
Isabella County	*1*
Jackson County	*1*
Kalamazoo County	*18*
Kent County	*46*
Keweenaw County	*n/l*
Ogemaw County	*3*
Ontonagon County	*n/l*
Osceola County	*3*
Oscoda County	*n/l*
Otsego County	*n/l*
Ottawa County	*3*
Roscommon County	*14*
Presque Isle County	*1*
Saginaw County	*33*
Sanilac County	*22*
St. Clair County	*22*
St. Joseph County	*11*
Shiawassee County	*25*
Schoolcraft County	*n/l*
Tuscola County	*10*
Van Buren County	*5*
Washtenaw County	*4*
Wayne County	*12*
Wexford County	*6*

It is interesting to note that while some counties are lacking mound listings entirely, others seemed to have far more than their fair share. Just how did your county compare?

So let's back up a bit historically to see how certain turn-of-the-century historians defined some of these Michigan mound discoveries:

W.B. Hinsdale's PRIMITIVE MAN IN MICHIGAN mentions several mound sites (pages 64-69);

1. In the 1930s only one mound in the state had been preserved, that being at Bronson Park, Kalamazoo.
2. There are two mounds on the larger of the Dickson Lakes near Brethren, Manistee County. One mound situated on the SE ¼ of the SW ¼ of Sec. 10, W½ of Dickson Township, measures 53-feet from trench to trench, east and west, by 41-feet, north and south. The surrounding trench, a feature not always associated with Michigan mounds is 36-inches deep. The other mound in the NE¼ of the NW¼ of Sec. 15, on the eastern shore of the Lakes, is slightly larger.
3. Mr. W.L. Coffinberry, reporting upon Grand River mounds, speaks of eight groups, consisting in all, of 46-

mounds. The mounds vary from 2-feet to 15-feet in height, and from 10-feet to 102-feet in diameter. Materials found were human remains, fabrics, pottery and drinking vessels, stone, bone and copper implements.

4. The Great Mound of the Rouge River at Delray was an imposing structure several hundred feet long and 40-feet high. During later times, this mound was probably a central burial place for Indians bringing the bones of their dead. The lower part of this mound must have been built before "historic" times. One mound still remains inside the grounds of old Fort Wayne.

5. A Mr. H.D. Post describes groups of mounds and inclosures upon the Rabbit River, Allegan County. In the same vicinity as the enclosures were mounds surrounded by circles. Some of the numerous mounds here were destroyed by road equipment, the plow and relic hunters.

6. Upon an island comprising 90 acres in the Kalamazoo River, 6-miles above the City of Kalamazoo, is a hill imagined to be an Indian mound. The hill rises abruptly 14-feet from the level of the island. The outline of elevation is triangular and upon it are 6-parallel shallow depressions or ditches running the entire distance of its longest axis, a hundred feet.

The following excerpts are taken from Bela Hubbard's *Memorials Of A Half Century:* (pages 228-9)

1. In 1837 a mound stood on the banks of the St. Joseph River. It was of small size, and so well defined that I could not pass it unnoticed. This was a tumulus on Climax Prarie, south of the mound and in the edge of the timber, on the highest part of a hill, there was an excavated ring, which formed the whole of a perfect circle, and enclosed 1½ acres. The excavated hollow was about 1-rod wide at the bottom and between 2 and 3-feet deep. Circles of this kind are very rare!

2. Tumuli or burial mounds, single and grouped, are very common in all parts of the peninsula. Many and perhaps the finest, occurs on the Grand River, 3-miles south of Grand Rapids. They were still perfect in 1874. The largest of these mounds has a diameter of 100-feet and a height of 15-feet or more. Close by are 2 others of nearly equal size, all very regular in shape and conical. They are in a line about 100 feet apart and 500-feet from the river. Around them cluster 17

smaller tumuli without regular arrangement and varying in height from 2 to 8-feet. All are within 2½ acres. No relics were found when opened. Red-Ochre dumpings were found together with ashes and bone pieces...perhaps bodies were cremated. 7 of the tumuli were opened. Of the 6-smaller ones, skeletons were found. All in a sitting posture. With the bones were many relics, the lowest mound yielded the richest harvest. Stone arrows, spear heads, copper needles, axes, awls, stone pipes and marine shells.
3. On the prarie of White Pigeon, near the Village I saw a tumulus of considerable size.

Local libraries are a good source for locating information regarding mounds, earthworks and formal gardens that may have been located in your specific region. The following brief quotes were taken from county historical works, mainly from the eastern side of the lower peninsula:

From *History Of The Lake Huron Shore*, by W.R. McCormick (pages 32-33)
1. On the Saginaw River, towards the mouth, we find the site of 2-large mounds. They contained a number of skeletons, stone axes and other artifacts.
2. Fifty years ago (about 1830) I saw a mound that stood some 30-rods below on Water Street, Bay City. There was an area of about 1½ acres behind the mound where earth was removed to build it. At a depth of 11½-feet, 3 skeletons of very large stature with large earthen pots at their heads, were found. I was unable to preserve any of these skulls, as they crumbled to dust when exposed to the air. This mound is full of the remains of ancient pottery. These mounds were on the east side of the Saginaw River.
3. Now over to the west side near the mill of J.J. Smith, there was here in 1830 a mound just above the mill, about 100-feet across in a circular form and about 3-feet high. Originally it must have been higher. Early settlers say a great many stone implements were found in it.
4. The Birney Mound was located near the west end of the Detroit and Bay City Railroad bridge. The mound was not so large in circumference, but was much higher than the one just mentioned. Human bones including a skull with a hole in it were found in a good stage of preservation. It was a well

developed head, not of Indian origin. It lacked the high cheek bones and receding forehead of an Indian skull. Artifacts removed from this mound included a small silver canoe about 5-inches long. Also a rough copper kettle of peculiar shape and manufacture, having been wrought by hammering without any seams.

5. Mounds on Duck Island in Lake Huron contained broken pottery, bowls, etc.

6. Mounds also were located at the headwaters of the AuSable River. One of these mounds turned up a large skeleton of immense size, that an old Indian trader reported was 7-feet long with a skull twice the normal size.

7. The Rifle River Fort contained mounds on the inside.

Further reports come from the *Alcona Historical Facts & Stories*, by N. Hansen. (pages 4-9, 24);

> Hubbard Lake. There are 3-mounds at the Henney place, one has been destroyed. One was about 4-feet high, 21-feet wide with 9-feet of a slope on the sides and 30-feet long. Countless stone implements such as axes, arrow heads and skinning knives were uncovered. Ceremonial mounds have been desecrated by the relic hunters. (These mounds stood near the unusual stone idol mentioned in the chapter on "Image Stones.")

Other regional records indicate a mound being 4-miles east of Glennie, Alcona County, located on U.S. Federal Forest land. This particular mound had been previously ransacked of artifacts. All that still remained were two stone internment boxes with lids. Most interesting!

Other information reported mounds near the harbor at Beaver Island at the turn-of-the-century. Research did not indicate if they presently remain.

An imposing list of artifacts gleaned from these Michigan mounds from around the state include: Stone caskets, lamps, pipes, clay tablets, battle axes, knives, spears, daggers, arrow points, utensils, saws, chisels, spades, a variety of ornamental apparel made from copper, stone tablets, medallions, medals, skinning knives, various implements of strange design plus other inexplicable material. With the exception of stone hammers, no other tools formed of stone were found.

Now for the "big" question! Were there actually "pyramids" found in Michigan? Well, from time to time reports surfaced of possible pyramid structures reportedly in Ontonagon County at the far western end of the Upper Peninsula. Research into old documents turned up the following descriptions of what may or may not have been pyramids:

These words are taken from *The Ancient Miners of Lake Superior*, by Charles Whittsley: (page 45)

There has not been observed on Lake Superior any remains that indicate the existence of cities or permanent houses of earth or stone. Mr. Hill is of the opinion that he has seen two "mounds" or tumuli near the Ontonagon River, that are artificial and ancient.

The next report comes from *The American Antiquarian*, by T.H. Lewis and published in 1889. (VolXX)

1. Traces of tumuli, constructed in the form of mathematical figures, have been observed, but not sufficiently explored to determine absolutely whether they be the work of art, and if so, for what purpose intended. In the northeast quarter of Sec. 16, Township 50, Range 39, near a small stream, there is a mound which has the appearance of having been a work of art. Mr. Hill (surveyor) from whose notes much of the above information has been derived, states that from the want of tools he was unable to penetrate it, to determine if it was stratified or not. It is about 10-feet high, in the form of a square, the sides of which are 15-feet in length, flat on top and slopes regularly to the base.

2. There is another tumulus on the right bank of the Ontonagon River, 6-miles from its mouth, 40-feet high and nearly circular, which has been supposed to be artificial, but has not been explored with a view to determine this point.

3. Mr. Lewis made a personal trip to the Ontonagon country and his report indicates...The square mound described and illustrated above stood about 40-rods west of the post office of Rockland and about 2-miles east of the Ontonagon River (N.W.N.E. 16, 50, 39) near the edge of a deep ravine, on nearly level ground, and undoubtedly it was artificial. The excavations and long years of cultivation have so defaced it that, at present, the casual observer could not locate it without

assistance...Several parties did more or less excavating in it and whilst they agree human bones were found at the bottom, near the level of the surrounding soil...the finding of the bones and the position and shape of the mound, indicate that it was artificially constructed and leaves no room for doubt.

4. The other mound, located some 5-miles above the Village of Ontonagon, also on the east side of the river, and which has generally been considered to be artificial by the citizens of that region, is unquestionably of natural origin, it being an isolated portion of adjoining plateau. The north end is some 30-feet in height above the flood plain on which it rests, and if isolated would be nearly triangular in shape at the base, but extends to the north where there is a large irregular ridge or "hog back." The base of this hog back is surrounded in high water and the southwest side is being cut-away, showing the clay formation.

It is believed that the effigy mounds shaped as numerical figures were true mounds as well as the flat-topped mound so described in Mr. Lewis's earlier report. The second mound somewhat described as a pyramid, thought to be a work of nature, turned out *not* to be the Ontonagon Pyramids we were searching for. Positive information came from Mr. Rudy Saari of Ontonagon who was quite familiar with the objects in question. In turn, Mr. Saari advised me the mounds described in the preceding age-old reports were definitely not the Ontonagon Pryamids. The ones so described were actually located near Mills Creek above the area of the pyramids.

Mr. Saari described these enigmatic pyramids as follows: They are approximately 100 yards from the Ontonagon River about 1½ miles from the Village of Ontonagon. The height of one mound was 56 feet while the other was 67 feet. The natural cover is mostly trees of aspen, white birch, maple and some forest underbrush. The soil is sand and leaf mulch with additional small stones. The south or river base has an appearance of a canal.

Mr. Saari made many trips to these mound sites. Several years ago he escorted Professor James Schertz and a geomorphologist from The University of Wisconsin to the pyramids. At this particular time, the two scientists took laser measurements and infrared photos of both structures. On one of these scientific expeditions, professors from Michigan Tech

University also accompanied Dr. Schertz. Once again their guide proved to be Rudy Saari. At this date and time, reports indicate Dr. Schertz was primarily interested in finding a site that could have been a port city for the shipment of copper by miners from other parts of the world. He thought these mounds may have represented such a site. Scientists from both Michigan Tech. and Wisconsin came to the conclusion that the pyramids were natural and showed no evidence of man's handiwork. In the first anaylsis they assumed them to be "sculpted" by geological forces at the end of the last glaciation, several thousand years past.

The surfacing of this information seems to close the chapter on at least one of Michigan's prehistory mysteries, that being...the Ontonagon Pyramids. However, I would like to point out at this writing, investigations are still forthcoming from that same general area. A recent newspaper clipping came my way from Stevens Point, Wisconsin that states Dr. James Schertz of the University of Wisconsin has discovered unusual sets of stone rock piles arranged in giant circles, divided into degrees, along rivers in both Wisconsin and northern Michigan. He believes they could have been used by the "ancients" to determine the precise occurrence of the summer and winter solstices. Schertz terms them as being solar calendars. Schertz indicated he found three of these circles along the Ontonagon River and states there was virtually no chance of the rocks being arranged by natural means or by past farming endeavors.

Furthermore, he theorizes the calendars were possibly constructed by early Indians along the copper trade routes between Lake Superior and the Mississippi River via the Ontonagon and Wisconsin River systems. Large trade canoes could have traveled from the lake, up the Ontonagon River to the first falls, then cargos could have been transferred to smaller canoes with the journey continuing by means of portaging. Villages may have developed along these waterways, for additional, similar cairns or calendars have turned up in Wisconsin as well. Schertz also claims old surveyors' notes mentioned temple mounds in Ontonagon County of a particular style and type that was not believed to have been constructed north of the southern portions of Wisconsin.

So the old stories of the 1800s persist and investigations may turn up new, informative and exciting results. It is also quite interesting to learn that a Mr. John Ralston from Merriweather, located on Lake Gogebic near the mound sites, has excavated numbers of prehistoric relics. The ones most unique that caught my fancy were several ancient stone plows. They leave questions...did the Mound-Builders use stone plows? I find this fact even more unexplainable than the Ontonagon Pyramids themselves. Additionally, were the "flat top" mounds of ancient Mississippian origin? Were the Mound-Builders one and the same as the race of people known as the Copper Culture Clan who worked the ancient copper mining pits? Were the reported "effigy mounds" located in Ontonagon County constructed in the shape of the age-old mysterious number "7". Research turned up no further positive information, so the questions still surface. Many of the mysteries remain. Perhaps with more dedicated scientists, the like of Dr. James Schertz, further answers will be forthcoming. Maybe at some future date, a window on Ontonagon's prehistory past will suddenly open and we'll learn the answer to the Riddle of the Pyramids, the stone plows and the perplexing rock-pile solar calendars. Indeed, I hope so!

BIBLIOGRAPHY: MOUNDS, PART II

PRIMITIVE MAN IN MICHIGAN, W.B. Hinsdale, Avery Color Studios, MI 1983-87

MEMORIALS OF A HALF—CENTURY, Bela Hubbard, G.P. Putnam's Sons, 1888

PREHISTORIC COPPER MINING IN THE LAKE SUPERIOR REGION, by Drier & DuTemple, Publ. privately, Calumet

HISTORY OF THE LAKE HURON SHORE, by W.R. McCormick, publ. H.R. Page & Co. 1883

ALCONA COUNTY HISTORICAL FACTS AND STORIES, N. Hansen, publ. privately

CREDITS:

Rudy Saari, 517 Zinc Street, Ontonagon, MI 49953

Great Mound at River Rouge, height 40 feet. From Hubbard, Memorials of a Half-Century. Totally destroyed.

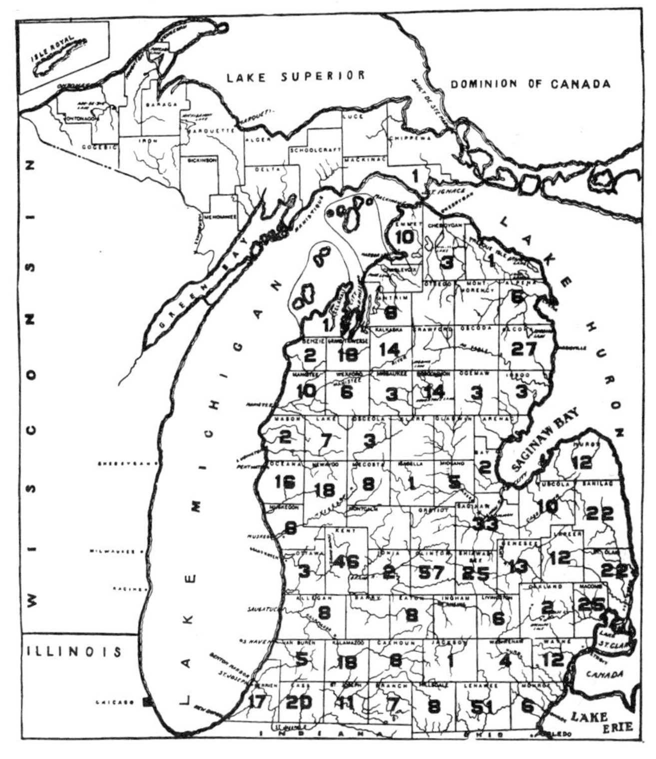

Base map of Michigan with number of authenticated mounds in each county indicated. 1924.

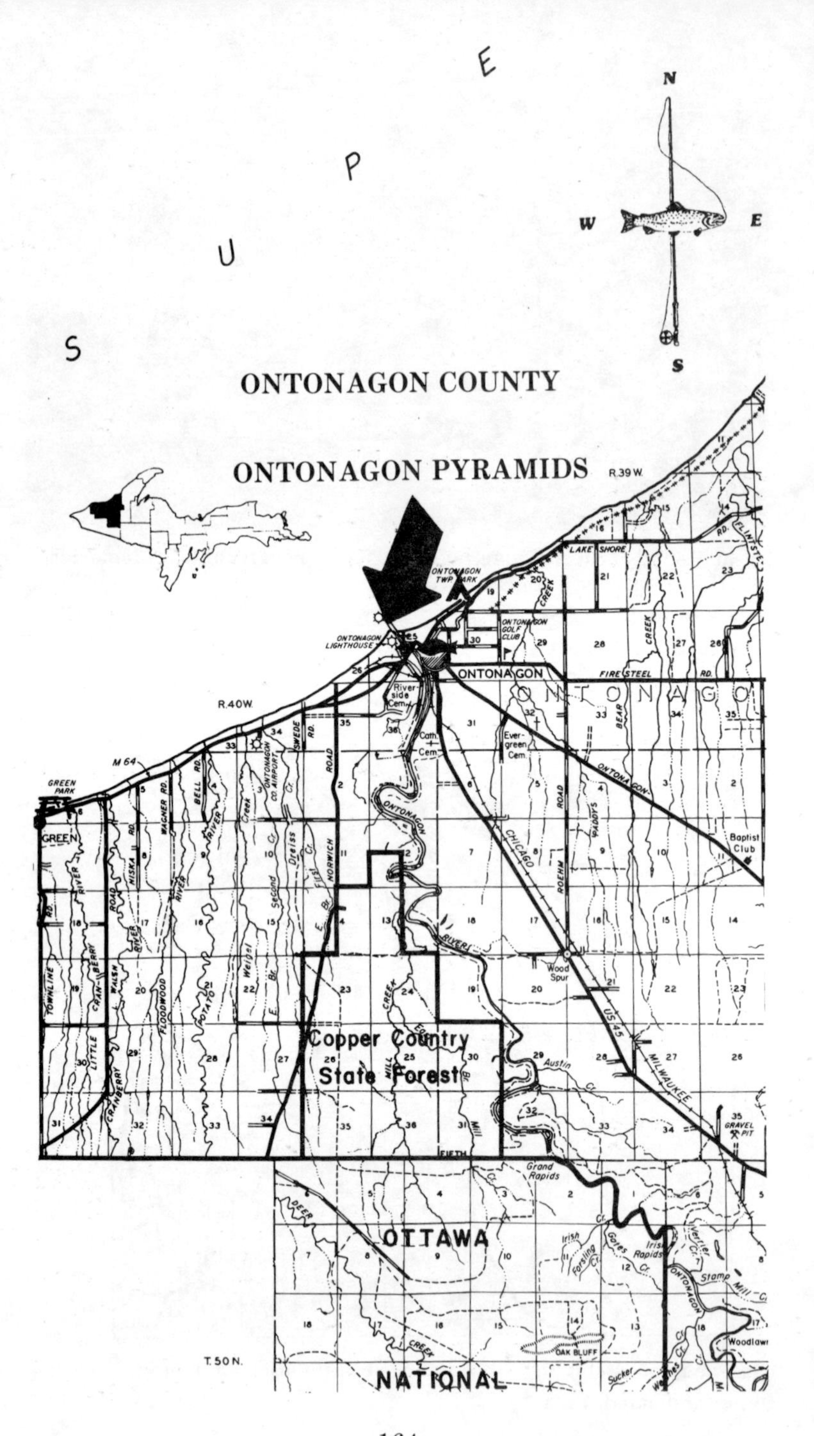
S U P E
N
W
E
S
ONTONAGON COUNTY
ONTONAGON PYRAMIDS
R.39W.
R.40W.
ONTONAGON
LIGHTHOUSE
ONTONAGON
TWP PARK
ONTONAGON
GOLF
CLUB
LAKE SHORE
FIRE STEEL
RD.
M 64
GREEN
PARK
GREEN
Copper Country
State Forest
OTTAWA
NATIONAL
Wood
Spur
Baptist
Club
GRAVEL
PIT
OAK BLUFF
Grand
Rapids
Irish
Rapids
Woodlawn
T.50N.

Prehistory Mounds - Pyramids - Earthworks - Gardens
PART III
Modern Day Excavation - Ancient Baraga County Mound

Has all this talk of prehistory mounds, historical artifacts as well as ancient life of a long-ago people stirred your imagaination? Don't you wish these early Michigan mounds had been preserved to at least some degree? True, most are gone, lost forever in the name of "progress!" But is there perhaps at least one place in our immense State of Michigan where we, the general public, can still observe such objects of ancient endeavor? Yes, I am pleased to report that in the Sand Point area near L'Anse in Baraga County in the far western reaches of the Upper Peninsula, a group of mounds still exists. Here mounds were located, where the experts denied tumuli to flourish...mounds do not belong in the U.P. scientific experts unanimously agreed.

Nevertheless, a group of dedicated Upper Peninsula amateur archaeologists eventually convinced proper authorities of the historical significance of the Sand Point Mounds. Furthermore the very site of these ancient mounds to all intents and purposes ties in well with the Copper Culture people that mined the copper pits of the Keweenaw and Isle Royale regions as far back in time as 2000 B.C.

The Baraga Historical Society has most kindly allowed us to reprint an article titled, "In Search of Baraga County's Ancient Past." This exciting rendition of an actual excavation of a Michigan mound was written by anthropologist Winston D. Moore. Moore's fine accounting was published in the *Baraga County Historical Book*, 1972-73.

Because this report gels so dramatically with other material presented in this book, the Baraga Historical Society felt it most important to include Moore's excellent article in its entirety:

In Search Of Baraga County's Ancient Past

When, in 1877, Chief Mack-aw-de-be-nessy (A.J. Blackbird) recorded the history of his people in his *History of the Ottawa and Chippewa Indians of Michigan* he began by commenting:

I deem it not improper to present the history of the last race of Indians now existing in the State of Michigan, called the Ottawa and Chippewa Nations of Indians.

..There were many other tribes of Indians in this region prior to the occupancy of the Ottawa and Chippewa Indians of this State, who have long ago gone out of existence. Not a page of their history is on record; but only an allusion to them in our traditions.

Here Chief Blackbird recognized that many Indian peoples had previously lived in the lands and along the shores where the first European explorers had found the Ottawas, Ojibwas and other great Indian Nations of the Great Lakes Region.

Chief Blackbird saw that a little information of these long ago times could be gleaned from what had been the unwritten history of Indian peoples--from the traditions, stories and lessons which parents and grandparents had taught the young for untold generations. But as the generations had passed, inevitably many of the details of the life of the people who were there before had been lost. And we might ask what knowledge has survived of the lives and accomplishments of those unnamed peoples who had passed this way even earlier? To know anything of them requires a detective optimistic enough to try to pick up a trail cold for 500 or 1000 or more years. Such a detective is the archaeologist.

Before the time when archaeologists began to piece the facts together to achieve an understanding of the true history of pre-Columbian America, there were many wrong guesses about the history of the first Americans. Some speculated that the Indians whom the first European explorers met had only arrived a few years before. When the ruins of great cities, temples, art works, and monuments were found there were those who speculated that the Indians could not have built them. Some other more advanced race had done this work, and that later, the war-like Indians had wiped them out.

But these were the speculations of the settlers who were involved in Indian wars and the land grab of a whole continent. In these wars which the whites brought to the Indians, psychological warfare and the germ warfare were more deadly than the actual armed encounters. The claims that the Indians were Johnny-come-latelys and warlike savages were parts of the psychological warfare. Ultimately, Indian children were taught in their victor's schools that American history began when Columbus "discovered" America. Anything before that was nothing but savages running through the bushes and would best be ignored.

Now that the dust of battling frontiersmen and Indians has settled, the record is being set straight. The painstaking detective work of archaeologists is proving that American heritage is a deep and rich history with only the most recent chapter documenting the coming of the White man. Ancestors of the American Indians have been in the Americas for many thousands of years, coming to the Americas from Siberia. They were living in areas to the south of Baraga County when the Upper Peninsula of Michigan and all of Lake Superior were nothing but a massive cake of glacial ice.

About 11,000 years ago Indian hunters

camped in an area not far from the present location of Detroit. On the beach of a glacial lake they cooked and ate a tundra-living caribou before moving on. That was a time when all mankind were hunters, gatherers and fishermen, before there was so much as a town the size of L'Anse built anywhere in the world!

Archaeologists have studied the ruins of ancient civilizations in North and South America marvelling at the skills of these bygone builders and craftsmen. In their studies they have always found that the work was not that of some mysterious lost race but was the work of American Indians. This is the true history of America and has replaced the earlier speculations.

Since no Indians in America north of Mexico are known to have made use of writing for all these thousands of years, their past is learned only through painstaking archaeological work. This work is carried out in areas where these ancient people lived and worked so long ago. The archaeologist carefully sifts through the ashes of a fire, cold for centuries, in a search for traces of the food of some long since disappeared people. An old garbage pile is a treasure to the archaeologist not because it may contain priceless relics, but because it may contain some equally priceless clues to the past.

While some parts of the United States are well known archaeologically, other areas, such as the Upper Peninsula of Michigan, remain largely unknown. So few locations have been found where Indian peoples lived prior to the time of European contact that for long periods of time nothing is known of them. As late as 1970 Professor James Fitting wrote in his book *The Archaeology of Michigan:*

..The largest (archaeologically) unexplored area of Michigan lies along the southern shore of Lake Superior. Even today, this is an area of low population density and little agricultural activity. Sites which would be brought to light by plowing in the lower peninsula remain covered with dense sod and underbrush in this region ... During one recent survey not one aboriginal site was encountered along the entire Pictured Rocks National Lakeshore.

This is not because people were not here, but as Professor Fitting indicates it is because much of the area is forest-covered and the sites have not been located. The search for man's past in the western Upper Peninsula has for the last several years centered on a very important site which has come to light in Baraga County. This site has been named the Sand Point Site after its geographical location.

The Sand Point Site came to light quite by accident. Dr. Louis C. Guy (a L'Anse dentist and real estate developer) who owns part of the property on which the site is located was in the process of filling in the swampy parts of his property with the higher sandy parts to ready the area for cabin sites. In the process of bulldozing a sandy knoll, human bones of ancient burials were disturbed. Dr. Guy suspended his bulldozing work and got in contact with another L'Anse man, Mr. Alf Jentoft, known to be interested in matters of the early Indian history of the region. Mr. Jentoft is the secretary of the Upper Peninsula Chapter of the Michigan Archaeological Society. This group is made up of people interested in early Indian history, mostly people who have other professions and who pursue archaeology as a serious hobby.

Mr. Jentoft and other members of the U.P. Chapter of the M.A.S. (as it is abbreviated) began the initial exploratory excavations at the site to determine exactly what was there. Through their work, they became convinced that this was, indeed, an important site. Attempts were made by the Chapter to interest the professional archaeologists at the University of Michigan and later Michigan State in the Site. But Baraga County is a long way from Ann Arbor and Lansing and besides that, sites reported to the professional archaeologists are seldom as important as they are purported to be. Further, most archaeologists have gone out 25 50 or 100 times to see what was explained to them as a mound only to find it to be a perfectly natural knoll or hummock. So when "Indian mounds" were reported from an area where mounds were not known to occur, there was some understandable skepticism.

Finally, a University of Michigan party came to see the site. But, as luck would have it, they arrived just when L'Anse, Baraga and the Sand Point Site were being flooded by the seiche of 1968. They looked at the tops of mounds protruding from the flood waters and went back to write their report. The report, while according some importance to the site, stated the "mounds" were build up by wind or wave action and were not anything constructed by man. Since the U.P. Chapter was excavating and keeping records of their works, no further work was planned, at least for the near future.

The Jentofts and the rest of the U.P. Chapter were greatly disappointed. That report might have meant that the history of Sand Point would never be recognized. Dr. Guy wished to get on with his development project and the Chapter members with other jobs to attend to could only devote a small amount of time to the project. Things might well have ended here except for another chance occurrence.

It happened that Mr. and Mrs. Larry Dorothy, members of the Kalamazoo Valley Chapter of the Michigan Archaeological Society, were vacationing in the western Upper Peninsula during the summer of 1969. They happened by the Baraga County Tourist Information Center and Museum, and stopped to see what was there. In the Museum the U.P. Chapter had provided a display of the artifacts from the Sand Point Site. After seeing the artifacts, the Dorothys looked up Mr. Jentoft and were shown and told about the site. When Mr. Jentoft indicated his great interest in getting professionals involved in the site, Mr. Dorothy said they might be able to interest the archaeologists at Western Michigan University in the project. Thus the Dorothys departed with photos and samples from the site.

Early that fall, Mr. Dorothy arranged to meet with myself and other archaeologists at Western to show and explain his photos and samples and to tell us about the Sand Point Site. Based on what we heard, two of us from the Anthropology Department made a trip to see the site and to talk with Mr. Jentoft to further ascertain what the U.P. Chapter had been finding. We soon determined that the Sand Point Site contained man-made mounds and that unless some large scale work was carried out on the site soon much would be irretrievably lost. If it were not lost to the bulldozer, it would surely be lost to relic hunters who had begun to secretly dig at the site when no one was around to protect it.

Thus in the summer of 1970 Western Michigan University began its archaeological excavations at Sand Point. Further excavations were made in the summer of 1971 and the analysis of the recovered material is still in progress. While much work remains to be done before the past of man at Sand Point is fully known, at least the broad outlines of the story are beginning to emerge. The information gathered at these excavations will add much to our understanding of the region's prehistory.

Text books will have to be rewritten because of our findings.

What exactly is there at Sand Point that makes it of interest and important? Already we have alluded to burial mounds at the site. Hundreds of years before the first European set foot in North America, people were living on Sand Point and casting their fishing nets in the rich waters of L'Anse Bay and Keweenaw Bay. Through the years these early resident fishermen constructed a series of memorials to their deceased friends and kinsmen, following the prescribed custom of reverence and respect of their culture and time.

Looking at their monuments today, we see a series of oblong mounds standing six to nine feet in height, twenty to thirty feet from side to side, and fifty to one-hundred feet long. Five such structures are clearly visible at the site today. It was a sixth such mound that was excavated first by the U.P. Chapter of the M.A.S. and then in the summer of 1970 by an archaeological group from Western Michigan University. Most of this mound is gone by now as the land development project has moved forward, but because of the archaeological work the lives and culture of these early residents will not go ignored and unappreciated.

The archaeological work has allowed us to understand how the one mound was built, and presumably how the others were built also. Sand was dug up nearby and piled to form a ramp-like structure. The sand used was not just any sand, but rather, special care was used to first scrape away all the sand stained by the dead vegetation at the surface. With this removed, the underlying clean yellow-orange could be scooped up to build a mound of the clean yellow-colored sand. As this yellow ramp structure was built, the bones of a number of people were laid to rest in the yellow sand. The burials here were all what are called "secondary burials". They are given this name because first the deceased was left on a scaffold or on a platform in a tree or possibly even buried elsewhere. Then after a time and after nature had taken its course, the bones of the person would be removed and placed in their secondary resting place. In many such instances, the final burial of the bones would mark the end of a formal mourning period which close relatives had been observing.

Certain features deserve special mention. At one point in the yellow sand five bundles of arm and leg bones had been left. A careful inspection of these bones show that each one had been struck with a hard, somewhat pointed object leaving a small hole near one end. A careful examination of the skulls also showed such holes. Further study has shown that this practice was also carried out at other sites from as far away as Ontario and North Dakota. What does it mean? We cannot be sure, but we believe it was a ritual act - possibly to release a spirit of the deceased for his journey to the after-life.

What of the color yellow used in the ramp? Again we must speculate, but we do know that different colors have special symbolic meanings among different peoples. We might suppose that the yellow color symbolically embodied the hope for a happy after-life. The orientation of the ramp rising toward the north may have also had symbolic meaning to the builders.

Over this ramp was constructed a wooden platform of rather heavy logs. Lighter wood was placed on this to form a funeral pyre. The remains of several individuals were placed on the pyre and the structure was set afire. When the blazing platform had finally burned its supports and collapsed, those assembled at the cremation ceremony gathered up sand (any sand was used at this point) Many people and many cubic yards of sand were involved. Not only did they cover the ramp, but they buried the highest part under three or more feet of sand and extended the mound (with a bend in it) to a length of 125 feet. Thus the monument was completed. Later it was used as the resting place for more secondary burials before it was finally left to the ages. As you can see, the people who commemorated their dead with these mounds must have been a deeply religious people with much concern for their deceased friends and relatives.
becomes necessary to excavate a burial area the archaeologist learns more than the burial practices and related religious ideas of the mound builders. He also learns much about the physical appearance of the former residents. There is no doubt for instance, that these people were American Indians. Still, these were by no means ordinary, as American Indians go. Our studies show them to be a very large people. Men were in some cases more than six feet in height, with the average height of adult men being 5'9". Women were also quite tall, averaging 5'6½" in height. While these figures may not seem extraordinary by modern standards, it should be remembered that Caucasian Americans have only reached these heights in recent years, under the influence of greatly improved diets.

We also are able to ascertain that the times in which these mound builders lived and died must have been rather peaceful times. In only one case do we have strong evidence of a death by violence. In this case an arrow or spear point embedded in a hip bone suggests a homicide. In more than fifty other cases there is no indication of foul play.

One aspect of the burial practices of these ancient mound builders deserves a special mention, because had it not been for this the mounds would have long ago been destroyed. The practice which saved the mounds to be appreciated these many years later was this: no grave offerings were left with the dead. No pots of food, no elaborate ornaments, no tools--nothing has been found which was unmistakably an offering left with the dead. In many other areas of the United States grave offerings were left with the dead; in these areas relic hunters have been busy hunting their treasures of pots and arrow points. Mounds have been totally obliterated, fields are pock-marked with craters from the digging and any chance of knowing and appreciating the lives of the ancient peoples has been lost forever. At Sand Point, however, the story is not so bleak. For the most part the mounds went unnoticed until recently; this saved them from destruction. But someone, sometime did get the idea that these sandy ridges were mounds, and whoever this was did dig into them. An inspection of the mounds today reveals depressions, slumped in remains of gaping holes--dug into every one of the mounds. This is where the lack of grave goods saved the mounds. Whoever it was, digging 20, 30, 50 or even 100 years ago finally quit when it became obvious that there was no rich booty to be found.

It might then be asked, why are the archaeologists interested in the site? Archaeologists are interested because their interest is not in relics but in history. The objects found are keys to understanding the past, not valuable commodities to be bought and sold. Thus, the Sand Point site is still of great interest and importance even though not so much as a single whole pot has been found.

Earlier, it was mentioned that the mound builders scooped up sand to smother the fire of an ancient cremation and went on to scoop up more sand to build the mound to its final, completed size. When they did this they were unknowingly scooping up the bits of broken trash and lost and discarded items which had fallen to the ground over the years as the people lived on Sand Point. They were, in fact, scooping up their own archaeological living site and piling it on the mound. Thus, in 1970 when the archaeological field crew was excavating the large mound in danger of destruction, they were finding in the sand of the mound the refuse and lost items scattered and misplaced as peoples had lived in the area. Bits of broken pots, lost arrow points, the broken rocks left over after an ancient craftsman had made a new arrow point, discarded bones from a fish dinner--all these things were found. All of this was certainly interesting; types of pottery were found which were very much unexpected in this region. But still, it was all jumbled up due to the fact that the people scooped up the sand and dumped it on the mound. The archaeologist can only sort out the clues to the past when they are found as they fell or were left. Thus, to understand more of the lives of the former residents it was necessary to locate and excavate living areas which had not been disturbed.

The main task of the summer session of 1971 was to locate such areas and to answer questions concerning the lives of the former residents and mound builders. What sort of housing did these people construct? What did the people eat? Did they farm? How many people were there? Did they live at Sand Point year round? Were there different peoples living at Sand Point at different times? These were all questions which excavation of living areas might help solve.

Thus, much excavation of the 1971 season was concentrated in an area of the site not particularly near any one of the mounds, but in an area along the road where some artifacts had been found. Although all the questions we had posed have not yet been answered, our work has yielded much information and further analysis of the material recovered may provide further answers.

We had hoped to find an area that the people had used for a refuse pile for a long time. In such an area we might find food remains along with broken and discarded earthenware pots piled up in layers with the oldest on the bottom and youngest on the top. Unfortunately no such layered midden was located. Had we found this we could determine what foods were eaten and what changes there may have been in pottery styles over the years.

We are, as archaeologists, greatly interested in pottery. Partly this is because it does not disintegrate even when buried for centuries, but more importantly, because pots can be made in so many different ways. Although there are exceptions, as a general rule, we could say that people made their pots following the traditions of their own people. Mothers and grandmothers taught daughters and grand-daughters. Change, nevertheless, did take place as styles of decoration and shapes of vessels waxed and waned in popularity. For this reason the pottery of one people differs from that of another and pottery of one time period differs from that of another. A great variety of decoration is noted on the pot sherds from Sand Point and it certainly would have helped in the study to have found them neatly layered.

Some answers about the everyday lives of the people have been forthcoming, however. Our study of the living area has unearthed roasting pits in which people cooked their food with the aid of fireheated stones. Carbon material taken from the roasting pits will allow us to establish when these fires were built. After much exploratory searching, almost at the end of the season's work, indications of a former house were discovered. All that remained was a series of stains in the sand where posts, once supports for walls, had been driven into the ground. This house was small, rectangular and probably bark, mat, or bough covered. This was probably the most easily built and efficient house type they could have constructed. While we would hope for further evidence to support this, it seems that large multi-family long houses or clay-mud plastered houses were not used.

We would like to know more about how the people lived, but we can say that fishing was definitely important in their lives. Not far from the remains of the house was a series of flat pebbles with curious nicks made on opposite sides. Most people would toss such rocks aside without a second thought. The trained eye, however, can recognize them for what they were--sinkers for fishing nets. The plant material from which the fisherman's net had been made probably was rotting and the net was discarded. Net sinkers are so easily made from any beach pebbles that there was little reason to salvage them. Hundreds of years later an odd grouping of nicked and notched pebbles is all that remains of the fisherman's net. Some fish bones, a copper fish hook and other probable fishing implements were also found; this supports the idea that there was an emphasis on fishing. For the most part, however, bones from the fish and game of former meals have been disintegrated by the acidic forest soil.

The acid soil and the passage of time have also obliterated almost all traces of implements and containers which had been made of wood, bark or plant fibers. We have every reason to believe that there once had been numerous handsome baskets, finely woven mats and well made tools. These are gone now; only the bits of pottery, copper and stone remain as clues to a past way of life.

The study of the lay of the land also helps us reconstruct the past. From this we can ascertain that when these fishermen lived at Sand Point the immediate area was much different than it is today. Where swamps now stand there was formerly open water, then later a sheltered, but open, lagoon. Probably when sand spits closed off the lagoon the former inhabitants moved elsewhere. Thus, long before Europeans came to Keweenaw Bay the living areas and mounds had been abandoned and forgotten. Only out along the present shoreline--some distance from the rest of the site--do we pick up evidence of more recent events. A gun flint recognizable as French in origin, a musket ball, bottle glass chipped by a person familiar with chipping stone--these are from a different page of history. The rest of the site is from an earlier era.

Returning now to a further discussion of what was found at Sand Point, I would like to indicate why the site is so unique and important to an understanding of Indian history in the years before the coming of the Europeans. A study of the pottery from the site shows it to be mostly Late Woodland types. Based upon this material it has been estimated that the site dates from about 1100 A.D. to 1300 A.D. Large burial mounds such as those encountered at Sand Point were not known to occur in Late Woodland times in Michigan. The most unexpected and amazing thing about the site, however, was the occurrence of Mississippian artifacts at Sand Point.

Let me digress to say a few words about Mississippian culture before coming back to the Sand Point artifacts. A recent textbook on American prehistory states: *"In areal extent of influence, ceremonialism, public works, technology, population density, and general richness, the Mississippian is exceeded by no other aboriginal American culture north of Mexico."* This culture centered on a great civilization in the middle and lower Mississippi Valley and dated from 600 A.D. to 1600 A.D. It influenced people as far south as the southern tip of Florida, as far east as Pennsylvania, as far West as Colorado and (now with Sand Point) as far north as Lake Superior. This culture is known primarily from its monumental earthwork mounds and pyramids. These pyramids had flat tops and were used as massive raised platforms for temples.

Probably the largest Mississippian city was at the present location of Cahokia, Illinois just across the Mississippi River from St. Louis, Missouri. This ancient city, called Cahokia, contained more than one hundred mounds and pyramids. The largest of these, called Monk's Mound, was and is the largest American Indian earthwork north of Mexico. It has been calculated to contain twenty-two million cubic feet of earth! The city of Cahokia was surrounded by a massive log wall or palisade. It has been calculated that it would have taken 10,000 soldiers to man the wall. On this basis, a guess at the population of Cahokia has been made at 40,000 people. This compares favorably in size with the ancient cities and civilizations of the Near East.

Another outstanding feature of the Mississippian culture was its ceramics. As people and influence of this civilization spread, the styles and means of manufacture of pottery vessels also spread. One of the key features of Mississippian ceramics which is detectable in even a single small sherd is the use of crushed shell as temper. This stands in sharp contrast with the sand or crushed stone of Woodland pottery.

Returning to the Sand Point material, we can see that finding pottery and other artifacts which are Mississippian definitely links this northern region to the great Mississippian civilization. We believe that we have found enough Mississippian material so that we would say that Mississippian peoples were once at Sand Point. Had only a few Mississippian things been found we might have concluded that the objects were traded in and that Mississippian peoples themselves were not there. But the material unearthed was such that the actual presence of Mississippian peoples seems more likely.

Besides shell tempering, the Mississippian pottery from Sand Point differs from the Woodland pottery in a number of ways. Decoration and shapes of pots differed considerably between Woodland and Mississippian traditions. Mississippian potters sometimes put handles on their pots; Woodland potters did not. Mississippian potters smoothed the surface of their pots; Woodland potters left rough impressions by paddling the damp pot with a paddle wrapped with a cord. Mississippian potters decorated their pots with broad or narrow grooves; Woodland potters decorated with cord and cordwrapped twig impressions. These are just some of the ways the two ceramic traditions differed.

Some of the outstanding examples of Mississippian artifacts and ideas at Sand Point include the following: a pot sherd recovered at Sand Point shows exactly the same design element as a pot recovered at the ancient city of Cahokia. A small arrow point is a typical Cahokia point in contrast with triangular Woodland points. A carved slate ear spool was found. This very carefully made ornament is much like ear spools found in the central and southern Mississippian Valley, never before found this far north. One must also look to the south to find parallels to the Sand Point mound construction. These mounds, in all probability, are related to Mississippian ideas of the appropriate treatment of the dead. The ramp, the burned structure, the use of the color yellow all find expression in burial practices at Cahokia.

The Sand Point site seems to be the farthest north location yet discovered which was an outpost of Mississippian Culture. Why would Mississippian people be at Sand Point? Here we must guess, but it seems reasonable that they came to the

Keweenaw Peninsula to procure the native copper not to be found elsewhere. Copper ornaments are commonly found farther south at Mississippian sites long distances from any source of copper. All right, you might say, but why a site near Baraga instead of near Rockland or Mass? I would guess the sites at the copper source have been destroyed by later mining or have gone unnoticed as yet. Probably Sand Point fits into the picture as an area where food was procured for the ancient copper miners. The rich fishing of the Keweenaw Bay (possibly in addition to farming) may well have provided the food so the miners could work full time extracting the copper. Of course, such a situation would imply considerable organization and division of labor. Sand Point may also have served as a port, a point of embarkation linking trails to the mining areas with water routes to the east. The miscellaneous lumps and chunks of copper as well as finished copper tools and ornaments which have been found might best be explained in this way.

What happened to these people and what happened to the whole Mississippian civilization is largely an unsolved mystery. It was just a memory when Father Marquette made his trip down the Mississippi. But even though the Mississippian civilization has fallen, as all civilizations eventually do, its richness and splendor are important parts of our American heritage and should not go unnoticed and unremembered.

For that reason let us come back from the past and consider the future of Sand Point. Most people would agree that this site should be preserved and protected for future generations to know and appreciate. Many Baraga County organizations have passed resolutions to that effect. These organizations include the Baraga County Board of Commissioners, the Baraga County Planning Commission, the Keweenaw Bay Indian Community, the Baraga Village Council, the Baraga County Committee for Overall Economic Development and Planning, and the Baraga County Soil Conservation District Board. With this strong showing of local support generated with the tireless help of Mr. Richard Breyer, I have been able to interest the State of Michigan in the protection and preservation of this site. Mr. James A. Bryant, Historic Preservation Coordinator in the Office of Planning Services of the Department of Natural Resources is currently working on ways to best protect, preserve and commemorate Sand Point. While precisely how best to do this has not been worked out, it is expected that plans would include an appropriate crypt for the return to Sand Point of the human skeletal material removed for study.

I have submitted the papers of nomination to have the Sand Point Site added to the State and National Registers of Historic Places. As a result of this, I do believe this site will eventually be declared a National Historic Landmark. Even now the site is protected by law from relic hunting, but when placed on the National Register as a landmark, its full protection will be even more firmly assured.

This is the developing story of Sand Point. Much remains to be learned, much remains to be done. Were it not for the generous help, hospitality and cooperation given to myself and the archaeology students from Western Michigan University by many Baraga County citizens and groups these chapters of the past would have gone unnoticed or destroyed. We can all be proud that we have had a part in bringing them to light.

****

UPDATE:

To bring things up to 1989 concerning the Sand Point Site, most analysis has been completed by now and the results published. A double issue of the MICHIGAN ARCHAEOLOGIST was devoted to coverage of this site in 1980 and another major article on the human remains by Larry Wyckoff, appeared in the same journal in 1981. Dr. William Cremmin of Western Michigan University has overseen the analysis and contributed an introductory article. The pottery was studied by Mr. Lawrence Dorothy, M.A., who brought the site to our attention in 1969.

Plant and animal remains were identified and reported upon by Terrance J. Martin and Deborah K. Rhead and the copper artifacts were the subject of a report by David Hoxie. Besides this, different parts of the excavated material were studied and reported upon in Masters' thesis and in papers presented at anthropological conventions. The stone artifacts were thus described by James Marek and the net sinkers and fishing technology at Sand Point studied by Donald Weston.

The ceramic artifacts and the human remains both point to links between the people at this site and prehistoric peoples of the Wisconsin area to the south. The age of the site has been confirmed by carbon dating methods at 1200-1300 AD. Food remains from Sand Point show a rather mixed forager's diet, more than a dominant emphasis on fishing. This could reflect the truth of the matter, or it may be more a reflection of what survived scavaging camp dogs and later acidic soils. In any case, there was no indication of farming in any of the food remains. Now that the site is in the professional literature, it will find its place as an important part of the overall prehistoric heritage left for us by Native Americans.

The plans for an interpretive center with displays of artifacts and an Indian Heritage oriented park development, painting, art and protecting the mounds...fell apart in the 1970s. The History Division of the Department of State took exception to the Department of Natural Resources (which runs parks) dabbling in the area of Prehistoric Michigan. The idea of returning the human remains to the site seems to have also fallen by the wayside.

Civilizations may rise and fall, but jurisdictional disputes seem destined to continue forever! Such is life! Maybe this book will help create or rekindle interests in Michigan prehistory which will solve riddles and bring more Native American heritage to light!

Winston D. Moore

Winston D. Moore

CREDITS:
The Baraga County Historical Society, (Ms. Irja Harju, Sec., Rt. 1, Box 97, L'Anse, MI 49946)
Winston D. Moore, Anthropologist, South Haven, MI - Author & Photographer
Shay Moore, St. Joseph, MI - Artwork

Stages of burial mound construction: A ramp of yellow sand is built.

A log platform is constructed over the ramp to serve as a funeral pyre.

The burned and collapsed platform is buried and the rest of the mound is built.

Excavation continues - Baraga Mound #1 - Sand Point, Baraga County.

(Above) Shards from the rims of Late Woodland pots.

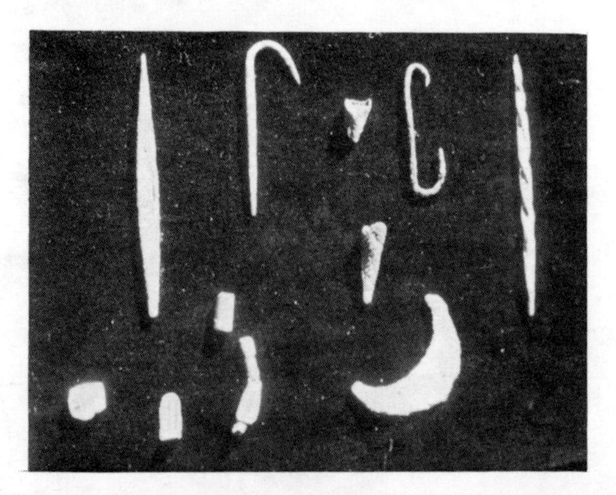

Copper artifacts from Sand Point. (Left to right, top) an awl, a fish hook or gaff hook, a conical bell, an unknown object, a twisted awl. (Lower) copper beads, a conical projectile point, a lunate ornament.

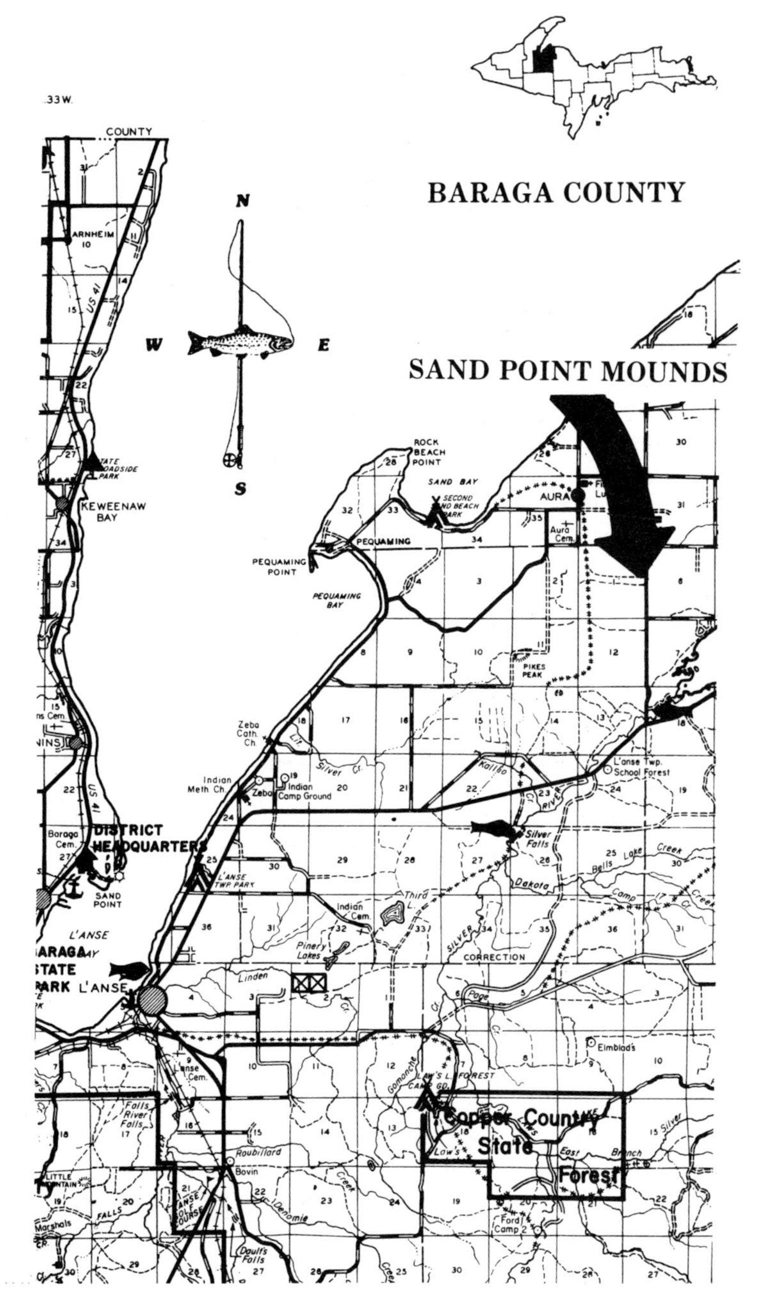
BARAGA COUNTY
SAND POINT MOUNDS
N
S
E
W
KEWEENAW BAY
PEQUAMING
PEQUAMING POINT
PEQUAMING BAY
ROCK BEACH POINT
SAND BAY
AURA
PIKES PEAK
DISTRICT HEADQUARTERS
SAND POINT
L'ANSE
BARAGA STATE PARK
L'ANSE
Zeba
Indian Camp Ground
L'anse Twp. School Forest
Silver Falls
CORRECTION
Copper Country State Forest
Bovin
Elmblad's
US 41

Michigan Mounds - Pyramids - Earthworks - Gardens
PART IV
Ambiguous Gardens & Earthworks

Of all the Michigan prehistory mysteries, perhaps less has been written of the complicated, ancient, formal "garden beds" scattered throughout the State in both peninsulas. Certainly no abstract conclusions were drawn. One positive fact, however, strongly indicates these anomalous garden plots were unique to Michigan, with only two other states reporting similar "garden beds," that being Indiana and Wisconsin.

What knowledge we have of them is detailed in the writings of Bela Hubbard, Henry Schoolcraft and others who traveled and reported from these regions many years ago. Of the very people who constructed them, we know little or nothing!

Accounts attributed to Bela Hubbard are provided to acquaint you, the reader, with some of these rare sites: *Memorials of a Half-Century* (pages 243-244-245)

1. "The earliest mention of these relics comes from "Archaeology of the U.S." by Haven. It is a report of Verandrier who, with several French associates, explored this region before 1748. He found in the western wilderness "large tracts free from wood, many of which are everywhere covered with furrows, as if they had formerly been ploughed and sown."

Author's note: Could the perplexing stone plows described in Part II, have been used in a "garden bed" endeavor?

2. Schoolcraft was the first to give to the world any accurate account of these "furrows." He is the only author of note who considers them a part of the Mound-Builders' culture. His observations were made as early as 1827. He lists two kinds of garden plots and states it was a fact that these "garden beds," not the mounds, form the most prominent and striking characteristic, antiquarian monuments of this district of the country.

3. In 1839 near Lake Michigan's western shore, a garden was found consisting of low parallel ridges, as if corn had been planted in drills. They average 4-feet wide and 25 of them have been counted in a space of 100 feet. With the exceptions listed in Wisconsin and possibly Indiana, they are confined to our State.

4. So-called "garden beds" were found in the valleys of the St. Joseph and Grand Rivers, principally in the counties of St. Joseph, Cass and Kalamazoo. They consist of raised patches of ground, separated by sunken paths, and were generally arranged in plats or blocks of parallel beds, varying in dimensions from 5 to 16-feet in width and 12 to more than 100-feet in length with a height of 6 to 18 inches. The tough sod of the prarie preserved very sharply all the outlines. These beds were laid out and fashioned with a skill, order and symmetry which distinguished them from the ordinary operations of agriculture and were combined with some peculiar features that belong to no recognized system of horticultural art.

5. A short distance from Three Rivers was a garden a half mile long by one-third mile wide, containing about 100-acres, regularly laid out in beds running north and south in the form of parallelograms, 5-feet wide by 100-feet long. Gardens of this kind were also found by early settlers at: Schoolcraft, the burr-oak plains near Kalamazoo, Toland's prarie, at Prarie-Ronde and elsewhere.

6. Schoolcraft speaks of "enigmatical plats of variously shaped beds with nearly all the lines of each area of beds being rectangular and parallel." Others admit of half-circles and variously curved beds with avenues, differently grouped and disposed. Beds also appeared in various fanciful shapes. Some in rectileal and curvilineal figures, either distinct or combined in a fantastic manner scalloped work with alleys between forming ample walkways leading in different directions. (*Author's Note:* Resembling formal pleasure gardens rather than corn beds or agricultural fields.)

7. Historians tell us of the Aztecs, that they had gardens in which were cultivated various plants, for medicinal use, as well as for ornament.

8. Gardens excavated turned up no aboriginal relics, no

pottery, no spears, no arrow heads, no implements of stone, not even the omnipresent pipes. Tumuli, or burial mounds of the ancients, are not uncommon, though not numerous in Western Michigan, but have no recognized association with the "garden bed" race of people.

9. The date of the abandonment of the garden beds may be fixed by the "Age of Trees" found growing upon them. One mentioned by Henry Schoolcraft, cut down in 1837, had 335 cortical layers. This carries the period back as far as 1502, or some years prior to the discovery of this country by the French. At the time of the arrival of the French, this country was in possession of Algonquian tribes, who emigrated from the St. Lawrence about the middle of the 16th century. They were ignorant of the authors of these garden beds and were not more advanced in the arts of culture than the other known tribes.

10. It is perhaps useless to regret that these most interesting and unique relics of a lost people have so completely perished, through the greed of the dominant race; or that they could not have received while they yet remained, the more exact and scientific scrutiny which is now being applied to the antiquities of our land. Much that might then have been cleared up, must now remain forever involved in mystery, or be left to conjecture.

W. B. Hinsdale in his book entitled *Primitive Man In Michigan* (pages 86-87) related the following paragraphs:

1. The garden beds of Michigan have been entirely destroyed, sad to relate. Had they been preserved, they would today rank among America's striking relics of a distinctive aboriginal trait, like the "great serpent mound" of Ohio and the numerous effigies of Wisconsin. Beds are reported to have been located in several counties east from a line running from the south-western corner of Berrien County to the head of Saginaw Bay. At least 23 of them have been described. There were also a few in Indiana. In extent, they varied from the "wheel" of Kalamazoo, 90-feet in diameter, to rectangles of over one hundred acres...It is said the beds had the appearance of being very old. Schoolcraft says several hundred years, based on vegetable growth upon them must have passed. Someone has suggested that they may have been the work of

the Mascoutins, a tribe of Indians that disappeared from this region very early in "historic" times, but their authorship is nothing more than a guess and depends upon no more foundation than does the theory that the mounds of the Ohio Valley were built by the Cherokees.

2. Upon an island comprising 90-acres in the Kalamazoo River, 6-miles above the City of Kalamazoo is a large mound outlined by ditches and shallow depressions, parallel, and some 12-feet apart...One with some imagaination and a not too critical attitude of mind might convince himself that here there is still remaining a small garden bed.

3. If one were to mention the outstanding peculiarities of prehistoric Michigan he would say the garden beds and the copper mines were the most conspicuous. The garden beds are destroyed, but the old mining pits may yet be studied...and should be protected against unintelligent despoliation. (page 139)

Beaver Island, in Lake Michigan, also was a source of "garden beds" as described in *The King Strang Story*, by Doyle C. Fitzpatrick, National Heritage, Lansing, MI 1970. (page 268)

More than a century ago, there was evidence of 200 year old plotted gardens on Beaver Island. When some of the trees were cut down at that time, they were found to be over 200 years old. Having grown on banked areas indicated the soil was previously cleared of trees. This remains proof that some early civilized explorers settled here.

Author's Note: C. Fred Rydholm, historian from Marquette, also told me personally that there was evidence of huge ancient Gardens on the Island. He located them on a recent trip while investigating the Beaver Island "Ring of Stones" discovery. See map from that specific chapter, showing the location of these garden beds, as well.

Furthermore a report from the Marquette County Historical Society gives a short description of additional Upper Peninsula gardens:

In Burt's original survey of 1842, old Indian garden beds are shown in this locality, indicating long term Indian occupancy, but unfortunately, they are located within the grounds of the Marquette Prison. Old beach levels are evident near the prison, that have been the source of a number of old copper artifacts here at our museum.

A reporting from the eastern side of the lower peninsula comes to us from W. B. Hinsdale's, *First People Of Michigan.* (page 156)

1. In some places, pits seem to show a degree of studious arrangement in Alcona County. Here a circular arrangement exists. In another location, in the same county and township, to the northeast and a mile from the shore of Lake Huron, is an arrangemnt of pits on the top of a hill in three rows so dug that in the middle row the pits come midway between or alternate with those of the other rows as do the pattern of pits observed in Isabella County. It has been said that one can locate over a hundred pits in Harrisville Township, which is immediately south of Haynes Township.

2. The most common evidence of Indian work in the ground to be found in Michigan, whether mound, embankment or other diggings, unless it be burial graves, is pit holes. They are found in great numbers in the vicinity of the old cornfields as well as in other parts of the state. On a knoll northeast of the fields in Haynes Township, Alcona County, are 7-pits arranged in a circle 20 feet across. In the center of the circle is an old fireplace...It is 7-feet across the top of each pit. The side walls go down 5-feet into the gravel perpendicularly. The pits are flat upon the bottom with a smaller pit in the center 8-inches in diameter and 12-inches deep. Other pits were found over the clearing which comprised at least 100 acres. All contain fragments of decayed and charred wood and ashes. (page 154)

Authors Note: Even though Hinsdale described the above pits along with his garden and cornfield descriptions...they seem to resemble the Black River stone cairns described in the chapter "Questionable Rocks With A Prehistory Past", Part II, "Black River Cairns & Walls."

Still another form of earthen structures were the so-termed "earthworks" or "fortifications." The largest of these inclosures found in the United States was termed Fort Ancient, located on the edge of present-day Wilmington in Warren County, Ohio. Here walls rise like a fortress some 270 feet above the plateau. The total distance around the irregular walls was close to 3 miles. It was surrounded by a moat some 25 feet deep in certain places. It contained banks some 20 to 30 feet high and covered a span of ground totaling approximately 100 acres. Archaeologists do not term this an actual fort. One, however, must agree, Fort Ancient could rank as one of the "wonders" of the New World!

Nothing quite so "grand" ever appeared in Michigan. Here what we term as "earthworks" were more or less fortified villages with possible palisades, as old post molds often indicate. Many of these unique fortifications were roughly circular while a few took on the form of say, a horseshoe. Other unique shapes also existed, such as an earthwork discovered in Ogemaw County that was built like a "square" with one side missing.

Gerald Haltiner in a booklet called *Long-Ago People* described still another form in a chapter entitled, "Earthworks Show Evidence Of Early Fortifications." Haltiner recalls a fortification found in Lenawee County near the town of Tecumseh, that was circular and also was connected to a square enclosure by a passageway. He also states many such structures of varying size and pattern, are found in a narrow band extended across the state from Glennie in Alcona County through West Branch and Lake City to Manistee. One he specifically calls our attention to as being a part of this corrider of forts, is located in Sec. 19, Mikado Township, Alcona County about one-half mile west of the south branch of the Pine River. It is known as the Mikado Earthworks. He considers it a fair example of most of the enclosures that lie in the aforementioned narrow band.

Archaeologists would define a typical "earthwork" or "fortification" as having a diameter average of 400-feet with perhaps 30-foot wide walls and ditch area, with 4 or 5 gates or openings in the wall. Basically there were two types of forts. One had curved walls forming a circular area while the second kind implored nearly straight line construction. Perhaps they belonged to two different cultural periods.

In *Primitive Man In Michigan*, once again W.B. Hinsdale presents some worthwhile fortifications located around Michigan. (pages 71-82)

1. In the summer of 1923 the University of Michigan

received a tract of land of 120-acres in Sec. 14, Aetna Township, Missaukee County upon which stood two well preserved inclosures. The elevation of the embankments of the circles on the outside average over 5-feet. The width on top of embankments is 7-feet...A small mound nearby also yielded a skeleton and artifacts...A third earthwork was later discovered six miles west by south of the above mentioned forts, in the SW¼ of the SE¼ of Sec. 26, Reider Township, Missaukee County. It is approximately circular, 165-feet east and west. There is a moat about the outside of the embankment, the walls rising from 5 to 8-feet above its bottom.
2. There were numerous rumors of another earthwork in the same vicinity of a horseshoe shape; and of another fort formerly existent near the Village of Falmouth.
3. Directly east from the Missaukee Preserve, across Roscommon County lies Ogemaw County. Through the center of Ogemaw County flows the Rifle River which empties into Saginaw Bay. Ten miles east of West Branch is the hamlet of Selkirk, in the township of Churchill. Churchill is in the same tier of townships as Aetna in Missaukee County, 40-miles away. Within a mile and a half of Selkirk are 4 inclosures; two north, or up the Rifle River; the other two down the river. This location is NW from the north shore of Saginaw Bay. It is about 15-miles from the SE corner of Ogemaw County to the northeast shore of the bay. Iosco County lies between Ogemaw and the shore of Lake Huron...See Sections 33 and 34, West Branch Township.
Inclosure #1 has the pathways leading from the openings of nearly all the inclosures that are quite narrow and consist of the original earth that was not disturbed in digging the trenches. In several places the gateways are as much as 12 feet in width.
Inclosure #2 is the largest of the group, being 300-feet east and west of 280 feet north and south. It may have had 5 openings.
Inclosure #3 indicates 8-openings, one for each cardinal and one for each intermediate compass point. It is well preserved.
Inclosure #4 was not completed. It has a more rectangular outline than the others, with an open side some 206-feet facing a narrow swamp. It contains some 400-feet of earth construction.

4. Other forts are listed in Kalamazoo County as being a perfect circle. Other principal ones have been located along the shores of the Detroit, Huron, and Raisin Rivers; and occasionally upon Lake Erie, between the Detroit and Maumee Rivers...Another is reported on the bank of the Detroit River in Wayne County.
5. Irregular outline forts were also reported in Bruce Township of Macomb County on the Clinton River's north fork. Similar earthworks were located in Kalamazoo County and near the Village of Marshall in Calhoun County. Macomb County in Bruce and Armada Townships also reported irregular outline fortifications. Near the Village of Boone in Wexford County is a remnant of an extensive earthwork, in the form of a horseshoe.
6. Embankments, circles, squares, breastworks, and other forms of earth construction, not described as mounds, are reported also from Antrim, Branch, Huron, Kalkaska, Keweenaw, Osceola, Saginaw, St. Joseph, Sanilac, Tuscola, and Wexford counties; probably not half of them recorded.

One of the most interesting and well known forts is called the "Mikado Earthworks" located in Mikado Township, Alcona County. Dennis Morrison reported on this find in an article written for the *Harrisville Review* called **"Mikado Earthwork Still Fascinates Scientists."** He describes a journey he and his wife Kathy made some years ago. "*We journeyed about 5-miles back into the woods. We braved swamps, barbed wires and angry posters on "No Trespassing" signs to reach and see what is probably one of the most mysterious places in all of Alcona County. It was discovered in the 1800s and is located in the Huron National Forest. It was first excavated in 1966 under a federal permit.*

The "earthwork" is an Indian fortification, more to the point, the remains of one. Currently all that is there to be seen is a mound of dirt, that runs in a horseshoe formation with a gully in the center. Post molds, dark stained dirt, where posts once stood, have been found along the top of this prehistoric "foundation". This indicates that the fort was palisaded, enclosed by wooden stakes. Along the mound are three openings which were quite likely entrances and exits. The circumference, the distance around the top of the footings, is 1000-feet. The earthwork has a total enclosed area of 96,000 square feet.

The north end is completely open and overlooks a small bluff...Arrowheads and other stone relics have been excavated from this site, they are by far out numbered by pot shards. These early Alcona cooking vessels were made most likely from local clays that were mixed with crushed rock...The pots used at the Mikado Earthwork were most likely not much different than the Late Woodland pots, found at other spots throughout this area.

While most earthworks in Michigan have been destroyed by construction and farming, the workers for the Alger Smith logging endeavor, who originally discovered the earthworks in the 1800s, were astute enough to leave this one intact. We can be thankful for this rare relic that reveals much about a vague and dark chapter in our nations history."

Actually, the long list of earthworks listed in this chapter forms quite an imposing list. Oftentimes the average Michigan citizen is more or less totally unaware of the extensive magnitude of collected prehistory events that took place right here in our home-state of Michigan, ranging as far back as 5000 years ago.

When you stop and consider the variety of ancient endeavors covered so far in this publication, all located here in Michigan, one just has to be in awe!

BIBLIOGRAPHY: MOUNDS, PART IV

MEMORIALS OF A HALF—CENTURY, by Bela Hubbard, G. P. Putnam's Sons, 1888.

PRIMITIVE MAN IN MICHIGAN, W. B. Hinsdale, Avery Color Studios, AuTrain, MI 1983-87

THE KING STRANG STORY, by Doyle C. Fitzpatrick, National Heritage, Lansing, MI 1970

FIRST PEOPLE OF MICHIGAN, W. B. Hinsdale, publ. Geo. Wahr, Ann Arbor 1930

LONG—AGO PEOPLE, by Gerald Haltiner, publ. privately, Alpena, MI

CENTURIES OLD, "MIKADO EARTHWORK" STILL FASCINATES SCIENTISTS, by Dennis Morrison, Harrisville Review, Harrisville, MI

CREDITS:

Marquette Historical Society, Marquette, MI

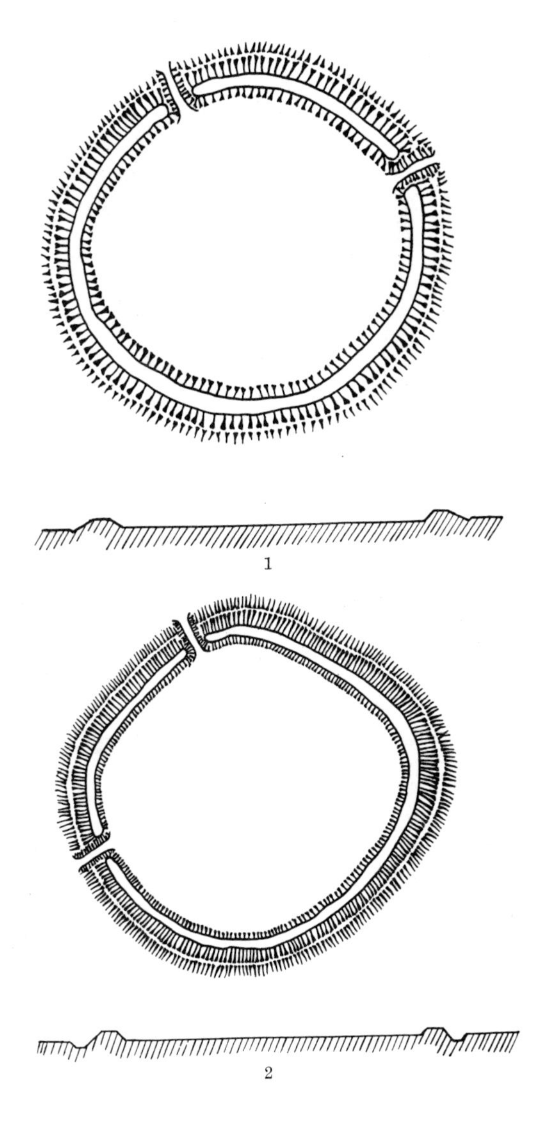

Fig. 1., Inclosure on the Missaukee Preserve. Greatest diameter 177 feet, height of embankment about 5 feet, width of embankment on top about 7 feet. Cross-section below. Fig. 2., Inclosure on the Missaukee Preserve. Greatest diameter 156 feet, height about 5 feet, width of embankment on top about 7 feet. Distance from Figure 1, 30 rods. Cross-section below.

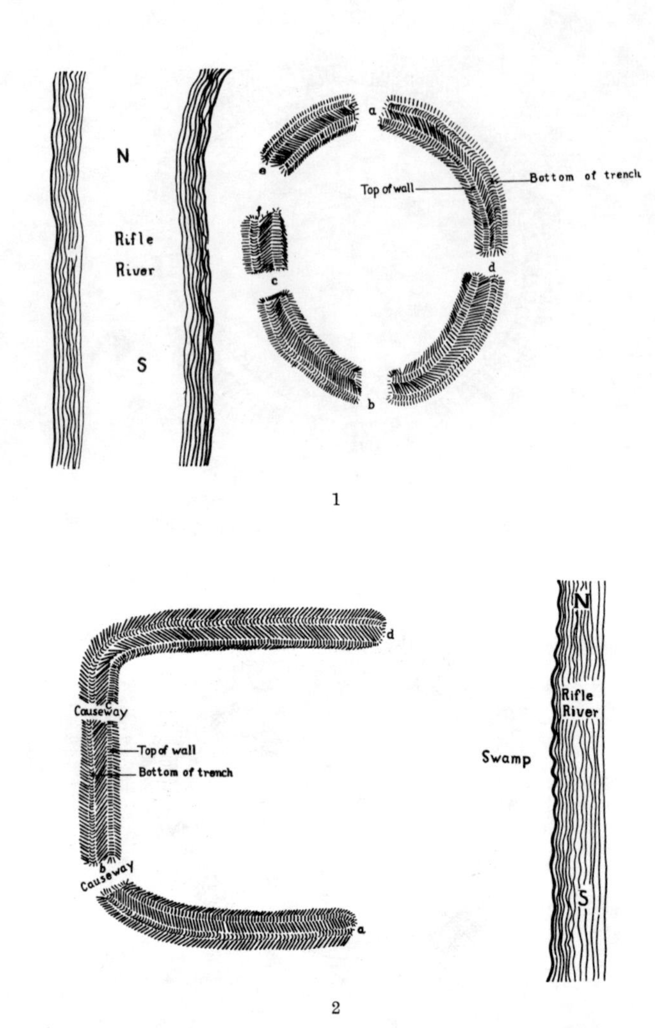

Fig. 1., Rifle River Fort No. 3: a,b,c, and d, original openings in walls of fort; e-f opening probably made by lumbermen. Fig. 2., Rifle River Fort No. 4, Ogemaw County.

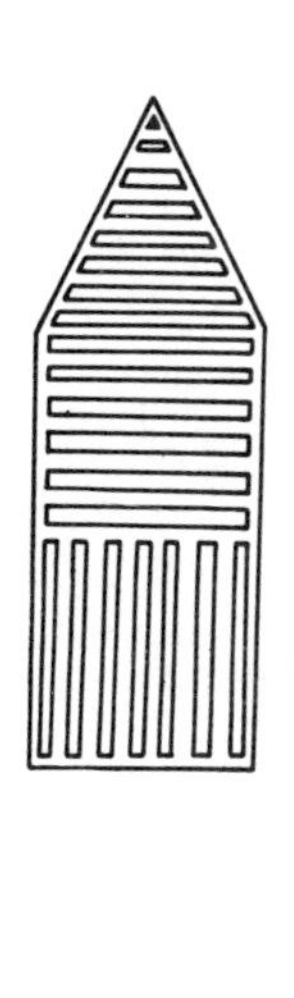

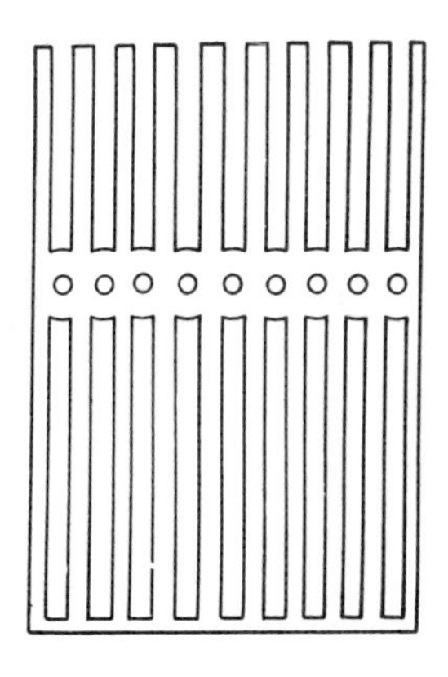

Diagrammatic sketches of ancient garden beds near Kalamazoo.

ALCONA COUNTY

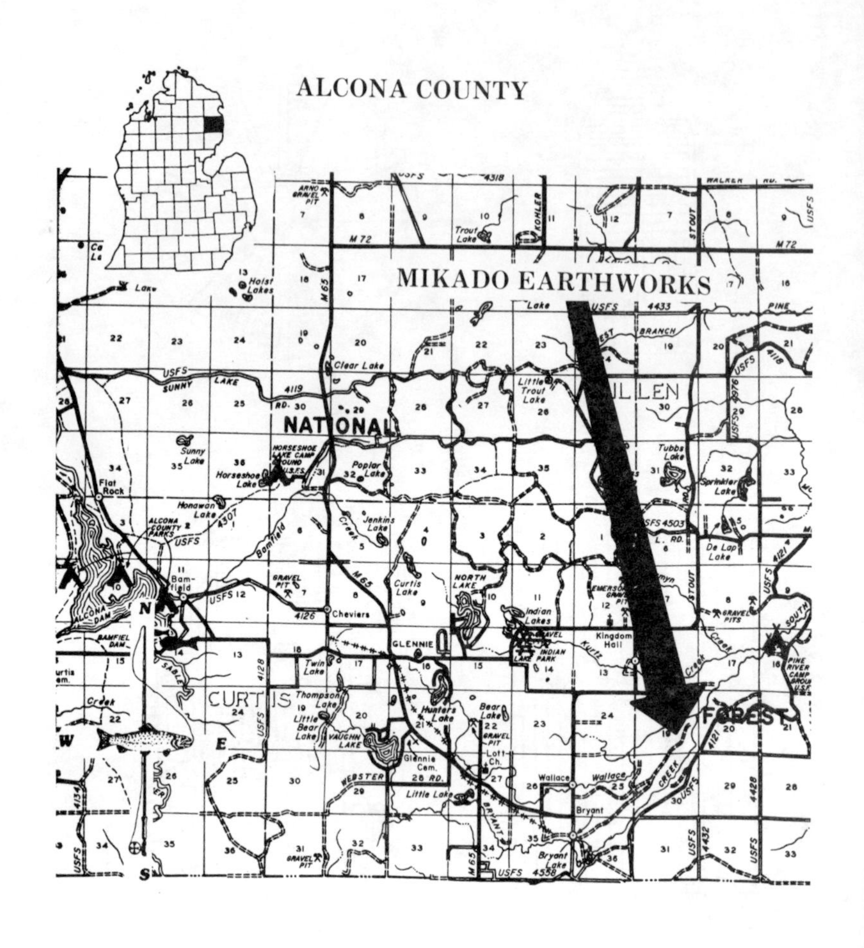

McGruer's Gods & The Newberry Stone
A Michigan Mystery
PART I
The Discovery!

The inadvertent unearthing of a strange archaeological discovery nearly a century ago remains virtually a Michigan prehistory mystery today. The legend began in 1896 in the Upper Peninsula just north of the village of Newberry, where unfathomable artifacts were found hidden under the roots of a fallen tree. Over a span of years they became known as the "McGruer's Gods" and the "Newberry Stone." The gods being three nearly life-size statues of a man, woman and child. The stone was, in essence, more of a tablet containing what appeared to be hieroglyphics believed at that point in time, to have been of an Egyptian persuasion. The origin of the McGruer's figures seemed to be as mysterious as the ideas they symbolized. Archaeologists of the day were totally unprepared for their sudden appearance, for very little sculpture of this specific nature had been discovered. There was never a question of them being American Indian...for that, they definitely were not!

Incidentally, the idols weighing together close to 1000 pounds were oddly manufactured of clay, even though early newspaper accountings from that 1896-97 period described them being made of sandstone. An excellent point to remember here is that "clay" was one of the most significant discoveries of the Archaic Period. In retrospect, clay can be broken, but the pieces will remain intact over thousands of years. Sooner or later, however, stone artifacts crumble and copper simply decomposes, but clay articles alone are comparatively immune from the so-called ravages of time.

This fascinating prehistory riddle unfolded when John McGruer employed two itinerant woodsmen to put up firewood on his "40" acres four miles north of town. The adventure climaxed when the lumberjacks noticed a mink slip under the roots of a windfall. Staring down into the tangled root structure, one of the pair saw what appeared to be the head of a statue quizzically peering back at him. Quickly the workmen used what tools were at hand, resulting in the eventual excavation of an idol of large proportion. Unfortunately, in their extreme haste, the figure was chipped and partially broken. Hurriedly, the two men dug up another statue. Still caught up with emotion, they searched the "cache" still further and turned up a third idol, plus a curious tablet carved or inscribed with 140 squares, each containing an inexplicable character or symbol.

Hurrying with their incredible finds to the small, turn-of-the century village of Newberry, the woodsmen quickly spread the word up and down Main Street. Most folks were simply confounded! Curiosity seekers as well as souvenir hunters, descended on the site of McGruer's woodlot by the wagonload, but in due course nothing of further interest showed up.

Naturally, as the artifacts were put on display locally, the townsfolk wildly speculated over their puzzling origin. Many questions immediately came to mind. How did heathen idols of this size and weight come to be found in a hidden pit at the edge of a swamp? What race of people manufactured these incomprehensible artifacts? Indeed, just the task of transporting statues of these proportions staggers the mind!

In the long run, as weird appearing as the statues seemed, with their plainly discernible features, it was the tablet that really generated the bulk of the excitement. Every learned man in Newberry offered a valued opinion or guesstimate of what the hieroglyphics were intended...ranging from say, an ancient Egyptian calendar to alphabetical letters of Greek persuasion, to perhaps a game board such as "chess" or "checkers." Ideas flowed like water. Yet others, however, were holding an opinion bordering on sheer folly or mere hoax.

Rumors ran rampant! Perhaps the furor of the moment could best be recaptured through actual early newspaper articles just as the events more or less unfolded. These picturesque publications ring out like voices from the past, actually seeming to bring the historical events to new life. *Author's Note:* Please be aware of the many discrepancies between articles.

The following excerpts were taken from the pages of the Newberry News, dated November 20, 1896 and December 11, 1896: *"Curious find...tablet of stone covered with hieroglyphics. One figure was 1 ft. 9 in. One figure was 2 ft. 8 in. One figure was 3 ft. 8 in. They are made of soft sandstone and resemble human beings in a stooping position (heathen idols). Stone slab is 19" x 26". There are 140 spaces divided by lines cut into the stone, with letters or characters in each space. The tablet was photographed and is on exhibition. A fee is charged. Jake Gordon and George Howe were the discoverers, raking in all the dollars from curiosity seekers. Also found, petrified remains of three persons. Fossils were brought to Newberry on exhibition. They are not Indian. The tablet is well preserved...only 3-letters are missing. It reveals a high order of intelligence."*

"After being exhibited at Stafford's old store on Helen Street, they were taken to the Sault, where they are attracting attention. The "Northwoods" are bristling with long-haired scientists, since Newberry hunters dug up three clay idols. Mystery tablet has not been deciphered yet!"

The following report written in January of 1897 appeared in a copy of the Sault Evening News: (Sault Ste. Marie, Michigan)

"The idols and tablet are of brown stone...the find was made by John Gordon and George Howe while cutting wood at the edge of a swamp. A large hemlock was uprooted and in the upturned earth the head of the largest of the idols was exposed...nearby found the rest of the collection, which weigh about 1000 lbs. Features are easily discernible...largest is about 4 ft. tall and in a sitting position with hands on the knees...next largest is standing while the smallest supposed to be in the image of a child, is sitting...tablet about 18 x 24 inches in size...marked off into 140-squares, upon which are inscribed hieroglyphic characters..."

The next article appeared November 28, 1896, in an unknown newspaper and included a hand-drawn facsimile of the man-idol as well as a drawing of the symbols found on the Newberry Stone. It was from the latter sketch that eventually the tablet was translated.

BY WHOSE HANDS

WERE THE IMAGES AND TABLET PLACED IN THE WOODS NEAR NEWBERRY?

THE IMAGES FACED THE EAST—THIS FACT POINTS STRONGLY TO SUN WORSHIP!

"The discovery found a few days ago near here promises to rank in importance, record to nothing yet unearthed relating to the prehistoric age in this country.

Jacob Brown and George Rowe, both residents of Newberry, were looking for deer, and in the course of their hunting started a mink, which made for a swamp nearby and took refuge in a hollow stump. In order to get at the mink, they struck stone, which bore evidances of the handiwork of man. Becoming interested they secured picks and spades and unearthed the stones.

As the result of their labors, 3 stone images were uncovered, also a large stone tablet. All four articles were cut from where the pictured rocks, great cliffs of sandstone, worn by wind and wave into fantastic forms, frown for many miles upon the blue water of the great lake. Of the 3-images, the largest is that of a man in a sitting posture, nearly lifesize. This statue is on a pedestal, formed from the same piece of stone. The second image from point of size, is that of a woman and is a trifle under three feet in height, while the third is the image of a child, and like the man, is postured in a sitting attitude, and is about two feet high! All three of the images were found placed with faces towards the EAST which may have been accidental, but more probably intentional, and points strongly towards sun-worship on the part of the unknown race that carved and placed the statues in times so distant that even an approximate estimate of the period is impossible.

Near these figures was found a slab of brownstone, averaging six inches in thickness and 18 by 25 inches on each face. One side was smoothed as carefully as the course structure of the rock had allowed. While upon the other face were engraved a series of inscriptions, each set in a square of approximately one and a half inches, there being 140 of these.

Those who have examined the images and the inscribed tablet are unable to assign them to any race or period, beyond being able to assert positively that they were not the work of Indians.

Those who saw the statues say they look like Egyptian idols, though the heads were those of human beings, and not of sacred animals with which the ancient race of the Nile was most in ornament of its carved images. These works bear strong relationship to the work of the Aztec and even more, the ancient "Toltec" races, remnants of whose work in stone are scattered so plentifullly about southern Mexico and the Central American states.

The look or length of the eyes noticed in the finds here, was known to the ancient inhabitants of Mexico, as well as to the Egyptians, and is noticeable in the findings of Mexico and other forms of the Toltecs and Aztecs.

The strange figures carved within the squares are also not without parallel, being found among the central American ruins. The Mexican idols were usually carved from obsedian, and the inscriptions which have so long puzzled the ingenuity of archaeologists were carved upon granite or rocks of equal hardness, which easily retained fine lines cut with such great effort, whereas the brown sandstone, indigenous to Lake Superior, cannot be made to take or retain lines of great fineness. Further excavations will be made and the find is rich in possibilities."

If you will notice, each article while being similar to the basic facts, provided individual new information that previous articles lacked. It makes you, the reader, seem a part of the action as each new bit of evidence unfolds. Actually an active member of the mystery.

While the last newspaper article originating from an unidentified source contained a sketch of the man-idol and the tablet, actual photographs were taken by the editor of the Newberry News and were in turn forwarded to the Smithsonian Institute at Washington, D.C. There they were lost! So for over ninety years these were the only reminders of what the artifacts once resembled. In 1988 another old article turned up that contained photographs of the man and the woman idol as well as one of the Newberry Stone. This was an exciting discovery for all involved in the mystery. It will be dealt with later in Part III.

In the meantime, yet another very important newspaper clipping came to light that brought forth new information as to how the diagram of the tablet was made. It is quite interesting. This particular piece had been in the files for some time but was in such poor condition that it was practically unreadable. With the aid of a magnifying glass the entire article was copied just as it appeared in a November 1896 Marquette Mining Journal.

THREE STATUES FOUND!

"A Marquette business man who returned from Newberry Tuesday says the town is all agog over a remarkable discovery made in the woods by two hunters. The authenticity of the find does not hang upon their words alone as others have been out and visited the site. George Rowe and Jake Gordon are the names of the hunters. They were out with their guns one day when they came upon a mink which they ran into a hollow log on the edge of a swamp. In digging to get at the mink they struck something hard and stoney. Further digging resulted in unearthing three brown sandstone images. They are in a state of good preservation and are of different and superior workmanship to that of the Indians who inhabited the peninsula before the whites came. The largest of the images or statues is that of a man in sitting posture, four feet high. The second is that of a woman standing. That is three feet high. The third is the statue of a child two feet high and in a sitting position. The man is on a pedestal but all of them are upright and their faces are turned toward the east. This leads to the belief that the statues were the work of a prehistoric race who worshipped the sun. Another point strengthening this belief is that the faces have strong Egyptian features.

With the images was found a tablet of stone. The face of it is 19 by 25 inches and is 6 inches thick. One hundred and forty characters, set in squares 1½ inches on a side. These characters are plainly not of Indian origin, but what they are, no one who has viewed the tablet, is able to say.

Rev. David Howell, missionary of the Presbyterian Church, stopped over in the city between trains Thursday. Mr. Howell is one of the best informed gentlemen who has seen the wonderful find near Newberry and he places full credence in the honesty of the discovery and considers it probably of great scientific and historical value. Mr. Howell is the only one who has yet made a copy of the inscriptions on the tablet. He intended to send a blueprint of the copy to the Smithsonian Institute and have it examined there by the great authorities and see if they can decipher the characters and shed any light upon the discovery. When Mr. Howell was to town yesterday he was interviewed by a Mining Journal reporter:

"There can be no doubt about the honesty of the men who made the discovery," he said. "Both of them are ignorant wood choppers who had a contract chopping near where they found the images. One of them started a mink and ran it in a hole under the upturned root of a fallen tree. They wanted to dig the mink out so one of the fellows ran over to a nearby settler by the name of Murray and borrowed a spade. He began to dig and after getting down a little ways struch something hard and stoney which proved to be the head of the largest idol. They kept on digging till they got the three images and the tablet.

The men are very ignorant, as I said, and they have an idea that the images and tablet are worth a hundred thousand dollars or more though they first thought that what they had discovered were the petrified bodies of human beings. Anyone who knows sandstone could tell that this was not right. The formation is very similar to that of the Pictured Rocks. The men are very suspicious and think someone is going to get the things away from them. They weren't even going to let me inside the railing of the vacant store where they have them to take a copy of the inscriptions. They have an idea that they can make a big thing exhibiting them around the country. I told them though they wouldn't be worth 15¢ to anyone out of Newberry, where there was some local interest attaching to the find. Unless the inscriptions were copied and sent to some place where they could be examined by men who were an authority upon such topics and their authenticity perfectly established... "Why," I said, "If you got away from here your exhibition people would say you were fakes." Then they couldn't let me over the railing quick enough!

I cleaned the tablet as well as I could and lamp blacked it and took an impression on a sheet of paper and then I made a tracing from that and when I was at Munising today the chief engineer of Munising Railway, Mr. Young, made these blueprints which showed clearly and distinctly the characters on the tablet." Here

Mr. Howell unrolled the two blueprints. As was told in yesterdays paper, the tablet is about 19 by 25 inches and divided into 140 squares, ten on one edge, fourteen on the other. A character or letter is inscribed in all but three of these small squares. The characters seem to have been effaced from these. Some of the characters appear more than once on the stone and a few of them bear a resemblance to Greek letters."

Both tablet and images, Mr. Howell says, were found just under where the tree would have been were it still standing. The trunk of the tree is 16 inches in diameter. This fact is worthy of note for while it does not preclude the possibility of the statues or idols having been buried there as recently as a hundred years ago, it would go to show that they had not been "planted" by some designing fakir to the last ten or twenty odd years.

This discovery was made on the twenty-ninth of last month."

As the initial excitement of the riddle of the ancient gods eventually died down, John McGruer hauled his mysterious artifacts to his farm on the banks of the Tahquamenon River, where he placed them for storage in an open carriage shed. A decade later they were more or less, laid to rest at the rear of his large hay barn. With the passage of time these ancient artifacts bore years of wear due to the elements and in turn at the hands of curiosity seekers. For many an adventuresome youth swam the clear, cool Tahquamenon on a hot summer day and ended an adventurous outing by peaking daringly into old Mr. McGruer's barn at the infamous heathen gods. Time took its toll! So did vandalism!

Ultimately, in 1929 the statue remains were gathered together along with the broken parts of the tablet and all were taken to a small museum or curio shop, called "Fort Algonquin," at St. Ignace, that was owned by Rev. H. Vaughn Norton. It seems hard to comprehend, but at some point during this transaction, the smallest figure, believed to have been the child idol, completely vanished. Mysteriously, no trace of its fate ever surfaced. With no existing sketch or photo of the child idol we shall never know its appearance and even its sex, ie. boy or girl. Also the question of who sold the artifacts to this private museum, similarily never came to light.

Part II of this fascinating tale of the ancient gods and the enigmatic inscribed tablet is picked up in the 1940s when Newberry historian, Charles "Sprague" Taylor reopened the McGruer Gods—Newberry Stone files and another flurry of interest began. Much of my material for the second part of this continuing saga comes from "Sprague" Taylor's widow, Carol. This author combined efforts with Mrs. Taylor in hopes that together we could find a possible solution to the age-old riddle that had remained such a mystery for the better part of a hundred years.

Please take just a moment and reread the INTRODUCTION of this book, and see if you too don't start to *"itch all over,"* just as Editor Fretz of *The Newberry News* so described when his interest was again sparked in 1958 by the mystifying legend of McGruer's Gods and the Newberry Stone!

CREDITS:
THE NEWBERRY NEWS, Newberry, MI Mr. Bill Fretz, Editor
THE LUCE COUNTY HISTORICAL SOCIETY, Newberry, MI
THE NEWBERRY LOGGING MUSEUM, M-123, Newberry, MI
Plat: supplied by Eino Saino, surveyor, Newberry, MI Plat shows McGruer owning 3 property parcels. All are outlined.

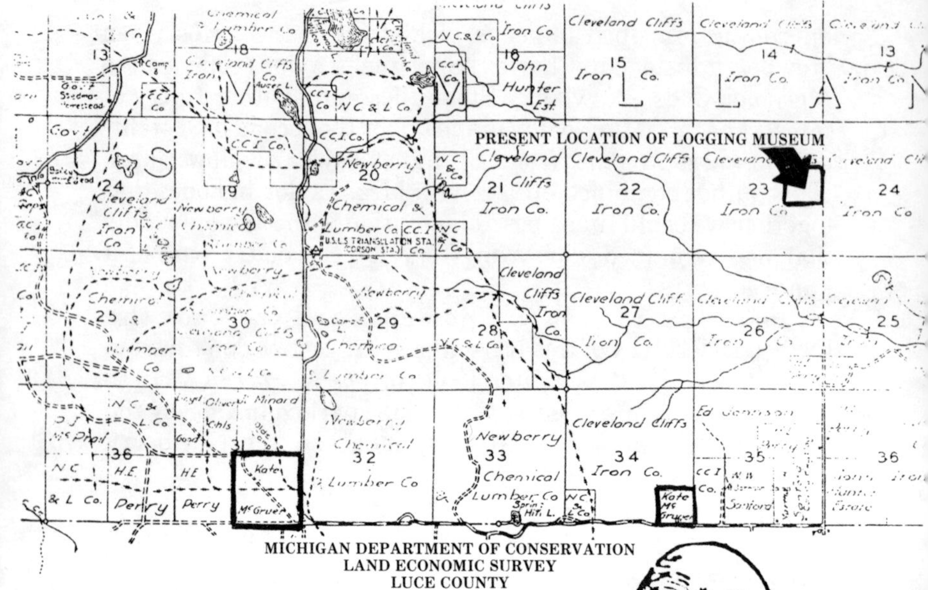

MICHIGAN DEPARTMENT OF CONSERVATION
LAND ECONOMIC SURVEY
LUCE COUNTY
1929

Plat shows 3 property parcels owned by the mcGruer's. #1, a "40 acre parcel" where the McGruer farm and home were located. Now the present site of the NEWBERRY LOGGING MUSEUM. #2, a "40 acre parcel" where the artifacts were discovered. #3, a "160 acre parcel" with no significance to the artifacts.

A hand-drawn facsimile of the largest statue, that of the man-idol. He is pictured in a seated position. His height is 4 feet tall.

McGruer's Gods & The Newberry Stone
A Michigan Mystery
PART II
The Translation!

As previously mentioned, the two idols and the inexplicable inscribed tablet were taken to a small private museum or curio shop at the east end of St. Ignace, called "Fort Algonquin," owned and operated by Rev. H.V. Norton. Charles "Sprague" Taylor contacted Rev. Norton in 1947. At that particular time, all that remained of the relics were the head and shoulder section of the man-idol, the head of the woman statue, and but broken pieces of the tablet. What a shame they had not been handled with proper care in 1896 and thus preserved to a better degree down through the ages. Again, may I also remind you, the child image was lost forever, before the private museum purchased the remaining artifacts in 1929.

Mr. Taylor went to the museum in 1947 and took marvelous photographs of the remains described above. These photos were in turn used in articles appearing in the Marquette Mining Journal and The Newberry News. Taylor also forwarded photo copies to the Smithsonian Institute at Washington, D.C. Up until these photographs were taken, just the hand-drawn facsimile that appeared in the 1896 newspaper article, was all researchers had to work from.

At the time of discovery, pictures of the idols and the tablet were forwarded to the Smithsonian by The Newberry News. At that time Charles Brebner was editor and that paper published a reply from the Institute that read as follows: "The photographs referred to in your letter of November 25th were duly received. We should be pleased to obtain all available information in regard to the discovery of the images and the tablet. At the present time we cannot offer an opinion or decipher the inscription. We will retain the photographs in accordance with your permission."

There was no follow-up of this in the paper. In 1947 Charles

Taylor sent his photos and a query to the Smithsonian. They could not locate the original pictures taken of this marvelous discovery of 1896. However they sent the following reply to the photographs submitted by Taylor: "Our archeologists doubt the authenticity of the pieces from the great Lakes area. Of course, we can certainly agree with the judgement that they are not Indian."

An article written by C.S. Taylor appeared in the April 7th, 1966 edition of the Newberry News entitled "The Riddle of McGruer's Gods". The following paragraphs are quotations from that newspaper piece:

"Time has dealt in its usual way with McGruer and all the wonderment about the curious "idols" that came from his woodlot. But it hasn't, apparently, served to solve very much of the mystery of their finding. Nor has it appeared to lessen, in the minds of the few who still recall the event or its aftermath, the conviction that neither McGruer nor anyone associated with him, was capable of perpetrating such a hoax.

In all the furor that resulted there is no indication that McGruer or the workmen Gordon and Howe, or a local jeweler, L.N. Forbes, who was said to be 'interested in the ownership' with McGruer, ever made any quotable comments on their good fortune. By this silence they seemed to be saying that they had brought the things to light by happy accident; they were as mystified as anyone about their origin or significance; and they awaited whatever scientific judgement of the day might be forthcoming.

(Here they differed markedly from relic peddlers who operated in the Lower Peninsula, especially near Detroit, in the following two decades, and who tested public gullibility with everything from copies of Noah's diary to prehistoric beer mugs.)

Clearly, no hint of connivance came into local print. Charles Brebner, editor of The Newberry News at the time, took a dim view of pranksters, whether they were announcing bloody attacks on woodsmen by timber wolves, or, more innocently, reporting the capture of a seventeen-foot 'sea monster' in Muskallonge Lake. He described the find as 'one of the wonders of the age, sent photographs of the collection to the Smithsonian Institute in Washington, and published a reply stating an inability to deliver an immmediate opinion on authenticity, and asking for more details.

Was, indeed, the whole thing nothing more than an engaging hoax?

Obviously so, some present-day archaeologists have said, studying the figures and the tablet...or photos of them.

Not necessarily so, said some older residents, questioned at length in the late 1940s. They had seen the find in 1896; they remembered it well; and to them there remained a certain irrefutable logic in their unanimous assessment of the finders: 'They simply were not ingenious enough to think it up!' "

Going back to the original point of discovery in 1896, these artifacts were then believed by some factions of the community to be no more than a "hoax" perpetuated by the men involved. But as time indeed passed, the men merely seemed to have found these items through actual accident rather than some ultra-devious planned plot. If it was a grandiose "hoax" well the three men so involved, certainly carried the "joke" to their graves...so in the long run...who then had the last laugh?

We must also remember here the early clipping that appeared in the Marquette Mining Journal that gave the testimony of Rev. David Howell, regarding the illiteracy of the two lumberjacks that found the idols and the tablet. In turn THEY, not McGruer, seemed to be the ones who thought a fortune was to be made. Another strong point brought to light by Rev. Howell, was that he went to the site where the artifacts were discovered. At that time he stated the tree's roots were such that they would have held the tree in place, had it not blown over. The size of the trunk also indicated these articles were not placed in the "cache" or "pit" for possibly several hundred years. All in all, was it "hoax" or "history?" "Fraud" or "Find?"

As with all prehistory mysteries, questions just tend to come to mind. Why were such massive idols and an unexplainable tablet placed in this seemingly wilderness pit? Research indicates early primitive man repeatedly placed numbers of items in a "cache," a "cluster" or a "hoard."* Circumstances

*W.B. Hinsdale - Primitive Man In Michigan.

often precluded the articles were hidden against possible theft. But no doubt many artifacts were probably put into pits while journeys were undertaken, secreted for the sake of safety. For on many occasions, artifacts have been discovered hidden securely under stumps, boulders, along river banks as well as in mounds...at times so isolated...so secret...only the original party responsible for hiding them, could have possibly located them, except through an accidental act.

Just as "Sprague" Taylor interviewed many of the old-timers of the village of Newberry who actually saw the three idols and the enigmatic tablet, your author, even at this late date, managed to find a man who had, as a child, viewed the ruins of the remains that were stored in the McGruer barn on the banks of the Tahquamenon. At the time of this interview we (husband and I), were actually living in the almost-century-old McGruer farmhouse. At that time we very carefully and thoroughly searched the premises for the lost child idol, with no success. But it was during this time period we talked to a Mr. John Bodi, senior citizen extraordinary from Newberry. Bodi recalled as a child of perhaps nine years of age, seeing one of the idols and a box containing blocks remaining from the tablet, in the old barn. John related that at that particular time, his family lived in the old McGruer turn-of-the-century homestead and he often swam in the river, and played in the big hay barn. Sadly, however, he could offer no further clues to the mysterious disappearance of the smallest statue. The site is now occupied by the Newberry Logging Museum, Newberry, Michigan.

Getting back to Charles "Sprague" Taylor and his years of research on the subject, I am sure Taylor must have indeed felt frustrated in his attempts to unravel the mystery of McGruer's Gods and the Newberry Stone...but now for the rest of the story!

On or about the year 1960 what small bits and pieces that remained of the original find, mainly torso plus heads along with chunks of the tablet, were transferred to yet another private museum in the area...Fort de Buade located downtown in St. Ignace. It is owned and operated in the summer months by Dr. Donald Benson and his wife. Fort de Buade Museum is a fitting place for the interment of the artifacts for it contains marvelous area displays from the eastern end of the Upper Peninsula. At this writing, to all intents and purposes, they remain there today.

After no little research and through various personal contacts, Taylor was put in touch with a prominent attorney from the Chicago area, Dr. Henriette Mertz. Ms. Mertz also was regarded as an eminent member of The Epigraphic Society, serving in the capacity of an expert on preColumbian archaeological forgeries. Her views on the artifacts are stated in a report of the Epigraphic Society, Vol. 9, #217, June 1981 listed in their *Occasional Publications* titled, "An Inscribed Tablet From Newberry, Michigan". Excerpts follow:

"The prehistory of the Copper Country, long haunted by tales of a by-gone race of people, has yet to be told. Comparatively few persons in our country are aware of the extensive mining activity taking place on Isle Royale in Lake Superior or along the Trap Range of the Upper Peninsula where approximately 500,000 tons of pure copper were mined out sometime between 1800 and 1000 B.C. No definitive study of this material has ever been published in spite of the fact that his extensive operation is known to have taken place and that artifacts recovered from mined out pits are comparable to those of Minoan Crete. Question may well arise as to whether or not the Newberry tablet once stemmed from that ancient activity and thus may provide a first clue to the origin of the miners themselves.

Discovery of these ancient artifacts (McGruer's Gods and The Newberry Stone) created considerable excitement throughout the region...archaeologists believing the story to be nothing more than a hoax while others who had seen the find in 1896 stood by their conviction that the finders were not ingenious enough to perpetuate a hoax. For several weeks the statues and the tablet were on display in a Newberry store and speculation ran rampant as to the meaning or origin of the letters within the squares.

Photographs of the four pieces were sent to the University at Ann Arbor and to the Smithsonian. Smithsonian replied indicating inability to recognize the inscribing and requested further time for study. No further response appears to have come at a later date from them.. The university convinced that the find was a hoax, failed to reply.

My own interest in the Newberry tablet started in the early 1950's. Sometime around 1953, while attending a meeting of the local archaeological society in Peoria, a group of ten or fifteen inscribed artifacts, noted above, uncovered from mounds in the Detroit area were submitted to me for a professional opinion as to whether or not the material had been forged since I had experience in the examination of forged matters. The problem fascinated me and in pursuing the quest, I eventually made a trip to Michigan in the summer of 1954 at which time I met Clair Reynolds, a kindred spirit in tracking down information regarding ancient peoples who might once have inhabited the State of Michigan. It is to Clair that I owe my information of the inscribed Newberry tablet. After an exchange of a few letters, he sent me a yellowed newspaper clipping headlined from Newberry dated 28 November 1896 which I quoted above and from which I copied the inscribed letters.

...The matter rested there until April 1977 when I received a letter from Barry Fell enquiring about the Newberry tablet and referring to my publication of a small portion in THE WINE DARK SEA in 1964. I then sent him the copy I had previously made of the entire tablet as published in 1896. Pursuant to that, I wrote Mr. Taylor on 8 July 1977 and received a reply from Mrs. Taylor saying that her husband had passed away but that she remembered the visit of Clair Reynolds. She said that her husband had had a small fragment of the 'pinkish clay' which he showed to Clair, but the piece had no markings on it of any nature. Insofar as I am presently aware, no other material from Newberry exists."

Allow me to refute Ms. Mertz's last statement for as it has already been established, some material does exist, basically torso and head of the man-idol, head of the woman, chunks of the tablet all on display at Fort de Buade in St. Ignace. In that respect, we can indeed be fortunate Mertz's accounting was in error.

Are you anxiously awaiting the translation of Michigan's oldest known inscribed tablet? They well may prove to be the first written words ever produced in Michigan. Professor Barry Fell translated the Newberry Stone and it is contained in Vol. 9, no 218, June 1981 of the *Occasional Publications* of

The Epigraphic Society in an article called, "Decipherment and Translation of the Newberry Tablet from Northern Michigan," by Barry Fell. Fell retains the title of professor emeritus at Harvard University, is president of The Epigraphic Society, and is the author of *Saga America, America B.C.* and *Bronze Age America.* His report and translation follows:

"As reported by Dr. Henriette Mertz in the preceding article, a drawing was sent to me by Dr. Mertz, at my request, showing the form and arrangement of the symbols observed on the ceramic tablet when it was excavated. I informed Dr. Mertz that the syllabary, for such it is, a variant of the well-known Cypro-Minoan script, comprised an omens text similar to that of the Phaistos Disk (OPES vol 4). The language comprising the text appears to be a creolinized form of Minoan, having vocabulary similar to that of Hittite, but lacking the formal declensions and conjugations of Hittite.

The vocabulary of this American omens text from Michigan invites comparison with that of the Cherokee language as well as with that of the Linear A tablets of Crete, and the Phaistos Disk.

The syllabary of the tablet has already (OPES vol 8) been compared with other known Cypro-Minoan syllabaries, and requires no further discussion here.

The contained vocabulary is given in full later in this paper. A sample of the similarities of the vocabulary to the other languages I have just named may be illustrated by these examples:

meaning	Hittite	Minoan	Newberry	Cherokee
grain	ziz, še	zi	zese, seyase	selu
son	uwas	not known	owa	uweji
father	un	not known	unu	udoda
man	lu	lu,ru	lu, lo	different
omen	kuš	kasa	kose	not known
honey	lal	lala	lole	-lisi
water	mu	mu	ma	ama
pay, price	killam	not known	kili	akwiyiha

Wyoming Tablet engraved in Cypriot script and language Deciphered by Fell

In his report Barry Fell states: "This inscription may be compared with that from Newberry, MI reported in ESOP vol

9, pt 2 (1981). Both tablets are magic quadrangles, to be read both vertically and horizontally, in alternate directions; both are magical charms, apparently copies from an import from the eastern Mediterranean, not later than Hellenistic times.

National Decipherment Center

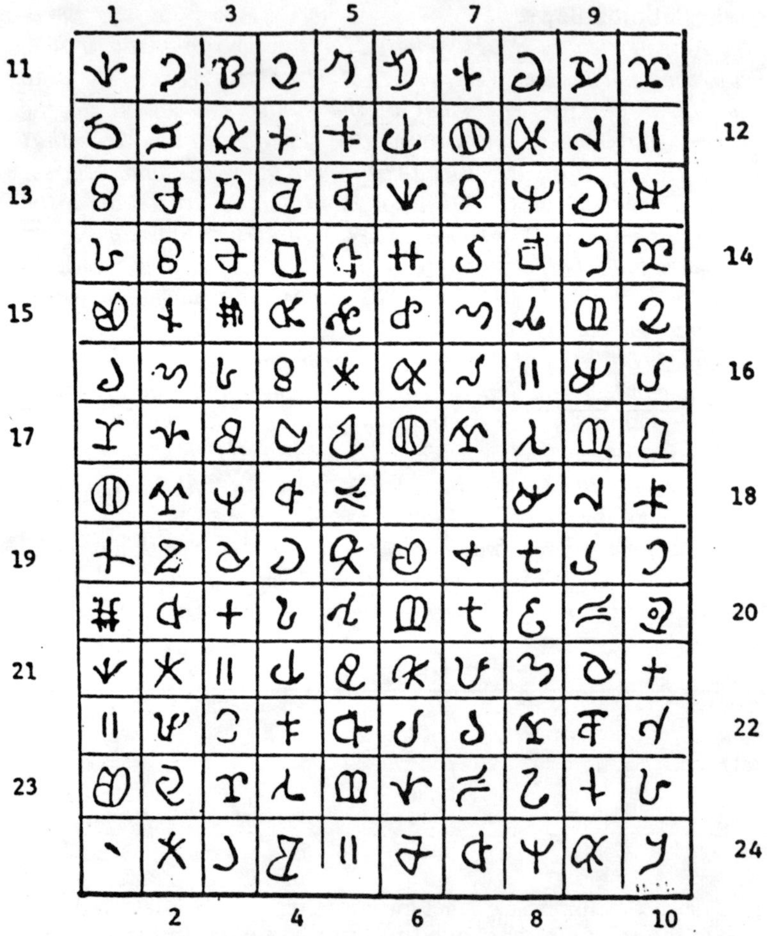

Newberry, Michigan   Henriette Mertz col.

The syllabary of this inscription, derived from Cypro-Minoan, is tabulated (Fell, 1980) on page 78, OPES vol 8, part

1. The numerals indicate the order, and the reading direction, in which each line is to be read. Thus the tablet is written in boustrophedon, alternate lines to be read in opposite directions. The tablet is also composed as an acrostic, to be read vertically as well as horizontally. The vertical reading logically precedes, thus line 1 is read downwards, line 2 upwards, and so on until line 10 is completed. Line 11 is then read horizontally, from left to right, line 12 from right to left, and so on to the end of line 24.

	1		3		5		7		9		
11	Pu	nu	si	wa	ko	se	lu	ya	ti	u	
	zi	ki	wa	lu	ta	li	ma	la	ta	wa	12
13	le	na	ko	li	li	pu	ri	se	ya	se	
	sa	le	na	ko	ze	no	po	li	nu	u	14
15	mu	so	no	ze	si	to	mi	li	lu	wa	
	sa	mi	sa	le	i	me	sa	zo	se	po	16
17	nu	pu	le	iya	le	mo	ki	li	mi	si	
	mo	ki	se	ze	we	(ma)	(sa)	la	ta	pa	18
19	lo	le	o	wa	me	lu	lo	lo	po	nu	
	no	ze	lo	sa	li	lu	ta	le	ke	re	20
21	pu	iya	zo	li	se	mu	sa	mi	o	so	
	zi	se	le	pa	ri	sa	sa	ki	na	ta	22
23	mu	sa	ki	li	lu	pu	na	sa	lo	sa	
	(sa)	na	sa	le	zo	pa	ze	se	si	ko	24
		2		4		6		8		10	

First stage in the decipherment of the Newberry Tablet. The phonetic values of the Cypro-Minoan signs have been substituted for the original elements. Three signs are inferred (for lacunae in the original text) and these are placed in parentheses.

On the next page the lines are taken in the numerical order

inferred above, the reading direction of all the lines is rectified to flow from left to right, thereby yielding an intelligible sequence of Hittite-Minoan elements that are linked by hyphens to form recognizable words and language. See next page.

The vertical text, as now rendered in left to right horizontal lines

1. Pu zi-le-sa mu-sa-nu ma lo no. Pu-zi mu-sa-
2. na. Sa se-ya-ze le-ki pu mi-so le-na-ki nu
3. si-wa ko-na no sa-le-se 'o-lo-zo le-ki sa-
4. le-li. Pa-li-sa-wa ze-ya-le-ze-ko li-lu wa-
5. ko-ta li-ze si-j-le we-me li-se-ri la zo-
6. pa mu-sa mu lu-lu ma mo-me to-no pu li-se
7. lu-a-ri po mi-sa ki-sa lo te-sa sa-na-ze
8. se-sa ki-mi-le lo-la li-zo li-li se-la ya-
9. li ta iya. Nu lu-se mi ta-po ke o-na lo si-
10. ko sa-ta so-re nu pa-si po wa u-se wa-u

The horizontal text, as now rendered in left-to-right horizontal lines.

11. pu-nu-si wa ko-se lu ya-ti u-
12. wa-ta-la. Ma-li-ta lu wa-ki-zi
13. le-na-ko. Li-li pu-ri-se ya-se.
14. U-nu li-po-no-ze ko-na. Le-sa
15. mu-so-no ze-si to-mi li-lu-wa
16. po-se-zo. Sa-me-i le-sa mi-sa
17. nu, pu-le Iya-le mo-ki li-mi-si
18. pa-ta-la-sa ma we ze-se ki-mo
19. lo-le o-wa me lu lo-lo po-nu
20. re-ke-le-ta lu. Li-sa lo-ze-no.
21. Pu-iya zo-li-se mu-sa mi-o-so
22. ta-na-ki-sa-sa-ri pa-le se-zi.
23. Mu-sa ki-li lu pu-na-sa lo-sa
24. ko-si se-ze pa zo-le sa-na-sa.

The Hittite-Minoan roots can all be found in Sturtevant's or Friedrich's Hittite Dictionaries, as already described in detail in the various papers already published in OPES vol. 4. On account of the exigencies of the acrostic structure, many vowels are inconsistent, this may either be due to the irregular spelling found in all American (and many North African) inscriptions, or it may indicate that the syllabic signs were treated by the composer as merely consonants. These vowel variations are self-evident, so a detailed vocabulary is not here given, for it can easily be ascertained from the dictionaries cited, and from the papers in OPES vol 4.

The Newberry Stone - Translation
By Barry Fell

1. To obtain an omen from birds when a man is worried, the sign is given
2. by birds. Put down grain, let it lie where it falls, but see
3. that it lies secure, is not blown away, or destroyed as it lies
4. on the grass. Protect it and drive away from the prairie
5. any sheep that may come to crop the grass or feed on man's seeds.
6. A flock of birds, however, is a good omen. Allow them the grain,
7. for good or bad fortune they deliver in this way. If they eat the grain
8. on the grass, and also eat it immediately on the prairie, it is a good omen,
9. for the gods speak by this sign. If they do not peck at it by this same token the man knows
10. he is divined to be a victim, so let him be reconciled for to obtain an omen for his son and heirs
11. ask an oracle for the boy. The man is to go to
12. the Seer. The man is to recite a prayer
13. and swear an oath. To the place of oracles on the prairie.
14. The man is to scatter grain. If peck
15. the birds the grain, the child will prosper,
16. and that is the omen. If the birds refuse to peck,
17. a libation to the gods, imploring aid by the licquor
18. the priest is to pour on the grain on the grass
19. made from honey, pleading for the prosperity of the man
20. in entreaty for the man. If they peck at it, he will prosper.
21. In this manner are given omens by the birds of oracules
22. at the sacred precincts when a libation and grain are given
23. for the birds. A fee the man is to pay for the service is
24. in grain. He must deliver it to the oracle for the safe omen.

After reading Barry Fell's translation how can denial of foreign intrusion be so lightly dismissed. Obviously this tablet either came from the Mediterranean area or was a copy manufactured here in this country...a copy of an original. The tablet was inscribed in the Hittite-Minoan language. Early forms of the Hittite (which many believe was the forerunner of the Minoan Greek language) were presumably spoken by other ancient cultures, many of which were copper-culture people. It is interesting to note, many Neolithic, copper-working clans not only worshipped household gods of clay, but also manufactured large gods and goddesses for religious worship. Is there a tie-in here between the idols and the tablet?

Charles W. Bailey of Duluth, Minnesota, is an expert on artifact fraud detection. Mr. Bailey has done extensive research on the three statues and continues with his investigation as this chapter is being written. We will discuss his theories and findings in Part III. However, I requested Bailey's opinion regarding the possibility of "hoax" or "history" conjecture. His reply was, "Barry Fell's translation of the Newberry stone appears plausible and certainly takes the find out of the realm of a hoax. I do not believe the knowledge existed at the time the stone and statues were found (1896) to fabricate a Hittite-Minoan tablet."

Perhaps the most important piece of research regarding the idols and tablet came to light in 1988. The museum at Marquette was contacted in hopes of turning up additional old articles regarding the artifacts. When their reply came, containing a newspaper clipping dated January 1, 1898, that included actual photographs of both the man and woman idols plus a clear picture of the Newberry Stone, the small group of dedicated McGruer's Gods people, were ecstatic! Words cannot express our feelings when we first viewed what these two idols actually looked like the day they were first discovered!

Furthermore, to date, none of the group had the slightest idea of what either the woman idol or the child would have resembled. Remember that hand-drawn sketch contained in the early 1896 newspaper article? That plus the drawing of the tablet's symbols was all that was available with the exception of the heads, torso, and tablet chunks located at Fort de Buade Museum. We all had goose bumps and yes indeed, we "itched all over."

The museum was contacted and we arranged for photographs to be taken from the original newspaper. Good results were obtained. The photos in turn were sent on to Barry Fell and at a slightly later date, to Charles Bailey. Fell immediately replied, "Thank you for your letter of June 28, 1988 and the enclosed clipping from the Marquette Mining Journal of January 1,1898. This latter is new to me and the three statues are quite a surprise...I have never before seen the photographs given in the Mining Journal, and it is excellent news that such photos were made."

Barry Fell examined the photographs and confirmed his earlier analysis of the Newberry Stone. He could shed no further light on the origin of the curious idols and promptly put me in touch with Charles Bailey of Duluth.

Bailey suggested two or three excellent approaches. First we would begin extensive research into the Gods and Goddesses of Mythology, especially of the copper-culture Tisza Culture of Neolithic Hungary. His second course of action was to forward samples of the clay from both the gods and tablet to laboratories for carbon-14 testing or a thermoluminescence test used to date the firing of ceramics. In turn, two samples were forwarded by Mr. Bailey to: Crocker Nuclear Laboratory, University of California, and to the research center at San Jose State University. The samples were provided from the files of Mrs. Carol Taylor of Newberry. One particular piece held a human or animal hair and it was so noted by Bailey when sent to the research center.

The third course of action Mr. Bailey asked me to pursue was to have the clay analyzed. It just so happened a geologist from Lake Superior State University was extremely interested in the McGruer's Gods and the Newberry Stone over a long period of years. In time we received the following report from C. Ernest Kemp, Dean Emeritus: "The material I have is definitely clay but I have been unable to ascertain the source. It has not been fired and appears to be mixed with coarser material. I could not determine either the age or the source and I remain intrigued by this enigma. It would please my sense of the dramatic to know these artifacts were genuine but at this point I am afraid I cannot shed much light on the problem."

Once again the clay sample came from Carol Taylor. It also should be mentioned here that it is indeed amazing that anything at all is left of the gods and tablet because, as this report indicates, the articles were made of "unfired" clay.

In Part III we will quote from the 1898 newspaper article that appeared in the Marquette Mining Journal, from which the photos were eventually reproduced showing exactly what the man-idol and woman-idol resembled when first discovered. We will continue following Chuck Bailey's research into the origin of the statues. Also, perhaps we will be able to publish reports from the two California laboratories that should appoint a "time-date" once and for all, for the artifacts. So...stay tuned for the latest results.

CREDITS:

Charles "Sprague" Taylor, deceased, Newberry, MI
Carol Taylor, Newberry, MI
Barry Fell, President, The Epigraphic Society, 6625 Bamburgh Drive, San Diego, CA 92117
Henriette Mertz, deceased, Chicago, IL
Charles W. Bailey, Duluth, MN
The Newberry News, Newberry, MI
The Newberry Logging Museum, Newberry, MI
The Luce County Historical Society, Newberry, MI
C. Ernest Kemp, Dean Emeritus, Lake Superior State University, Sault Ste. Marie, MI

Photos taken in 1947 of the McGruer's Man-idol find.

1947 Remains - McGruer's Woman-idol

1947 Remains of the Newberry Stone

1947 Remains - Newberry Stone

McGruer's Gods & The Newberry Stone
A Michigan Mystery
PART III
The Conclusion

As discussed in Part II, the discovery of the long-lost photographs from the 1898 Marquette Mining Journal article was certainly our first big breakthrough. Now we knew what two of the statues actually resembled, we knew somewhat of their composition, and we had a positive source of origin for the Newberry Tablet. Before getting into our research tracking on the McGruer's Gods, let's take a moment to see what this last 19th century newspaper clipping had to offer. Excerpts follow:

Relics In The Lake Superior Country Of A Prehistoric Race

"We present photographic reproductions of the tablet and two of the Gods, exhumed at Newberry, Michigan, in November 1896; the following description of this most interesting discovery is taken from the Newberry News of November 20th, 1896:

"Last week we called attention, briefly to a curious find said to have been made in this county a few miles north of Newberry. Since then we have examined more closely into the matter and find that the discovery is likely to turn out to be of great historical value and importance. Three figures of stone have been unearthed. They are made of soft sandstone and resemble human beings in a stooping position. They are supposed to be heathen idols or images, as they bear a close resemblance to similar specimens found in other countries. Along with the images was a stone slab or tablet measuring about 19 x 26. This tablet is divided into 140 squares by lines cut into the stone. In each of the spaces is a letter or character, which in all probability record the history or religious creed of some prehistoric people. Some of the characters are very much like letters of the Greek alphabet, others resemble Egyptian hieroglyphics.

A party consisting of Dr. H.C. Farrand, Messrs. W.T. Crocker, D.N. McLeod, Wm. Trueman and Charles Brebner, drove out to the place where the find was made with the intention of doing a little exploring. They found the upturned hemlock root where the figures and tablet were dug out, but owing to the recent thaw the hole was filled with water and the surrounding territory also covered with water to the depth of several inches and digging was out of the question. However several test pits were sunk and rock struck every time and the party were of the opinion that further important discoveries would yet be made.

Just what the explorers' pick and shovel may reveal is hard to surmise. Some are of the opinion that the site of some religious edifice belonging to some pre-historic people will be brought to light. The work on the tablet is too artistic to be ascribed to any of the Indian tribes. It must have been done by some people of a higher order of intelligence. The tablet is remarkably well preserved, every square stands out clearly and only three letters or characters are missing. With the aid of a magnifying glass these may yet be made out.

The find may turn out to be a rich prize to the antiquarian and the archaeologist. The tablet no doubt contains the key to the mystery and until that is deciphered only wild guesses can be made."

The old article went on to describe the Mound-Builders plus the old Copper-Culture mining pits of the Keweenaw Peninsula, as well as Isle Royale. In turn, it attempts to draw a conclusion between the Mound-Builders, the Copper-Culture and the makers of the statues. The final paragraph of the article reads as follows:

"Is it not more than probable that these people who wrought the copper mines set up these graven images on the south shore of Lake Superior, and inscribed their history on tablets of stone, are the same as those who built, in old Mexico, the wonderful pyramid of Cholula (one hundred and seventy-two feet high with a base of thirteen hundred and thirty-five feet, nearly double the size of the great pyramid of Egypt) and all those other temples, palaces and piles stupendous, of whose builders, Reau Campbell makes the ancient Chronicle say:

They are the work of a people which has passed away, under the assaults of barbarism, at a period prior to all traditions, leaving no trace of their existence save these monuments, which, neglected and forgotten by their successors, have become the riddle of later generations to solve."

Had the early writers of that day been privy to the 1981 decipherment of the Newberry Stone, they would have indeed been quite surprised to learn the tablet did not in reality offer a "clue" to the mystery of the idols.

Actually, our research regarding the statues has taken several completely different aproaches. We kept an open mind throughout. One man in particular, Roger Jewell from Sault Ste. Marie, held a very unique hypothesis. It has been quite evident from the several quoted newspaper articles from 1896 to 1898 that these artifacts have consistently been termed as having been made of "sandstone" or "brownstone." Mr. Jewell offered the suggestion that the figures we know of today formed of an unfired clay, may be but replicas of the original finds. He strongly feels the original sandstone figures are secreted somewhere in the eastern U.P. still awaiting their "second coming!" This too, is a possibility.

My research into the statues' origins, combined with that of Chuck Bailey's work took us down several never-before-trod paths. One was to trace a correlation between the McGruer's Gods idols and the "image stones" that once stood at various hidden spots around the shorelines of the Great Lakes. This research was more or less described in the chapter entitled "Image Stone-Spirit Stone." Our main highlight here was first the description of the copper idol of the Lake Superior region, that wore a Mediterranean-style beard. Secondly, many other large stone statues were described by early 17th century Jesuits. It is a known fact, early Indians did not work stone. Lastly, the finding of a replica of a small statue at a private museum near Oscoda, was carved in a similar manner to one of the Gods...namely, the man-idol. It was said the replica was produced from a drawing found in one of the 78 volumes of the *Jesuit Relations.* These ancient records are still being searched at this writing. If the sketch can be located in the *Relations,* it may serve to indicate that other statues made in the same style as our McGruer's Gods would have been positioned by foreigners at strategic sites around Michigan. The large stone statue that once stood on the shores of the Detroit River plus the idol near Green Bay may have been one of these idols.

The other tack our research developed was the Neolithic European connection, especially the Tisza Culture of Hungary, 4000 B.C. A drawing of a seated man-idol from this period compared to a side view of the existing head of the woman-idol shows a definite similarity. This particular idol was termed "the Sickle God" and represented a dominant male deity. The figure was discovered in south-eastern Hungary during the excavation of a neolithic settlement called Szegvar.

This very distinctive sculpture seemed to be wearing a mask affording a flat profile. The statue holds a sickle in his right hand that extends over his shoulder. Bracelets are carved on both arms while a belt simulation occurs around the waist of his robust body.

Experts tend to agree the Sickle God may perhaps be an ancestor of the Greek God, Kronos. The sickle itself gives him status for it duly represents a power insignia. Furthermore these implements were also featured as ornamental ritual objects. Incidentally some were actually produced from copper as far back as 5000 B.C. found in east central Europe. An outstanding example was a huge copper sickle, 54 cm long found in Hungary. Although this sickle was merely an isolated find, its shape resembles the one found on this particular male deity statue.

The seated Sickle God, masked, male and holding the sickle was found with legs broken off below the knees, as well as a damaged nose. Its registered height was 25.6 cm. In retrospect this icon is relatively smaller than the McGruer's Gods but in turn it could have been a clay househould god. Larger statues were used for public worship.

Many of the Tisza Culture Gods and Goddesses represented an agricultural endeavor. Their female goddess of vegetation was usually portrayed nude (as our female Newberry find) and hales from 6000 B.C. Presently, other books of mythology from Europe and surrounding Mediterranean countries are being searched. Let me tell you a little about the Tisza culture.

The Tisza culture centered in the middle Danube Region in Hungary about 4000 B.C. It was one of the first metalworking cultures, predating those in the Mediterranean basin. The people probably spoke an Indo-European language similar to the Hittite language, which some experts feel was a forerunner of Greek. (The Hittite-speaking peoples are thought to have conquered Greece and their language, mixed with the local idiom, became the Mycenean Greek of Bronze Age Greece.)

The Newberry Stone, written in a Hittite-Minoan language would therefore, fit with the statues which are of an art style similar to that of the Tisza peoples. From that point wild conjecture takes over. We know little of these people and their civilization. It is assumed they had no written language, but somehow they reached a high state of culture which included agriculture, and metalworking without it. Perhaps we will one day also find evidence of their writing.

How the McGruer's Gods and the Newberry Stone came to be in the Upper Peninsula is a question which requires assimilation of many facts which are just now coming to light. Reexamination of items formerly discarded for lack of explanation by archaeologists in the past, must also be considered. If the puzzle pieces do not fall into proper perspective, say within the next few years, the necessary breakthroughs in understanding will come and that the answers exist in the archives and memories available to us. (The above paragraphs are attributed to Charles Bailey's research.)

This final chapter of the McGruer Gods-Newberry Stone conclusion is being written as material surfaces, so you, the reader, can share in the excitement of our discoveries, be they a "detour" or on the right path. For sake of review, let's briefly state our research results at this particular writing: (It will be the last chapter written before publication and will hold the "key" to our success or failure in this regard.)

1. Three statues found in the U.P. associated with a tablet which has been authenticated by Barry Fell, president of Epigraphic Society.
2. Tablet in the Hittite-Minoan language.
3. Early form of the Hittite (which many believe was the forerunner of the Minoan Greek language), presumably spoken by ancient Tisza culture in Hungary c. 5000-3000 B.C.
4. Statue from that culture bears superficial resemblance to the Upper Peninsula statue. The seated masked god holding a

sickle also has what might be described as a cowl around the head. The face is triangular rather than round like the McGruer statues, as are the faces of smaller associated clay statues from the Neolithic Era. 5. The Tisza culture people were an agricultural people. The tablet translation is an "omen" relating to a farming-type endeavor of sowing seeds. The birds partaking of these seeds brings forth the good luck required by the "omen."

6. Some type of stone statues still being worshipped by the native population in the Great Lakes region found by early Jesuits of the 17th century were destroyed by the religious priests as sacrilegious idols.

So we leave this "mystery" here at this point until further results of our combined research materializes. Charles Bailey and your author also are anxiously awaiting the results of the dating process from the two formerly mentioned California laboratories. We will keep you advised as reports filter in...

****

Received letter from Charles Bailey dated March 28, 1989 regarding progress of determination of our pet project, the McGruer's Gods. Bailey reported as follows:

"I stopped at Hamlin University library in Minneapolis where they have the complete set of the *Jesuit Relations* in both French and English out on the shelves. (Remember here that Jerry Wagner, owner of a private Indian museum near Oscoda had carved a statue quite similar in several respects to the male McGruer idol. Wagner claimed he made the replica from a drawing found in the *Relations*.) There are no illustrations other than a couple of maps. There is naturally speculation that this Oscoda replica did not come from data found in this source.

Still not a word from the two laboratories I sent letters to regarding the dating of the idols. At the recent Upper Great Lakes Basin conference, I asked several experts about dating the find. One told me the best method would be to try to date the hair embedded in one of the pieces but that the cost is very high because the sample is so small. We might try to get an expert to give an opinion on the type of hair through microscopic examination."

In the meantime I contacted a friend, Gerry Blair, of

Flagstaff, Arizona for some time back he was researching "Kachina Dolls" from Indians of the southwestern areas. While at Jerry Wagner's museum talking about the replica that seemed to resemble our male McGruer's God, he made mention of a relationship between this statue and the Kachina dolls. Perhaps this small clue will yet offer a reward for our never ending detective work in tracking the origin of our now quite famous "gods!"

Received reply from Gerry Blair regarding a possible connection between the replica resembling one of the McGruer's gods to the "Kachina Dolls" of the southwest. Blair stated: "The photo seems to be similar in the respect that it looks a little like some of the very primitive Hopi Kachinas I have seen; the kind they give to their children, not the kind they sell to the tourists."

Blair advised he also would forward several reference books on "Kachinas" to me for comparison study.

A letter dated April 18, 1989 arrived from Charles Bailey of Duluth regarding a study done on the hair contained in a fragment from either one of the "gods" or the Newberry Stone. May I again take the liberty to quote: "...The lady from the UMD/DNR Archaeology Laboratory here made a slide of the "hair" which clings to one of the pieces to determine what it is. After careful comparison with several human and animal hairs, cotton fibre, and other common fibres, the answer is...we still don't know. It may be a root hair of some sort. The cellular structure is somewhat similar to wood. It is thicker than human or animal hair and is smooth without cilia. Sue, the lady from the lab, who is an expert on plant pollens believes she can detect a cytolith within the sample. I left the slide with her. She will try to get an expert plant biologist to give an opinion.

Knowing what it is and dating it are two different things. It might be possible to date it using a new technology which dates small amounts of organic substances. Unfortunately the cost is prohibitive at $1000 per sample."

Previously I mailed additional samples of clay from the McGruer's artifacts to Mr. Bailey advising him of another foreign particle that I questioned. In reply Charles Bailey stated: "The pebble visible in the large piece of the clay is granite with a large amount of quartz. Also the sample of clay showing what appears to be a surfacing of sorts, does not seem to have been fired. The finish may be due to degredation weathering or perhaps paint."

The month of May found Charles Bailey in Washington, D.C. While there he checked with the Smithsonian Museum in hopes of finding the original file on the "gods" as well as perhaps an update. However, the building was undergoing renovations and was closed. He did learn that the pictures taken of the tablet and gods in 1896 were not in the files.

While in Washington Bailey discussed carbon-14 dating techniques with a scientist at the U.S. Geological Survey Lab. He was sure a thermonuclear dating of the hair that was found in one clay sample could be done for around $600. Still too cost prohibitive, working without a grant. On the very crude description furnished him by Charles Bailey, he thought it still might be a human or animal hair based on the computer printout furnished.

In the meantime the books on "Kachina Dolls" arrived from Gerry Blair, Flagstaff, AZ. The modern versions of the Kachina relics are too stylized for our McGruer Gods connection. The text supplied indicated the kachina cult existed prior to the Spanish explorations in the Southwest. Archaeological evidence of pottery designs links kachina similarities to the late 1300 A.D. Some murals worked on cave walls and slab ruins have been excavated in both New Mexico and Arizona. Earliest finds of the kachina concept have evolved over thousands of years. Many unexcavated areas still are prevalent in the Southwest territory.

One interesting facet of the kachina production is that the wooden dolls or figures are coated with clay. The clay is located in various locations near the Hopi mesas. Large chunks are transported, then broken up into a container of water and soaked. This process softens the coarse grit which in turn, sinks to the bottom. The finer, minute clay particles are thusly caught in suspension. As the water evaporates, the remaining fluid turns to a thick, creamy clay which when coated on the statues offers a gray-white base upon which to paint.

The initial Kachina finds were quite crude from what has

been offered in the past century. They are but fragments of a lost culture with no documentation. Little is known about the prehistory kachina.

At one time large kachina dolls proved popular; some being almost lifesize. This would have been similar in fashion to our "gods." Research indicates photos do exist of some early kachinas being extremely large in the three to five foot height bracket.

I found the eyes and nose similar between the Michigan statues and some modern day examples of the kachinas. The mouth, however, proved completely different. Some early aspects showed similar body style, especially the arms. But no definite conclusions could be drawn...it seems as though the "kachina connection" proved to be a detour, if not an absolute dead-end.

As publication deadlines approach, I find it necessary to close the book on McGruer's Gods and the Newberry Stone. Up to this very moment, both Charles Bailey and your author, strongly held out hope that word would come from one of the California laboratories regarding the carbon-14 dating process of the clay samples from the McGruer idols. But, to no avail...grant research takes time! The answers will be forthcoming and at that time, they will be published as an update should publication reprints prove necessary.

The answers will surface at some future date. Since the Newberry Stone has been accepted as authentic in scientific circles; surely, the statues made from the same material and hidden in the same cache, too will have their day of glory. Who knows, just perhaps an archaeologist, historian, anthropologist or epigraphist has a clue or two gleaned from prior research? The publication of this book, *Michigan Prehistory Mysteries*, might tend to "jog one's memory!" Let's hope so! But in the meantime, the dedicated followers of McGruer's Gods will continue their, "search for the truth!"

****

The following information crossed my desk after the close of these three chapters regarding McGruer's Gods: Nextdoor neighbors to the Hungarian Tisza culture were the people of Lepenski Vir, the Starcevo Culture centering around presentday Yugoslavia and Romania. They were an agricultural community of the Mesolithic or Middle Stone Age of prehistory. Their time era extends some 3000 years ranging from 8000 BC and 500 BC. Why am I mentioning this culture? I have just learned that when Lepenski Vir was discovered, each of the huts contained an altar. Behind the altar of one such home, stood two large upright boulders. When the mud and debris was cleaned from one of them a human face plus a torso appeared. They were made of red sandstone. The interesting facts here are that these people manufactured lifesize gods of stone and clay. Furthermore the godlike stone described above had an almost similar face (round, not triangular) to our male McGruer's god. The set of the eyes and especially the nose are startling. While this culture produced statues mainly resembling fish people, they have on at least one specific instance created one god in the near likeness to our McGruer find. Only the results of the carbon-14 dating will prove if there is a relationship here. The photographs I mention can be verified in the March 1975 issue of the *Smithsonian* magazine, page 36.

CREDITS:

The Marquette Mining Journal, Marquette, MI
The Marquette Historical Museum, Marquette, MI
Roger Jewell, Sault Ste. Marie, MI
Charles W. Bailey, Duluth, MN
Crocker Nuclear Laboratory, University of California
San Jose State University, San Jose, CA
Gerry Blair, Flagstaff, AZ

Woman-idol

Man-idol

Photos discovered in 1988 that depict for the very first time, what the artifacts resembled at the time of discovery. The photo of the woman-idol is the only record to date of what this goddess looked like.

Photo discovered in 1988 that depict for the very first time, what the Newberry Stone resembled at the time of discovery.

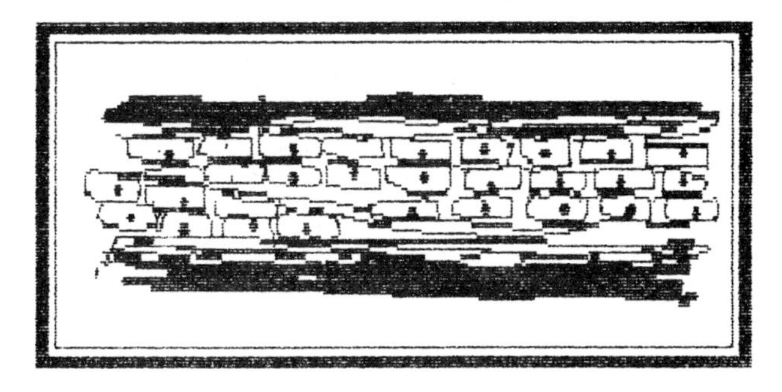

Cross section of hair found in one of the artifacts.

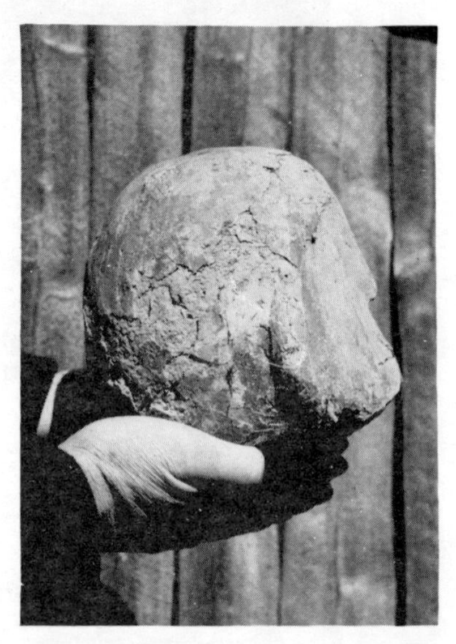

A comparison of the head from the McGruer's woman-idol profile to that of the Tisza Culture, Sickle God.

The Kachina Connection! Jerry Wagner suggested there may be a connection between the McGruer's Gods, his carved replica and the Kachina dolls of the American Southwest.

The Mysterious Symbol Stone

A timeless Native American legend exists regarding a mystifying disappearing copper kettle that serves to "set the stage" for the presentation of our next subject, the mysterious symbol stone. The fable is reported as follows:

The tale is named the story of "Manitou-Au-Kick" (God's Kettle), and this particular relic was purported to have been left behind by the inexplicable people who so populated Michigan before the time of the Pottawatomis, the Ottawas or the Chippewas. It is so thought this anomalous kettle stemmed from that enigmatic race responsible for not only the mounds, the unexplainable garden-beds and the copper mining prehistory pits, but as well, many other unascribed antiquities from Michigan's long-ago past.

The legend states that almost 400 years ago Chief We-Me-Gen-De-Bay while hunting in what we now term Grand Traverse Bay country, came upon an enormous copper kettle partially buried in the earth and anchored there by the root system of a large tree. When the chief dug it out he noticed the kettle appeared to be new, probably never used, and contained an unusual bright spot at the very bottom. Believe it or not, this magnificent pot was so immense, an entire bear or deer could be cooked in it at one boiling!

Indians placed great store in whatever could be termed "mystical," thus Chief We-Me-Gen-De-Bay used this kettle only for special ceremonies believing it a gift supplied by the "gods." As soon as a religious feast came to an end, the prize kettle was quickly secreted for safety's sake, with the hiding spot being located some distance from the village site. The Indians further thought the kettle to have been the work of a "manitou" who fashioned it from copper outcroppings, say from the Keweenaw-Isle Royale prehistory mining pits.

Still more surprising was the fact that this remarkable pot contained no bail or rim when first discovered. Much later, in 1840, these missing parts were added by one Andrew Blackbird, an Indian blacksmith. At this point in time, the kettle was no longer used primarily for ceremonial purposes, but in its stead provided a boiling vessel for the manufacture of maple syrup and other year-round cooking needs.

Then, as suddenly as the kettle appeared to old Chief We-Me-Gen-De-Bay, some 300-plus years ago, it simply vanished for well over a half a century! Mysteriously it turned up in the possession of an Indian chief from Keewadin who in turn, displayed this unique copper vessel at fairs and exhibitions around Michigan. When this chief, named Ma-Ma-Go-Nis passed away, the inscrutable kettle once again vanished. True, it was a fact that a copper pot remained in the dead chieftain's earthly possessions but in essence, it was not *the* mammoth original copper kettle of this legend.

Will the future bring new sightings of this mystifying enigma? Only time will tell!

Author's Note: Remember here the unusual copper kettle, containing no seams that was excavated from a Bay City mound? It too was very large and the bail and rim were absent. I wonder if this early 1800 find was the one and same kettle.

Now you may ask, how does a mysterious here-again, gone-again copper pot tie in with a mystic symbol stone, which is the main subject of this particular chapter? Actually it is quite simple, the relationship being that while the entire kettle appeared and disappeared over a period of hundreds of years, the mystic symbol stone had characters or symbols that came, went and changed over a 14-day period. Impossible, you say? Maybe so, but many, many unexplained events of a similar vein, have occurred all over the world and have been properly documented. Parapsychology is the investigation of psychic phenomena such as extrasensory perception, telepathy, etc.

A most reputable group exists that delves into just such reported phenomena. The name of the organization is The Early-Sites Research Society and its diagnostic center's address is: Long Hill, MASS 01969. The phone number is (617) 948-2410. The Archaeological Director's name is James P. Whittall. You will find mention of Mr. Whittall in both Trento's and Fell's books as a very learned, respected and able scientist. Their investigation of the Michigan mystic-symbol stone will be presented later in this chapter.

Before you, the reader, cry loudly..."Bah, humbug!", let the facts be so presented just as they mysteriously unfolded...then form your own convictions. Try to keep an "open-mind." Remember, there is today a strong trend towards paraphysical presentations. With these points in mind we will present an actual case that developed in Michigan, fully documented as not merely being the work of an overstimulated imagination. Here...documentation, is the key!

Let's tell this fascinating event just as it happened from beginning to end. Later we will discuss opinions of the scientific community. However, we will omit the names of witnesses, maintaining those of the principals. Full disclosure of all participants can be provided to any and all interested parties.

Dennis Morrison, formerly of Oscoda, now living near Greenbush, along with his wife, Kathy, are the main pair involved in the "happenings."

For months on end, Dennis dreamed almost constantly of unearthing Native American artifacts. He had been an amateur archaeologist for some time, but now these dreams or visions seemed to strongly persist. He regards the dreams as the beginning of a possible psychic connection. In July of 1986, Dennis's dog, Samson, dug up three pottery shards near his doghouse. Incidentally, it was located directly next to the small building the Morrison's turned into their Indian artifact museum. Dennis always believed where you find one piece of pottery, you will locate more. In August the young couple began a carefully planned excavation, and in no time at all they unearthed a grand total of 1500 pot shards. Some were decorated (mostly rim shards), but the majority were plain surfaced body pieces. In one particular area, many large pieces were found, giving the impression the pot had more or less collapsed on itself. The artifacts were located approximately 10-inches below the surface. It is interesting to note, this was a former garden plot and it had previously been rototilled to a depth of 5 inches, with no ancient items surfacing.

Additionally, other artifacts were recovered...chert debtage from possible tool production, a broken scraper as well as considerable fire-cracked rock. The mysterious symbol stone was also unearthed here. It proved to be a most common, plain, unattractive looking rock, somewhat resembling that of a "celt." *Author's Note:* A celt is actually the head of an ungrooved stone ax, and it is a fact that all "celt" stones are of ancient origin, dating back to prehistory times. Because of its celtic shape, Morrison set the rock aside on a small table near Samson's doghouse. And there it so remained until November.

Dennis Morrison continues the interview. He states that in early November he developed a nasty toothache which on one night in particular kept him from sleeping. Being in pain and exceedingly restless, he decided to stay up and reconstruct the largest pottery vessel described previously. The pottery project went well and 17 pieces forming a 12- by 7-inch section were assembled like an ancient jigsaw puzzle. Being quite pleased with the results, Dennis, on the following day, took the pottery pieces to a nearby friend's house to obtain his archaeological opinions. This man had never seen as large a pottery vessel from this specific area and was most anxious to view the reconstruction of the pot itself. So Dennis and Kathy packaged the shards carefully for transportation and at the very last moment, Dennis also decided to bring along the "celt." The two old friends, along with their wives, spent a pleasant evening viewing the pottery artifacts and talking at great lengths of the early people of both Alcona and Iosco counties.

Now when Dennis picked up the stone to take to his friend's house, it was exactly as he first found it back in August...a plain, small rock of little significance. When he displayed the pottery pieces, he used the stone to prop up the largest assembled section of the clay pot. As the two men were once again repacking the artifacts, his buddy remarked, "Dennis, what are these symbols on this rock?" At first, Dennis Morrison thought his friend to be joking for earlier when he had examined it, there were not strange markings visible. However, now this stone indeed held strange symbols! In fact a whole string of inscriptions appeared across the stone and still more amazing, was the fact they seemed to be raised. Both men felt 80% positive a psychic event was actually occurring at this point...the other 20% was reserved for the possibility of it being attributed to a natural phenomena.

The Morrison's took their stone home and made an attempt to photograph it but each try merely seemed to fog the camera lens. The mysterious symbols slowly faded until by morning they were all but lost and by evening, they were completely absent.

The story continues when on the afternoon of November 28th the "celt" stone had its most active period to that date. Dennis and his archaeological companion had been invited to another friend's home at Comins for dinner and scientific conversation afterwards. The main topic during the meal, naturally, was the unusual qualities of the stone. The trip to Comins took the men 45 minutes. Throughout dinner, the stone remained in the car. After the meal the host, along with his guests, wanted to view this unique rock, so Dennis went out to the car to bring it in for all to see.

As soon as Dennis Morrison opened the car door it was quite apparent the rock was again working its own peculiar brand of magic. There was now a dark circle forming that actually appeared sticky, but in retrospect, was not. It also gave the appearance of being excreted from the rock, but again nothing could be felt by the touch. This time, however, the figure that appeared was not raised but instead was very dark and most clearly defined. When Dennis took the rock into the house the people there were amazed beyond words. Over a period of one hour, many signs were witnessed.

An open 4 appeared along with the numbers 2 and 7. *Author's Note:* Remember the fact mentioned in a previous chapter that the #7 had appeared in many prehistory incidents and settings worldwide. Right before the witnesses' eyes, the open 4 changed to a closed 4 in a phantasmagoric manner. The action of this numerical change was comparable to how the numbers change on a digital watch. The original large circle now changed from a plain circle to one with 2 lines extending out of it. This resembled an eye. At the time, Dennis wondered if this indicated he should be seeing or watching something. But what? Indeed, that was the question!

All the above symbols faded rapidly. At 7 P.M. the two friends left Comins and were now 90% convinced that a psychic happening had taken place. Halfway home they stopped along their route to check the stone for further action. The formerly mentioned dark circle still existed but now had an eyebrow-like mark above it, reminding them of a "face in profile." Once again photographs were taken at this point.

Upon reaching home one further event occurred, this time in the presence of Dennis's wife Kathy, and his mother Lorraine. The circle was still evident with the alleged eyebrow placed above it, but just beyond this point a symbol appearing as a stylized number "8" had formed. In turn, this figure faded quickly. The stone then rested until the 30th of November.

The symbol stone had been placed in the Morrison's small private museum but on the above mentioned date, Dennis again brought it into the house. After perhaps an hour, symbols resembling a 715 seemed to appear. Shortly afterwards, a diamond with a tail could easily be seen. Please note here as in the other previous circumstances, the stone had gone through a temperature change...that being, from cold to warm...when the symbols started to appear. This fact may or may not be significant.

The stone again took a rest period with no noticeable action until the 5th of December. What took place at this time was quite different in scope than the previous marking action. On this particular instance, toward the end of the celt, (if in reality it truly is a celt) at the cutting edge of said tool, there appeared light veins of gold and one vein of silver. By the 17th of December this veining process was still visible but additionally a spotting pattern had broken out on both sides of the stone. Up to this point, the symbols were always located on the darker side of the rock. Now most of the action was apparent on the stone's opposite side.

Dennis Morrison asked the following questions during this part of our interview: "Why would symbols resembling our alphabet and numerical system, appear on a pre-Indian artifact?" "Why do my fingers tingle when I hold this rock?" "Do I have to be present personally for the mystic symbols to appear?" It seems so!

Most of the photographic work resulted in pictures of a very poor quality, even though Morrison is an able newspaper reporter and photographer. But the photos taken the night of

November 25th were extremely overexposed. Due to this inadvertent process, the markings can be seen, but not quite distinctly enough for positive identification. However, with the aid of a magnifying glass, some symbols Dennis previously had ignored, were now visible for the first time. What he and Kathy had previously regarded as an "omega"-type symbol was in reality, a "stick-man." Located nearby were other undiscernible figures. He later had this photograph enhanced further, resulting in at least three human-like stick figures faintly coming in view. One resembled an archer...similar to the bowman of the Sanilac Petroglyphs. Other symbols were not unlike other figures and signs found in prehistory culture for say, the sun and the moon. Sadly, however, all but one of the photographs were of such poor quality they could not successfully be reproduced for use in this publication.

Dennis Morrison consulted ancient writing symbol charts and determined eight symbols could be attributed to the prehistory Iberian script of Spain and Portugal. In turn, he also picked six symbols from the stone that resembled Punic inscriptions. Furthermore, from Native American culture sites one could perhaps attribute six signs to the "Adena" and six symbols to the "Aptucret." To all intents and purposes the stone seemed to be a bilingual mix of symbols, almost to the point of actually resembling a "Rosetta Stone."

Dennis wished to recall here, that the mysterious symbol stone had been taken in relationship to a site containing other Indian artifacts. Still, it is indeed odd as to why the signs appeared and disappeared seemingly at will, while additionally, the rock at times held both Indian and non-Indian (Mediterranean) inscriptions.

Further questions were addressed here by Morrison: "Why did the specific symbols appear but once, never being duplicated?" "Are they perhaps time-released in some unknown manner?" "Was it so planned to appear in this manner as say, a pattern?" "What is the unknown substance acting as the catalyst?"

Certainly it cannot be overlooked that this phenomenon may be of a spiritual nature! In fact the Native American culture held many spiritual rocks as we have already witnessed from the "Image Stone-Spirit Stone" chapter. But the subject of "magic" rocks was not actually discussed in that particular chapter. For example, the Sioux Indians (with a possible co-mingling of culture with Ojibwas from Michigan) referred to "magic" stones they called the Yuwipi. These unusual magical stones were found by medicine men in anthills. It was said they had a glistening quality or luminescence about them. Indeed, they were deemed "sacred!" The Yuwipi contained a "power." Other magic rocks were obtained from high mountain plateaus, being termed "Inyan Wasicun Wakan" and were basically employed by medicine men to cure an illness. It has further been written that these "magic" stones oftentimes held a message which they often revealed...invisible writing for those who read with their hearts. The medicine men were believed to have the power to "talk" or communicate with these sacred rocks.

Additionally, ancient religious men of the Sioux Nation emplored "Yuwipi" stones to locate lost items. They fully regarded a medicine stone to be the work of the gods...a rock had "no beginning" and "no end". The "Yuwipi's" power was eternal. These "magic" rocks were also termed "thunder-stones" for most Indian cultures believed they were placed beneath the earth by "thunder-bolts." Furthermore, they should be left alone, never to be disturbed, unless you were a special medicine man, a "Heyoka." To non-Indian races and cultures this discussion of Native American culture beliefs seems unreal and strange. But the Indians regard us as having short memories, and over the centuries the white people have simply forgotten the ultimate power contained in the rocks.

At this point, Mr. Morrison asked the following question: "Perhaps the Caucasian Race has lost the communication power with these "sacred" stones, but could a racial memory from my archaeological buddy, his wife, my wife Kathy or myself have acted as the catalyst to trigger my mystic symbol stone into action?"

Dennis Morrison's brother-in-law, Marlin is a respected, recognized water-dowser and has been most of his adult life. Dennis remarked that sometimes artifacts can be located with metal dowsing rods. His relative was totally surprised with the introduction of this information. Nevertheless, Marlin was more than game to give it a try. The men bent two coat hangers and took them outside. Dennis had the stone in his pocket. The results from the very start were most peculiar. For one rod pointed towards Dennis and the stone while the second one aimed in the opposite direction; then they both returned to their original positons. Marlin seemed stunned and remarked, "I have never seen dowsing rods act so strangely."

At this point Dennis suggested they go to the backyard where the stone was excavated. When they approached the very spot where the stone was uncovered, the rods quickly crossed. Time and time again, both men tried the same procedure, and each attempt brought the two dowsers in a crossed position. When they would move to other areas not previously excavated, then the rods would uncross.

In January of 1987 Mr. Morrison contacted *The Early Sites Research Center* in Massachusetts. James Whittall, ESRS Archaeological Director, replied to his inquiry on the 20th of January. May we quote from his reply:

"I sent a copy of your letter on to Terry Ross, past-president of the American Dowsers Society. Inclosed is a copy of his reply.

Certainly the lettering is familiar and the symbols could represent a sun and moon symbol. It is possible that this is someone's "talisman," but with the unusual nature of the appearances of the markings, I would suggest it is from a "Shaman's" kit. Strange artifacts of this nature do show up all over the world and although most might shake their head and cast the item out, I am inclined to believe that their reality is yet to be understood by the "European Christian mind."

It certainly was recovered in the right context to be "something." I would be interested to know what else results either from the stone or from the site. I will keep your material on file and keep an eye open for any material which has something similar.

I hope I have been of some help to you: items like this take time to jell into the mind and system."

The enclosed report from Terry Ross that James Whittall spoke of read as follows: (It was written to Whittall)

"The first thing is a check on Mr. and Mrs. Morrison. They are both okay.

The second thing is to check the backyard at their address in Michigan. It has a confluence of five lines-of-force ('leys'), over a very large water dome, with a standing wave over it.

The third thing is to compare the scene with what Ginny and I ran into at 12,000 feet in the Andes at Cocesqui, where three slides of my automatic camera produced a golden fogging, with a humanoid form faintly discernible...somewhat of a corroboration of my questioning of the Quechuan as to whether he knew the "dos phantasmas" (spirits) that had been following us around all p.m.? "Si, I know them well," he said. and described what I had seen, and presumably what came out on the slides back in the states.

The fourth thing is to ask if Mr. and Mrs. Morrison have a "contact" going.

The fifth thing is to ask, if they do, is this series of imprints a "message," and if so, is it one with meaning, and valid?

The sixth thing is to determine if someone can make out the imprints.

The seventh thing is to check the area with instruments, add the azimuth of the lines for solar, lunar and stellar orientation."

Dennis Morrison additionally contacted John R. Halsey, State Archaeologist, Bureau of History, Michigan Department of State at Lansing. Excerpts from his report follow:

"Thank you for your recent letter concerning the "stone with symbols." I am not a geologist, but I do believe there are probably physical reasons for the appearance and disappearance of the letters, numbers and symbols. I suspect, as you suggest, that it probably has to do with the change of temperatures. Why don't you contact the geology department at Central Michigan University or Alpena Community College and take it in?

On another matter...that being, a "blind man fetish." There is a great gulf between the *possibility* of a natural stone having been used as a fetish or charm and the *likelihood* of it having been so used. In this case we will probably never know."

And that is just about that...the case remains open at present. The facts have been presented. The mysterious symbol stone has given forth no further signs, inscriptions or designs. This entire documented affair remains an enigmatic parapsychological experience.

Now...What do *YOU* think?

CREDITS:

Dennis and Kathy Morrison, Greenbush, MI
John R. Halsey, State Archaeologist, Michigan Dept. of State, Bureau of History, 208 N. Capitol Avenue, Lansing, MI
Early Sites Research Society, Long Hill, MA. James P. Whittall, Archaeological Director.
Terry Ross, past president, American Dowser's Society

SUGGESTED FURTHER READING

MYSTERIES OF MICHIGAN'S LONG-AGO PEOPLE, "Indian Legend an Enigma, Does God's Kettle Exist?", Gerald Haltiner, publ. privately.
LAME DEER, SEEKER OF VISIONS, "Yuwipi Little Lights From Nowhere", John Lame Deer, Richard Erdoes, Washington Squire Press, 1976.

Symbol stone showing what is thought to be an eye and an eyelash.

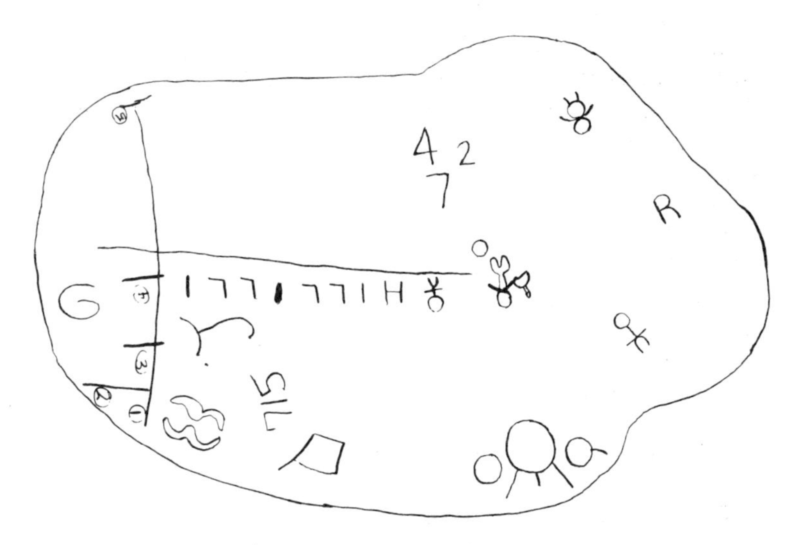

A composite drawing of all the symbols that appeared over a 14 day period to the mysterious symbol stone.

Hoax or History- Fake or Find?

As with any prehistory artifact, one must always keep an open mind, but one also needs to be aware that over the collective years, fraudulent schemes and artifacts lacking proper authenticity have been foisted on the general public as the genuine article. The reasons unscrupulous people attempt to pass off counterfeit historical treasures are multiple, ranging from publicity to profit. Some, you can be assured, are clever schemes with first-class reproductions offered, while others are but sloppy re-creations of famous works with no eye for retaining even a semblance of historic merit.

An early example of such a fraud would have been the discovery of the "Kinderhook Plates," so called because the artifacts were unearthed near Kinderhook, Illinois...the date for this fraudulent deception is listed as 1843. The discovery comprised six inscribed copper plates or tablets on which were engraved authentic-appearing Chinese symbols. Upon translation by the proper authorities, they were declared to be nothing more than a copy of the engravings that appeared on a Chinese tea tin of that particular era. The village blacksmith, seeking notoriety, cut the inscriptions into the copper plates spuriously.

Doyle C. Fitzpatrick, author of *The King Strang Story*, wrote of a similar bronze plate scheme that took place in 1850 when James J. Strang crowned himself "King" making Beaver Island the only kingdom ever to exist in the United States. This self-appointed monarch claims to have dug up inscribed bronze plates or tablets from under an oak tree near Voree, Wisconsin. Strang claimed he found these plates known as the "Voree plates," as well as a second group termed the "Plates of Laban," through the divine intervention of God. These inscribed plates were believed to be God's laws.

The Voree plates were brass, each 1½ by 3 inches. On all six sides were engravings...a man with a scepter; an eye, sun and moon with 12 stars; 12 larger stars, 3 pillars and 70 tiny stars. The remaining plates held hieroglyphics. Strang claims to have deciphered the plates through the use of his two miraculous stones, Urim and Thummin. The Voree plates have long been lost and the followers of Strang believed they returned to a heavenly depository as did the two stones. These mysterious rocks which James Strang claimed to have used to translate the two sets of plates are referred to in the Bible, EX 28:30. Still further back in history, the Jews claim to have known of Urim and Thummin's existence.

A cloud of doubt remained over "King" Strang's purported brass plates containing messages from God. Hazel Strang McCardell, granddaughter of James Strang, once remarked that Strang was smart and well educated and had most likely written the plates himself. Thus it seems as though the Voree plates figured into a religious "power ploy!"

Michigan was not immune by any means from sordid attempts to dupe gullible individuals or credulous experts alike, regarding relics of antiquity relating to that mysterious race of people we have already discussed, termed the Mound-Builders. The best known of these so-called "relic peddlers" was classified as "The Soper Frauds." In reality, this 1890-1925 bunco scheme was recently laid to rest once and for all, by the Epigraphic Society. Over the years these bogus artifacts simply surfaced again and again as genuine articles.

The principal figure in this case was an energetic prehistory artifact collector named Daniel E. Soper, who incidentally served at that particular period as Michigan's secretary of state. A well-known victim of this deception was a most loved clergyman by the name of Rev. James Savage. While dean of the eastern Diocese and pastor of Holy Trinity Catholic church in Detroit, he was also regarded as a respected eminent archaeologist. Rev. Savage was so completely duped during the course of the purported scam, that over a period of years he actually purchased some fifty plus relics that he fully regarded to be historical artifacts of the finest quality and degree.

Other notables similarly taken in by Soper's grandiose schemes were the most respected Dr. R.B. Orr and Major James of the Provincial Museum of Toronto, Canada, along with Bishop Etzenhauser, leader of the areas Latter Day Saints.

How could such upstanding community leaders be so foolish? Perhaps they merely failed to do their "homework." Or just maybe the fakes and frauds were so cleverly done, that indeed detection bordered on the impossible. The counterfeiters were dubious men to a degree, but as the story unfolds you will also learn they were careless. It is not surprising, however, that the artifacts kept surfacing as authentic, for the relics were so expertly contrived that even the astute Dr. Henriette Mertz fully believed in their credibility. a book published shortly after her death entitled, *The Mystic Symbol* so indicated these beliefs.

Gerald Haltiner in a booklet called *Mysteries of Michigan's Long-Ago People*, describes the Soper frauds in the following manner: "These relics were found only in the period mentioned and the finders may have been influenced by Mr. Soper, who seemed to have an uncanny knowledge of where they might be found. Many were 'discovered' in mounds and graves in Montcalm and Crawford counties, and near Detroit (Highland and Palmer Park areas) and Traverse City. They are relics of unusual size and beauty and many are covered with cuneiform letters resembling those used by the ancient Chaldeans.

Some are inscribed with a Greek cross. Another bears the figure of an angel in prayer. Still another has a scene depicting 'The Flood' and with a dove on the reverse side. Many bear inscriptions of Biblical characters and events.

However, since the discovery of these controversial artifacts long since ceased, in the light of superior techniques of investigation, the bulk of evidence concerning them has shifted sharply to the support of University of Michigan scientists and other experts who are unswerving in denunciation of their authenticity.

If they were 'planted' as many believe, how was it done so as to defy detection by such experts as the Rev. Mr. Savage? He gained nothing financially, for he sold nothing. Dr. Orr and Major James were connected with the University of Toronto and their interest was purely scientific. They gained nothing for themselves. Mr. Soper himself stoutly maintained that he sold nothing, while eagerly purchasing any such items he located.

The questions remain unanswered. If these relics were 'planted' then how and why and by whom?"

Now after all these years this mystery that so bothered Gerald Haltiner, has finally been brought to a satisfactory conclusion. The report solving this riddle was forwarded to me by Barry Fell, president of The Epigraphic Society and is published in full in their *Occasional Publication*, Vol. 17, Oct. 1988. The article is termed, "The Michigan 'Relics'."

This excellent report describes the Michigan Relics" scam as an extensive massive production of professionally forged artifacts that took place between 1880 and 1911. On August 10, 1911, Dr. James Talmage, geologist from the University of Utah and director of the Deseret Museum in Salt Lake City, published a report on extensive investigational work done on hundreds of artifacts from the Detroit area. Talmage demonstrated that many of the copper pieces excavated were actually made in more modern times from sheet copper alloy. Furthermore, the actual engraving marks appeared fresh, viewed under a microscope. In other words, they sorely lacked the "patina" of age.

An unpublished diary of Dr. Talmage's recently came to light through the efforts of Professor Paul Chessman. This diary indicates that the able doctor had located a Mrs. E.H. Riley who was the stepdaughter of the counterfeiter, one James O. Scotford, a housepainter by trade. This man along with his two sons, Charles and Percy, supplied the fake artifacts to the reputable Daniel E. Soper.

These relics of antiquity included a variety of artifacts, such as small caskets, copper ornaments, tools and weapons, tablets of both baked and unbaked clay, pipes and pottery vessels. The false hieroglyphics were a combination of miscellaneous alphabets and symbols that could be found in various places from the encyclopedia to the Moabite Stone and the Norse rune stones. It is interesting to note that almost all of the artifacts were inscribed, the clays while still wet by impression, the coppers by hammering, and the slates by engraving tools.

It was earlier brought to light that Mr. Soper seemed to know where to find these seemingly genuine articles in the barren, deserted fields located in the Highland and Palmer Parks areas of Detroit. It was also mentioned that Mr. Soper bought as many of the counterfeit pieces as he could lay his hands on. Why? That is the question Gerald Haltiner hoped would someday be answered. Well the reason Soper was buying his own fraudulent material was because he also owned and operated a reputable mail-order relic business dealing in just such objects. This front gave him the respectability needed. By the year 1911 it was believed Daniel Soper most likely possessed between 200 and 300 of these cleverly contrived fake antiquities.

Dr. Talmage also noted in his diary that Mrs. E.H. Riley, stepdaughter of the relic manufacturer, Scotford, signed a declaration that the objects were indeed forgeries made by her stepfather. She further recalled watching Scotford bury the counterfeit artifacts, then later excavate them, claiming the items to be the genuine article. By an agreement executed with the venerable Dr. Talmage, Mrs. Riley asked the declaration not be published until after her mother's death.

As matters came to pass, it seems as though Dr. Talmage died before Mrs. Riley's mother. However, on the 10th of August in the year 1911, Talmage issued a public report in which he branded these artifacts as fraudulent material and considered them to have been manufactured to "dupe" the general public for monetary gains. The diary remained unpublished until recently brought to light in 1988 by Professor Chessman.

Shortly after the Talmage Report was released to the press in 1911, two reporters from the Detroit News turned up the following information. They located a neighbor of Scotford's who granted them an interview. This lady indicated the house painter and his sons often worked into the small hours of the morning noisily hammering in their garage workshop. She also stated the two Scotford boys held no regular jobs and often informed her they had no need for one. Further investigative work turned up the fact that James Scotford once owned and operated his own relic-peddling business in the town of Big Rapids. Additionally, he and Soper were both involved in alleged excavation efforts of fraudulent items recovered in Montcalm County in 1891.

So...this matter has finally been laid to rest!

Are we immune from such schemes, dupes and devious practices in today's modern world? Certainly not! Unscrupulous individuals are always waiting in the wings eager to make a quick buck with a seemingly easy "con." All the factors must be evaluated with any archaeological discovery. Extensive research should be in order. Again, do your homework. Seek professional help. You may in turn get several different viewpoints, but actually, that is not all that bad either. Archaeology is indeed a mystery science and detective work of the first degree is in order. Good advice here...learn your facts, know your facts and assemble your facts carefully! If you do not, your artifacts may be deemed worthless.

An example of a modern-day fraud that quickly comes to mind was termed "The Los Lunas Hoaxes." It dealt with a trail of forged engraved stones and artifacts recently replicated in a similar fashion to the "Los Lunas" stone itself. The perpetrators were eventually exposed and brought to trial in Albuquerque, New Mexico. They received a jail term.

Charles W. Bailey from Duluth, Minnesota, has been detecting "hoax or history" "fake or find" artifacts for over 30 odd years. Recently he informed me that some articles of dubious origin turned up in the State of Illinois, known as the "Burrow's Cave Artifacts." Bailey wrote an excellent report bearing the same title, that appeared in The Epigraphic Society's *Occasional Publication,* Vol. 17, Oct. 1988.

BURROWS CAVE ARTIFACTS

Editor - ESOP Forum

Having recently had the opportunity to examine pictures of stone carvings and artifacts alleged to have been found at a place called "Burrows Cave" in Illinois, I can understand why their authenticity has been questioned. I am, however, familiar with ancient art forms, having done considerable research in this area over the past 30 years. When the collection is viewed as a whole, several things about it send warning signals:

1. There are many faces depicted in both line and relief carvings. When pictures of these faces are compared, it is evident that they were largely carved by the same person, exhibiting the same "lantern-jawed" profile. They are dressed in armor, clothes and headgear from several different epochs-from 2000 BC by 1000 AD - certainly beyond the timespan of a single artist.

2. The carvings are extremely crude and hastily done. When you look at most art produced by ancient civilizations, the attention to detail and craftsmanship are striking with a real feel for the medium on the part of the artist. These are crude copies of everything from Egyptian and Babylonian tomb paintings to gargoyles from Notre Dame and dragons from the Book of Kjells.

3. Not only is the art work crude, it is also amateurish. Much of the relief carving follows the contours of the stone the carver picked up - lending credence to the suspicion that it was done in a hurry and without any feeling for the religious symbols and figures represented.

4. Many of the objects appear to have no utility other than to represent objects found elsewhere. Arrowheads, spearheads and knives are crude depictions rather than working tools. Plummets are crudely shaped. Lamps are only roughed out. One picture even shows a stone knife blade with a stone handle - anticipating our modern-day table knives by several centuries!

There may be a cave somewhere in Illinois that these objects came from but I strongly doubt it - especially if these pictures show what is supposed to have come out of it. It appears more to me that a prodigious effort has been made to manufacture a bunch of stuff to hoodwink the unwary.

My research has lead me to the conclusion that there were many contacts between the Americas and Europe, Africa and Asia in ancient times and certainly credit the Society for stimulating awareness. Much evidence of these contacts exists and has been documented already. I do not believe that this particular "find" is at all helpful in this regard.

Charles W. Bailey

A good example of just how well they police their own efforts came about over this very same Illinois find, the Burrow's Cave artifacts. In 1976 Barry Fell inadvertently placed an incorrect copy of the Cuenca elephant tablet taken from an excavation at the airport near Cuenca, on the cover of The Epigraphic Society's *Occasional Publications*. It contained a misshapen "ya" symbol, and incidentally, was so copywrited by the Society. It should also be stated at this time, that a corrected version of this error was later published, and that both drawings were done by Professor Fell. Well, at any rate, perhaps you have already guessed the outcome. The counterfeiter made a replica of the famous Cuenca elephant tablet using the incorrect Fell-Epigraphic Society drawing. As Fell reports on this unusual happenstance in vol 17, 1988 of ESOP, "Thus the ludicrous situation arises that the "antique" from Illinois has infringed the registered copyright of a drawing first published in 1976." What further proof was needed regarding these "Burrow's Cave" artifacts? Surely,none!

Just how does all this talk of fraud, hoax, deception and trickery ultimately affect the McGruer's Gods and Newberry Stone discoveries? Well, as previously indicated, the authenticity of the clay inscribed tablet is presently well established by the respected translation of the astute Barry Fell. Further research should also, in turn, prove the idols of great archaeological merit as they are comprised of the same medium, that being clay. Please remember here the source and analysis of this unusual "pinkish-reddish" clay was not able to be determined. Once the final tabulations are in, they may well prove to be of the utmost historical importance. But you must remember from the very onset of this discovery, the cry of "hoax" and "fake" did surface. This fact can be attributed in part to the controversy that developed during that particular time period with fraudulent material recovered from downstate mounds, perpetuated by the likes of one, Daniel Soper and the now famous, "Soper Frauds." Many of the learned townspeople of Newberry bore a shred of skepticism...many carried it to their demise. But as we discussed in the chapter on McGruer's Gods, no sign of a plot, devious or otherwise, ever came to light. And indeed, had there actually been one, the three individuals so involved must have certainly carried it to their graves. No one made a fortune! No one gained scientific notoriety. No one prospered from the discovery in any way, shape or form.

As indicated previously, even the editor of The Newberry News, who knew the principal subjects involved in the gods and tablet being discovered, thought otherwise. He felt the lumberjacks lacked the proper intelligence to carry out a scheme of such proportion. Editor Fretz also remarked that McGruer himself was a rather simple-minded old coot with no capacity for such a stunt, and, when properly lubricated, told all he knew anyway. As Fretz so indicated, he personally "lubricated" John McGruer to no avail. It should be noted that the many people interested in the scientific aspects of the McGruer's Gods and the Newberry Tablet, do not believe this event was one of a "relic peddler's" persuasion.

The site location itself where the artifacts were cached, gives credence to the idol's and tablet's authenticity. The facts are still surfacing, but to date they strongly point to the fact that the gods and the tablet are genuine antiquities.

While unanswered questions still arise regarding many of the artifacts and cultural achievements described in this book, including the image stones, the dolmens, the "rings of stone", the "wagon wheels", the ancient garden beds, stone cairns and rambling rock walls, the petroglyphs and pictographs, as well as the mounds and the prehistoric mining pits, in time, future archaeologists, anthropologists, geologists and epigraphists will supply the answers to the remaining problems that still exist. Remember in the "Introduction" you were advised accordingly that this would be a publication of many unanswered questions.

Perhaps a proper way of closing the book on *Michigan Prehistory Mysteries* would be with a quotation from Robert Haltiner, Chief of Resources for the Jesse Besser Museum in Alpena. Mr. Haltiner's advice follows:

"Archaeology has always been most fascinating...especially the mysteries it presents. I hope most of the mysteries will remain so...for that is what makes the study of the early people so intriguing."

AND SO BE IT!

CREDITS:

Robert E. Haltiner, Chief of Resources, JESSE BESSER MUSEUM, Alpena, MI.

MYSTERIES OF MICHIGAN'S LONG—AGO PEOPLE,

Gerald Haltiner, publ. privately, Alpena, MI.
The Epigraphic Society's OCCASIONAL PUBLICATION. Vol. 17, Oct. 1988.
"The Michigan Relics," Barry Fell
"Burrows Cave Artifacts," Charles W. Bailey

SUGGESTED FURTHER READING

MYSTERIES OF MICHIGAN'S LONG-AGO PEOPLE, Gerald Haltiner, publ. privately, Alpena, MI
THE KING STRANG STORY, by Doyle C. Fitzpatrick, National Heritage, Lansing, MI 1970 (70-140603 cc)

BETTY SODDERS

If hermits came in 'pairs', surely Bill and I would qualify. We prefer the solitude of a forest, the cry of a loon, a visit from a black bear, raccoon or white-tail deer to all our modern-day environment has to offer.

Having retired at the early age of 46, both Bill and I have indeed had the time and energy to pursue our many varied interests. Our retirement has taken us to many wilderness northern Michigan areas where our love of nature, wildlife and the total outdoor scene has led to my late-in-life writing career. My animal study and nature articles have regularly appeared in the popular magazine, *Michigan Out-Of—Doors* since 1984. Furthermore, many of my wildlife and historical articles have also been published in an Upper Peninsula, Michigan magazine, so aptly named, *Above The Bridge.*

While I am busy pounding the typewriter, Bill keeps occupied in his workshop turning out 'working' duck decoys as well as creating unique 'burl' art.

Our other interests include a deep love of our state's early history, both ancient and pioneer. When I recently came face to face with the prehistory artifacts termed "McGruer's Gods," I knew I was hooked, and this book just naturally evolved.

Bill and I have raised four children: Terri, Bruce, Bonnie and Billie. Presently we reside with our 15-year-old Siamese cat called Tigger, near DeTour Village at the far eastern end of the U.P. Here we nightly feed a gang of raccoons a diet of popped corn. All our local wildlife partake in this venture from deer, bear, fox, rabbit, squirrel and occasionally a shy bobcat or two. IT IS A GOOD LIFE!

Photography & Artwork Credits

Copper pits on Isle Royale — taken from Primitive Man In Michigan, by Hinsdale.

King Crowley — Artwork by Diane Tedora, Avery Color Studios.

The Haltiner Collection —Robert E. Haltiner, Chief of Resources, Jesse Besser Museum, Alpena, MI 49707.

Worked Copper from Michigan — taken from Primitive Man In Michigan, by Hinsdale.

Ontonagon Boulder — unknown source.

Early Indian mining — Artwork by Francis Moses, St. Ignace.

Part II

Mass Copper — Artwork by Diane Tedora, Avery Color Studios, from a xerox copy of 1896 article. Credit to: Marquette Mining Journal, Marquette, MI (Marquette County Historical Society).

Mining hammers — taken from Primitive Man In Michigan, by Hinsdale.

Mining tools — taken from Primitive Man In Michigan, by Hinsdale.

Fluted Celt — taken from Primitive Man In Michigan, by Hinsdale.

Part III

Keweenaw County and Isle Royale maps — created from Michigan Natural Resources "Mapbook Of Michigan Counties."

A Puzzling Prehistory Disc Factory!

Five photos entitled; Engraved discs — Robert Haltiner, Chief of Resources, Jesse Besser Museum, Alpena, MI 49707, Photo reproductions by Dennis Morrison, Greenbush, MI.

Perplexing Pictographs & Petroglyphs!

Spider Man — Artwork by Francis Moses, St. Ignace, MI

Two men in the act of urinating — Artwork by Francis Moses, St. Ignace.

Big Man — Artwork by Francis Moses, St. Ignace, MI.

Problematical Burnt Bluff Pictograph — Artwork by Francis Moses, St. Ignace, MI.

Grid — Artwork by Francis Moses, St. Ignace, MI.
Elongated Man — Artwork by Francis Moses, St. Ignace, MI.
Bowman — Artwork by Francis Moses, St. Ignace, MI.
Sanilac and Delta County maps — created from Michigan Natural Resources "Mapbook of Michigan Counties."

Questionable Rocks With A Prehistory Past!

Diagram of ring of stones — Artwork by Avery Color Studios, re: The Detroit News.
Ring of Stones — Artwork by Francis Moses, St. Ignace, MI.
Five photos of the Beaver Island discovery — The Beaver Island Historical Society, St. James, MI., Alvin Lafreniere, President, Beaver Island Historical Society, Phil Becker, photographer.
Beaver Island map — created from a Beaver Island Historical Society map. Site location done by, Fred Rydholm, Marquette, MI.

Part II

Black River Stone Cairns and Rock Walls placement sketch — Artwork by Avery Color Studios, source Dennis Morrison, Greenbush, MI.
Three photos of Black River cairns — Dennis Morrison, freelance writer-photographer, Greenbush, MI.
Alpena County map — Created from Michigan Natural Resources "Mapbook of Michigan Counties."

Part III

Escanaba Stone — Artwork by Avery Color Studios, created from a xerox copy of a photograph provided by Marquette County Historical Society, Marquette, MI.
Photos of dolmen found in Minnesota — Charles Bailey, Duluth MN.
Huron Mountain dolmen — C. Fred Rydholm, Marquette, MI.
Marquette County map — created from Michigan Natural Resources "Mapbook of Michigan Counties."

Image Stones — Spirit Stones

Copper effigy — taken from Primitive Man In Michigan, by Hinsdale.
Photos of a replica of a statue that may have stood in the Great Lakes country in the 1600s — The replica was carved by Jerry Wagner of Oscoda for his Native American Museum — Jerry Wagner.

Spirit stones — Artwork by Avery Color Studios, re: The First People Of Michigan, by Hinsdale.
Smiling sandstone sculpture — Artwork by Francis Moses, St. Ignace, MI.

Prehistory Mounds—Pyramids—Earthworks—Gardens

Pottery— taken from Primitive Man In Michigan, by Hinsdale.
Pipes — taken from Primitive Man In Michigan, by Hinsdale.
Artifact collection — taken from Primitive Man In Michigan, by Hinsdale.
Bird - Stones — taken from Primitive Man In Michigan, by Hinsdale.

Part II

River Rouge Mound — taken from Primitive Man In Michigan, by Hinsdale.
Map of Michigan showing mounds — taken from Primitive Man In Michigan, by Hinsdale.
Map of Ontonagon County — created from Michigan Natural Resources "Mapbook of Michigan Counties."

Part III

Photos on modern-day excavation — Winston D. Moore, South Haven, MI.
Baraga County Sand Point Mounds — Artwork by Shay Moore, St. Joseph, MI.
Baraga County map — created from Michigan Natural Resources "Mapbook of Michigan Counties."

Part IV

Earthworks — Missaukee Preserve — taken from Primitive Man In Michigan, by Hinsdale.
Earthworks — Rifle River — taken from Primitive Man In Michigan, by Hinsdale.
Ancient gardens — taken from Primitive Man In Michigan, by Hinsdale.
Alcona County map — created from Michigan Natural Resources "Mapbook of Michigan Counties."

McGruer's Gods & The Newberry Stone — A Michigan Mystery!

Drawn facsimile of man-idol statue — taken from newspaper article, unknown source, Article titled, "By Whose Hands

were the Images & Tablet Placed in the Woods Near Newberry?"
Plat — Michigan Department of Conservation, Land Economic Survey, Luce County, 1929.

Part II

Photos taken in 1947 of the McGruer find — Carol Taylor, Newberry, MI.

Part III

Photos of the McGruer's Gods — The Marquette County Historical Society Museum, Marquette, MI.
Tisza Culture, Sickle God — Artwork by Diane Tedora, Avery Color Studios.
Photo of woman-idol — Carol Taylor, Newberry, MI.
Photo of carved replica located at Jerry Wagner's private Indian Museum, Oscoda, MI — Betty Sodders
Cross section of hair — Charles Bailey, Duluth, MN.

The Mysterious Symbol Stone

Symbol Stone — Dennis Morrison, Greenbush, MI.
Composite drawing of symbols — Artwork by Francis Moses, St. Ignace, MI.

We at Avery Color Studios thank you for purchasing this book. We hope it has provided many hours of enjoyable reading.

L[illegible] an and the Great Lakes a[illegible] nge of titles that cover [illegible]s, early Indians and t[illegible] es shipwrecks, Cully [illegible] ders (full of laughter [illegible] ss), and full-color [illegible] by and the natural [illegible] is land.

[illegible] autiful full-color [illegible] ote stationery.

To obtain a free catalog, please call (800) 722-9925 in Michigan, or (906) 892-8251, or tear out this page and mail it to us. Please tape or staple the card and put a stamp on it.

PLEASE RETURN TO:

Avery **Color Studios**

Star Route - Box 275

Au Train, Michigan 49806

Phone: (906) 892-8251

IN MICHIGAN

CALL TOLL FREE

1-800-722-9925

Your complete shipping address:

____

____

____

Fold, Staple, Affix Stamp and Mail ____________

Avery COLOR STUDIOS

Star Route - Box 275

AuTrain, Michigan 49806